FEARLESS

A DISSECTION OF JAMAICAN SPIRITUALITY

*A Path to Unity and Triumph
for the African and Non-African Diaspora*

BIANCA ROSE

Edited by Tamara Tamu

Copyright © 2021 [Bianca Rose]

All rights reserved.

No part of this publication may be reproduced, distributed, or transmitted in any form or by any means, including photocopying, recording, or other electronic or mechanical methods, or by any information storage and retrieval system without the prior written permission of the publisher, except in the case of very brief quotations embodied in critical reviews and certain other noncommercial uses permitted by copyright law.

This book is dedicated to my mother and father,
Sherine & Earl, for igniting the fire.
To my brother,
Deon, for always keeping the fire blazing with me.

Thank you for loving me and others the way you do.
Thank you for setting a high standard of how to exist in this world.
Thank you for teaching me how to love, how to apply courage,
and express gratitude despite my environmental circumstances.
Because of you, all I know is love.

And to the rest of my Jamaican family in the US, UK, and Jamaica:
my siblings, cousins, aunts, uncles, grandmother,
grandfather, in-laws, and friends who became family; and all the
incredible Jamaicans around the world,
thank you for sharing your spirit with the world
and making this life worthwhile for all of those around you.

Preface

My mother has always been a true lioness in human form. Her energy dominates any environment despite systematic levels, economic barriers, and deep-rooted racial bias and bigotry. Like how a lion cub follows her mom to survive in the animal kingdom, I adopted my mother's energy to thrive in any environment. I witnessed her demonstration of perseverance and faith in extraordinary ways that ensured my siblings and I graduated college and healed from significant ailments. She exemplifies love, justice, and courage in her community by reflecting on the values she stands for. I would be remiss if I did not pay homage to my father as well. He demonstrated the same aura as my mother. His presence and poise in any given circumstance demanded respect. He was cherished in the community as a revered elder who spoke with wisdom. Present day, I regularly utilize my lioness energy in my experiences as I face inequalities in a western environment while creating a lifestyle. As a child, I developed a fearless paradigm that has worked in my favor, especially as I have moved through life phases. This paradigm is indigenous to other Jamaicans, which prompted my immersion into learning the full scope of this spiritual-lioness energy deep-rooted in Jamaica.

During my childhood, the magnitude of my parent's power and influence escaped me. The way they navigated circumstances, favorable and non-favorable, was of normalcy. In my young rationale, everyone's parents did what my parents did. Just as my parents received people with love and encouragement, everyone's parents did the same. This belief translated into the lessons I was taught about doing my best and treating people with respect; I thought the lessons in my household were the same in all families. I reached my mid-20s before I noticed how different my parents were from those of my peers, mainly regarding interpersonal connections and how they perceived life's challenges.

My mom is from St. Elizabeth, Jamaica, and my dad was from St. Ann. I grew up in Boston, and my family from Jamaica visited regularly. It was customary for my parents to send my relatives barrels of clothes, non-perishable food items, and other necessities that could serve as a buffer while navigating through their plights back home in Jamaica. My parents opened our Boston home for relatives and friends who migrated to America for the first time to help them get established. Without hesitation, my parents extended the same love and attention to non-family members as well. I recall Ms. Karen, whom my mother was a nanny to her three children for years. I watched how the relationship between my mother and Ms. Karen blossomed into a long-lasting friendship. My dad worked in the music industry to spread the reggae culture in places reggae didn't hold too much popularity in, and his working relationships also grew into friendships as he labored. My parents made personal connections of utmost importance because their focus was always on love, peace, and unity, not fear.

People looked to my parents for advice and guidance through various life situations. My mom is known to be a dedicated mother who cares for her household and does what she can to help other families. My father had a reputation for inspiring people to persevere by using fun, laughter, and positivity. Both were hard workers with at times having multiple jobs. My childhood was filled with family gatherings, big and small. These gatherings were used to create intentional relationships that keep my immediate and extended family connected today.

I emphasize fearlessness as the force that drove my parent's actions and how they approached life. To solidify this truth, even more, I want to share several vivid memories here of my mother putting her freedom and life at risk to extend love to another human being. Riding the school bus was a regular occurrence for most kids in our neighborhood. Every morning as my siblings and the other neighborhood kids and I huddled around the bus stop, my mother would accompany us. One morning, one of the kids was being bullied by three kids who were known troublemakers in the neighborhood. My mother immediately went into action and put her safety at risk to protect the young boy as if he were her child. This incident drew so much attention, prominent law enforcement was compelled to acknowledge her bravery. I recall another incident where my mother assisted a postal worker suffering from a gunshot wound after being robbed of the goods in his truck, a common occurrence during the holiday seasons. While waiting for the paramedics, she gave the man refuge in her car, not giving thought to the impending danger still possibly lingering nearby. Following the incident, federal agents questioned her to get testimonials during the court process. These agents asked my mother to lie and identify the suspects she did not see. She quickly asked them to leave her house. Those agents did not return to our home. I was utterly in awe of the courage I witnessed from one extreme to the next, and it all seemed so effortless. It did not matter whether the person was of familial relationship, friend, or stranger. It did not matter a person's background or the circumstance; the fearless energy never subsided. I started to notice, albeit slowly, the Jamaican spirit was of bold energy used strategically to exercise peace, safety, and happiness. My journey to creating this book started long before I conceptualized the idea. My dive into my roots has always been brewing.

Because I inherited this fearless energy, I always felt confident and secure when I was away from my home. Even though the families on the outside did not look like mine, I did not have concern for my safety. It was not until my father passed away when I was 19 years old when I realized I had taken my blissful life for granted. The passing of my father was the first real heartache I had experienced. Rather than relying on my inherited lioness energy, I searched for physical replacements only to be disappointed. After being worn with the disappointments, I embraced my need to grieve in healthier ways. The disruption of self-care discovery led me to this endless journey of discovering different dimensions and reigniting my spiritual heritage that encompasses the spirit of my ancestors.

Before the passing of my father, I was functioning in a constant state of gratitude, a dimension higher than the 3D physical plane. After my father passed, I realized he, or the event, was anchoring me in whatever this higher dimension was, also known as the 5D plane. As I addressed the impact of my father's death, I was more compelled to study the interaction between the death of a person who was of a positive and powerful force in life and how we function in life after the grief. We lose people we love, then after we have grieved "enough," we often go back to our regularly scheduled lives. But, instead of returning to a regular cycle of work and to-do lists, what if we go from grieving to discovering a higher purpose? What if we embraced the death of a loved one being an avenue to perceive unfamiliar plateaus and answer an inner call? What if, after grieving, we removed distractions to exist at a higher vibration by discovering forgotten ancient roots and tools? What if our discovery and knowledge of these ancient roots is the missing link in a world phenomenon? These are just a few of the questions that have guided me and my discovery of Jamaican spirituality.

This book is a dissection of Jamaican spirituality fueled by my childhood experiences. This book is not a history lesson as much as it is a plea for all of us to go deeper into our roots, our history, and our truth. I knew more profound factors existed than the surface-level characteristics that contributed to the Jamaican peoples' level of courage and bravery. Within the last four years, I have seen a sweeping chain of events ushering in a cloud of fear in America. These events stamped my voyage to find an intangible antidote that would counter this fear. Secure in my personal experience with spiritually powerful Jamaicans around me, I began to trace Jamaicans' history through as many generations as possible. This book culminated in three years of sleepless nights and countless hours in the Boston Public Central Library. I scoured information from books and documentaries highlighting ancient Jamaica. I have gained extensive insight from interviews with Jamaicans, non-Jamaicans, Jamaican historians, and other Africans with similarly high bravery vibrations. I visited historic sites across America to widen my perspective and draw connections amongst the African diaspora's most fearless figures.

My approach to discovering this "antidote" is based on my desire to uncover patterns in actions, attitudes, and practices amongst modern-day Jamaicans that connect to the first inhabitants of the Jamaican island. With experiential evidence from my life and now with rewarding research, I have dissected why Jamaicans are so fearless, and I intend to highlight the strengths the Jamaican people bring to the world. I also show the weaknesses we must work on relinquishing. I hope highlighting the Jamaican people's strengths and weaknesses will challenge readers to do the same with their native country and heritage. I believe when we all take on this challenge at any level, it can positively shift our evolution as human beings in today's world. This challenge is an unconventional approach to world peace and the global removal of the fear cloud.

Despite roadblocks that arose during this journey, I am pleased to share historical surprises and unbelievable findings. During my research, I often found information on Jamaican life to be vastly different from one source to the next, making it difficult to make connections. Where data was missing, incomplete, or confusing, I lean on my personal experiences to offer possible links. I will note that much to my surprise; there are growing numbers of writers, historians, archaeologists, and professors who desire to preserve Jamaican history by presenting a consistent flow of accurate information.

I invite you to join me on this spiritual awakening journey and the embracing of the ancestral heritage to be fearless.

CONTENTS

Preface vi

Part One: Where Do Jamaicans Come From? 15

    The Taínos 16

    The Jews 18

    The Africans 20

    The Maroons 23

    The Irish 26

    The Germans 26

    The East Indians 27

    The Chinese 27

    The Middle Easterns 28

    The Rastafarians 28

Part Two: The [R]Evolutionary Mindset Of Jamaicans Explained 31

  Chapter One: Fighting For Justice Is The Foundation For A Better World 35

  Chapter Two: Making The Best Out Of Reality 40

  Chapter Three: Love And Sound As Catalysts For Evolution 42

  Chapter Four: Dance Is A Powerful Force For Connection 45

  Chapter Five: Energy Is The Most Valuable Currency In The World 48

  Chapter Six: Poor Treatment Can Warrant War 54

  Chapter Seven: The Silent Killer 59

Chapter Eight: Peace Without Racism, The Possibilities 64

Part Three: Recurring Behavioral Patterns That Have Traveled Through Generations To Present-Day Jamaica 69

Chapter Nine: Jamaicans Don't Wait To Take Initiative 71

Chapter Ten: Jamaicans Make The Best Of Their Circumstances, So They Can Advance Closer To Their End Goals. 76

Chapter Eleven: Jamaicans Find And Show Joy In Reality, Despite Their Circumstances 115

Chapter Twelve: Jamaicans Use Sound As A Tool For Peace 121

Chapter Thirteen: Jamaicans Have Never Stopped Partying 144

Chapter Fourteen: Jamaicans See No Limits 154

Chapter Fifteen: Jamaicans Will Fight For Their Freedom Until They Win 161

Chapter Sixteen: Jamaicans Master Awareness 174

Chapter Seventeen: Jamaicans Believe All People Are Equal, And Everyone Has Something To Bring To The Table 189

Part Four: Controversy 200

Chapter Eighteen: Crime & Violence 201

Chapter Nineteen: Classism 207

Chapter Twenty: Colorism & Bleaching 212

Chapter Twenty-One: Rigid Mindsets 215

Chapter Twenty-Two: Society & Development 219

Part Five: Attentively & Courageously Entering Higher Dimensions 224

Chapter Twenty-Three: Trace Your Roots 225

Chapter Twenty-Four: Striving For Unity Amongst The African Diasporas 229

Chapter Twenty-Five: Evolving Pass Black Oppression 240

Chapter Twenty-Six: Executing The Steps For Ascension To Higher Dimensions ....
.... 250

Epilogue 272

Postscript 274

Acknowledgements 277

Bibliography 278

PART ONE

Where Do Jamaicans Come From?

Research regarding the origins of Jamaican people proved to be the most challenging part of this journey. Amongst the first story I was privy to was rebellious enslaved Africans from all over the Americas being sent to Jamaica from neighboring islands and countries as a form of punishment. I shared these findings during an interview with my Aunty Lark, my mom's youngest sister, born and raised in St. Elizabeth. She turned my attention to a video featuring a Ghanaian guide giving a tour of what appeared to be an enslaved African port in Ghana. After providing a brief history of the various countries enslaved Africans were taken to, he explained to the tourists, "slaves were not taken from any particular castle to Jamaica. Jamaica was founded due to individual enslaved Africans who rebelled against British and European plantation owners." I listened as the tour guide connected this rebellion to the behaviors and attitudes of Jamaicans today. "That's why the Jamaicans...up to today, the 21st century, they are not the easy type. They are very aggressive. That is why they say, 'Out of Many, One People.'" [1] While I was mesmerized by the story, I would learn quickly the tour guide's summary was barely a fraction of the origins, because before the Africans touched the island, there were people who had already created a life there.

The Taínos

The first inhabitants of the island of Jamaica were from the Taíno ancestors of the Ostionoid culture, who migrated from Central America approximately AD 650 & AD 700 AD. Very little (as of right now) is known before this period. The Ostionoid people were also known as the Redware people, a group known for their ceramics and regular use of the color red. They were known to settle alongside the coast of the St. Ann parish and along the shores of St. Elizabeth, Manchester, and Westmoreland, where they hunted for fish and turtles as their primary source of diet.[2] Although very little is known, it seems like evidence of their existence continues to emerge as more archaeologists move to the island to study the history. Initially, pottery marked with red was the only thing they left behind that we could use to identify their existence. Now, archaeologists are discovering new patterns — "significant features of Redware subsistence patterns and exploitation of the environment."[3] Unrelated, I realize St. Elizabeth people are sometimes called "Red", which I always thought referred to the fair complexions of Jamaicans residing in St. Elizabeth. It is possible this could have a connection to the Redware people, who were also known to inhabit St. Ann parish, as mentioned before.

About 300 years later, about 877 AD - 1490 AD, the Meillacan people appeared. They were also known as the White Marl culture based on their physical appearance & pottery style. It was believed the Meillacan people overcame the Ostionan people. New evidence now shows both cultures may have existed on the island. Evidence shows the Ostionans remained closer to the sea and slightly inland, while the Meillacan people inhabited various parts of the island. The Meillacans' sites were known to have the best panoramic views.[2] They engaged in hunting and agriculture and improved the existing cultivation of their co-inhabitants. They introduced corn cultivation and tobacco as smoking. Their pottery is distinguished from the Ostionans as having thinner widths and is found throughout the island. The Meillacan eventually evolved into the Taínos, who's descendants still exist on the island today, around AD 1200 until Columbus' arrival in 1494. The Taínos were just one of several subgroups of the Arawak tribe, a peaceful farming tribe dating back to prehistoric South America and the Caribbean, who settled mostly on the islands of Hispaniola (Dominican Republic and Haiti), Cuba, Jamaica, Puerto Rico and Lesser Antilles.

As the Taíno culture developed, so did social activity and systems in Jamaica. The Taínos were the bedrock of a spiritually renewed world. The Taíno created a social class where there were four different types of people: commoners (naborias) & nobles (mitaínos), chiefs (caciques) who governed the commoners & nobles, and healers/priests (bohiques) who advised the chiefs.[4] They had a profound love for women, as they held feminine consciousness in high regard,[28] like the way Jamaican men love women today. Women and men played sports with each other. One game popular to the culture was called Batey, reminiscent of today's netball, a very popular sport in Jamaica amongst women. They built rafts and canoes, and they were generous in gift-giving.[28] They did not write, but they spoke an Awarawkan language; Barbacoa ("barbecue"), Hamaca ("hammock"), Kanoa ("canoe"), Tabaco ("tobacco"), Yuca, Batata ("sweet potato"), and Juracán ("hurricane") were all common words indicative of their lifestyle. One can safely assume they lived in peace before the Spaniards arrived in 1494, with Columbus spearheading the voyage. His first stop was in the Bahamas in 1492.

Subsequently, when the Spanish came, Taínos became the first enslaved people on the island to the Spaniards. Along with being tortured, they fell deathly ill to diseases such as yellow fever, to which the Taíno, whom we now know took hygiene very seriously and baths very frequently as they did not like sweat on them for too long, had no immunity. Nearly 60,000 of the Taínos population died, except for a small group of survivors who most likely escaped to the mountains where future generations would be joined with their allies from Africa, becoming the Maroons some 300 years later. The first Africans didn't arrive in Jamaica until 1513 as enslaved Africans to Spanish settlers, though it is speculated that prior to that time, the Spanish did bring enslaved Africans with them who were already brought to Europe.

Here is where I would like to interject a brief look into how the island name *Jamaica* was derived. While there are disparities, I would like to address likely possibilities. A common possibility exists in the sources I gleaned information from; Taínos named the island *Xaymaca*, which means 'land abounding with springs'. Today, *Jamaica* is known to mean 'land of wood and water'. Based on evidence from Columbus' journal, Taínos called Jamaica *Yamaye*, but there was only one source I found that gives the name the following meaning: 'big western spirits'. Although not a popular angle, some sources mentioned Jamaica was also called *Jah-Mek-Ya*, meaning 'Jah [God] Made Here'.

The Jews

During the Spanish rule from 1494-1655, Jews arrived in Jamaica to flee from The Inquisition in Spain and Portugal, where they were being persecuted for not converting to Catholicism. They stayed hidden and concealed their religious practices by claiming to be Spanish or Portuguese while Jamaica was still under Spanish rule. When the British conquered Jamaica in 1655, Jews were allowed to remain on the island and openly practice their religion; it has been said they helped the British conquer Jamaica, perhaps to avail their own freedom. In the centuries to follow, Jews would come from Brazil, England, British Guiana, and Surinam between 1661 and 1673; and then Curacao and Germany in the 18th and 19th centuries before the influx of Jews arriving in the country ceased.[5] During the 18th century, there were over 1000 Jews in Jamaica, more than there were in all of North America put together.[9] The rich history of Jews in Jamaica, including Port Royal, can still be seen where Jewish sites remain.

The Shaare Shalom, originally built in 1885 and rebuilt in 1912, is the oldest synagogue in Jamaica, located in Kingston. The first Black millionaire, George Stiebel, was born to a German-Jewish father and an African housekeeper. His famous mansion now houses Jamaica's best and most famous ice cream, Devon House. Jamaica's oldest newspaper, The Jamaican Gleaner, was founded by James De Cordova, who was born to British-Jews. Jews have 350 years of rich history on the island. They are said to have been a significant contribution to Jamaica's economic and commercial framework. The first ultimate financial contributions to the country came directly from the slave trade. It's important to note Jews did own enslaved Africans, although with a limit of two per plantation, and only those with plantation ownership had the rights to enslaved people. Jews also introduced sugar cultivation techniques to Jamaica.[58] Still, they were always regarded as second-class citizens in Jamaica.

The Africans

The majority of African enslaved Africans in Jamaica came from West Africa.[20] Africans were first brought to Jamaica in 1513 from Spain, not directly from Africa, as enslaved Africans to the Spanish settlers and were freed by the Spanish when the British conquered the Spaniards in 1655. These Africans fled to the mountains in hopes of living a free life, where they joined the Taínos who escaped decades prior. After the British settled, sugar soon became Jamaica's most profitable crop and England's most sought-after commodity. Still, there was a labor shortage with the Taínos nearly wiped out and the presence of a small population of Africans. The need for more enslaved Africans for labor on the sugar estates, mainly because they were cheap to purchase and were perceived as hard-working, ignited the push toward Triangular Trade. Triangular Trade involved goods leaving England for Africa in exchange for enslaved Africans. These enslaved Africans were then brought to the West Indies to produce the goods England profited from, which continued the cycle; a 3-point system when mapped out. The Middle Passage, a voyage spanning from Africa to the West Indies, was the Triangular Trade product. Over 600,000 (at times estimated to be closer to a million) of the ten million enslaved Africans who crossed the Atlantic were brought to Jamaica. Of these, an estimated 250,000 were re-routed to other colonies.[90]

Jamaica was used as a holding port before enslaved Africans were re-directed to their final destinations. For this reason, Jamaica is comprised of all different types of Africans. Akan and Igbo/Ibo mostly made up the African population in Jamaica. Most came from West Africa in the late 17th and early 18th centuries. Africans from the Coromantee region, present-day Ghana and Ivory Coast, begin to arrive as early as 1663.[13] It should be noted at this point that the word *Coromantee* is the same as *Koromanti* and *Kromanti*, just with different spelling dependent on who is using it. Coromantee is derived from the Akan word Kormantse, which was a town on the Gold Coast that homed what was called Fort Cormantin under British rule and Fort Amsterdam under Dutch rule, a prison for enslaved Africans and the first of its kind on the Gold Coast. Enslaved Africans from this fort were referred to as Coromantee by Europeans. Coromantee is used throughout this book because it has become the dominant version in Westernized culture, not necessarily because it is the proper way to refer to the Akan people. The Igbo people, originating from present-day Nigeria, arrived in the late 18th and early 19th century.

Africans brought with them their traditions, but traditions were hard to maintain in oppressive environments. Africans soon began to rebel after becoming unhappy with their status and treatment. Many successfully escaped joining the Maroons in the mountains. More Africans on the island meant more miscegenation, which I found evident in my own DNA chart from Ancestry DNA (22% Benin/Togo, 20% Cameroon/Congo, 17% Ivory Coast/Ghana, and 12% Scandinavia, 8% Mali, 1% Nigeria, and the rest, white and Asian groups). Between 1690 and 1807, most of these aforementioned groups were brought from Africa to the Americas with their approximate numbers and corresponding regions below.[18] Although Africans from the Gold Coast were among the first Africans brought to Jamaica, Africans from the Bight of Biafara outnumbered those from the Gold Coast. Here is a minor breakdown of estimates from 1650-1810 taken from *The Links of a Legacy: Figuring the Slave Trade to Jamaica*, - beginning with what the countries we know today were once referred to during legal slavery.[90][91]

Bight of Biafra (306,492) - SE Nigeria, Cameroon, Gabon (largely Igbo people)

Gold Coast (252,513) - Ghana (largely Coromantee/Akan people)

Bight of Benin (108,873) - Togo, Benin, SW Nigeria

West-Central Africa (109,002) - Congo, Angola

Greater Senegambia (66,579) - Senegal, Gambia, Guinea-Bissau, Sierra Leone, Liberia, Ivory Coast (Windward Coast)

Southeast Africa (543) - Madagascar

To emphasize, between 1690 and 1760, most enslaved Africans in Jamaica came from the Gold Coast, according to the Transatlantic Slave Trade Database, a system essential to the development and wealth of each of the nations that dominated in it. There were four nations invested most heavilty into the Transatinctic Slave Trade that forced the migration of over 12.5 million African people from their home: Portugal (31%), the Netherlands (6%), England (40%), and France (18%). It is said Jamaica was the "largest single source" for enslaved Africans from the Gold Coast.[19] Jamaica comprises different African groups who contribute to its beauty and harmony, especially with Africans from the Bight of Biafra having the most imported at three-quarters of a million. Still, it seems as if the early arrival of those from the Gold Coast, specifically the Akan people, set a powerful tone for Jamaica and its' destiny. It was especially after the Akan arrived that the Maroon community grew and became more feared amongst Europeans.

The Maroons

The Maroon community developed as early as 1512, when the Spanish captured the Taínos in Jamaica. The African fugitives left behind in the mountains were already given the Spanish name Maroons, coming from the Spanish word *Cimarrones* before the British arrival. The name was given to the runaways, meaning 'unruly,' ,wild' or 'untamed'. At the time of Britain's successful capture of Jamaica from the Spanish in 1655, approximately 1500 enslaved Africans were imported to the island by the Spanish. Many of these Africans escaped from plantations, joined the Taínos in the mountains, collectively became the Maroons, and continued to be of trouble to the new English settlers. Some of these enslaved Africans were from present-day Clarendon, one of the fourteen parishes of Jamaica, led by a chief named Juan de Bolas (who later switched from being a Spanish Maroon to later aiding the British under Governor Edward D'Oyley's rule at the time). Bolas and another Spanish Maroon chief named Juan de Serras, along with additional Spanish hopefuls still on the island, still carried hope that they could recapture Jamaica from the British. The Spanish waged war on the British with the help of some Maroons, but were defeated and eventually diminished.[11] Both the Spanish and the British used Africans in their plight for the prized Jamaica. As Britain brought in more Africans to support the increase in demand for labor in sugar plantations, a prized industry, the Maroon community would grow and free the enslaved while ransacking plantations for food and resources for their own survival.

Jamaica before 1750 consisted of Africans mostly from the Akan region. In 1690, a group of runaway enslaved Africans called The Clarendon Rebels emerged, developing their distinguished reputation aside from the Maroons. This group eventually elected the famous Cudjoe to be their leader, who would later end up becoming the leader of the Leeward Maroons (currently close to Accompong in St. Elizabeth). These gangs would rebel against their masters and free the enslaved from other plantations to join them. Cudjoe's war against the white inhabitants of Jamaica earned him fame across the island. He adopted tactics for order once used from his tribe back home, the Ashanti tribe whom still exist today, as Queen Nanny (a notable leader also from the same tribe) would also do with the Windward Maroons in Nannytown on the opposite side of the island. As a result, a group called the Cottawoods, who once separated from the original Maroons before 1730, joined forces with the Clarendon Rebels under Cudjoe's leadership. Cottawoods came to reunite with their old family under him as well. Soon after, a group called Madagascar joined them, most likely from the country of Madagascar in Africa. According to Robert Charles Dallas, a Jamaican-born British writer who I've graciously come to acquaint myself with while scouting for valuable information for this book, these negroes were described as "distinct in every respect; their figure, character, language, and country, different from those of the other Blacks."[11] Furthermore, I found out there were about 2000 enslaved Africans imported from Madagascar to Jamaica between 1685-1719, specifically an area called Lacovia in St. Elizabeth, Jamaica where they ran away from to join Cudjoe. Under Cudjoe's leadership, these three groups, including his original gang known as the Kencufees before joining forces with the Clarendon Rebels, became known as the Leeward Maroons.[11] Between 1694 to 1704, a number of rebellions rocked Jamaica and prepared the Maroons for a war that would prove victorious in their favor between 1729-1740.[12] The influence and dominance of the Coramantee

(Akan) people forced other groups apart of the Maroons to adopt their language, which was evident in the Maroons' choice of using Akan names for new baby names in Jamaica.

As the importance of enslaved Africans from the Gold Coast began to decrease in the 18th century, Igbo people were being imported in large numbers after the 1750s. Where the Coromantee people became known as revolters, the Igbo people came to be known as resisters. They were known to forge significant resistance cultures instead of fighting back, which confused their masters.[95] They were often stereotyped as lazy due to their refusal to labor or subject themselves to something they weren't accustomed to. Some reverted to suicide. Resisting bondage is energy still felt in Jamaica today. Those who know of Jamaica's rich history of revolutions often only know and refer to the Maroons, mostly Akan-influenced, most likely due to their impact on colonizers during the Maroon wars. The Igbo people, who also fought back differently, are often forgotten though the resistance tactic was quite effective. One famous case of an Igbo group in Black River, where a 'King of the Eboes' was elected to lead about 250 Igbo people with a plan to kill all whites of Jamaica. The plan was discovered. Before the king was hanged, he confidently proclaimed leaving behind enough of his countrymen to carry out their initial plan and seek revenge for his death.[95] Another Igbo leader was jailed, escaped but was found in a notorious Obeahman's hut. When both leaders were captured, they were notably "calm and unconcerned" and admitted to their roles without hesitance.[95] There is no doubt the Igbo behavior, their nonchalant atttitude especially, has also contributed to the powerful spirituality and respect for freedom of the Jamaican people today.

Between 1834-38, after slavery was officially abolished, another wave of Africans came to the island but as free laborers, mainly from the Ashanti tribe in Coromantee present-day Ghana. With the increase of slave rebellions, religious groups, and humanitarian groups like the Quakers publicly protesting against the slave trade, slavery was finally abolished in 1834. An apprenticeship was enacted before being terminated in 1838 for being unmanageable.[6] The apprenticeship allowed Africans to come to Jamaica to work freely. This sparked a wave of about 32,000 West Africans coming in between 1841 and 1867. This indentureship required five years of labor in return for pay, free passage, and the option of returning to their country or finding another field of work.[7] This indentureship also gave way for non-African groups to migrate to the island.

The Irish & The Scottish

The Irish began arriving onto the island as early as the 17th century when the British took over and brought roughly 5,000 over from Barbados, a colony the British had already established in 1626 as they needed to populate their colonies. Presbyterians who were running from religious persecution in Ireland found refuge on the island. Various Irish people arrived on the island; sailors, servants, merchants, prisoners of war, the majority serving as indentured servants. The Scottish also is have said to come over as prisoners of war with the Irish after the British conquest of Jamaica and made up 1/3 of the white population by 1774.[44]

The Germans

Over 1000 Germans, farmers and trade people, who most likely practiced Catholicism, arrived between 1834-1838 in Jamaica. Germans intermarried with Jamaican Blacks through the 1930s, and their presence began to dwindle. However, heavily populated areas of people with German heritage like Seaford Town in Westmoreland made way for a 1990s documentary called *Seaford Town - German Settlement in Jamaica*, which highlights the history and modern image of the German-Jamaican. Some popular German surnames are still around and include Somers, Eldermeyer, Wedermeyer or Kameka.[8] Their infuence is still there as one can still find descendants with noticeable German attributes.

The East Indians

About 21,500 East Indians arrived between 1838-1917 to establish wealth through apprenticeships to take back to India. They became the replacement for enslaved Africans after the abolishment of slavery as they were treated just as harshly.[6] After their indentureship was over, many remained in the country, adding to the multicultural mix, and returned to their previous occupations and trades; some became money lenders. They introduced coolie plums, mangoes, jackfruit, and tamarinds to Jamaica, in addition to well-known dishes like curried goat, curried potato, eggplant, and okra. They are the largest minority on the island, Africans being the majority. Like the Chinese, Indians rarely went back to their country as the living and working conditions were often worse in their homeland than they were in Jamaica.

The Chinese

Between 1860 and 1893, about 5,000 Chinese came to Jamaica to work as indentured laborers.[6] Also, displeased with the work, they directed their energy towards commerce and food services by setting up grocery stores across the island. Many Chinese also remained on the island, and many went back to China to marry Chinese women before returning to Jamaica again. Chinese-owned supermarkets and restaurants remain popular on the island.

The Middle Easterns

During the last decade of the 19th century, immigrants arrived in Jamaica from the Middle East, mainly Lebanon. They were primarily Christians fleeing religious persecution from the Ottoman Empire. They did not come as indentured servants but expected to take advantage of opportunities as a result of the 1891 Great Exhibition, an attempt to promote Jamaica with its opportunities, and beauty, and awaken the world to the creative talent and industry of its people.

When the banana industry began to fail, they established dry goods shops. They brought various customs with them like all groups who arrived on the island, of which Jamaicans gradually adopted, while they inturn adopted Jamaican ways that had developed prior to their arrival. They contributed to the commercial development, as well as the industrial development of the Jamaican economy.[10]

The Rastafarians

Rastas are the last major group to emerge in Jamaica, and they didn't necessarily immigrate from anywhere in particular. The Rastafari movement, both a religious and spiritual lifestyle, began in the 1930s in Jamaica, with a strict belief that Jah (God) resides in each of us. They focused their attention on the African diaspora and their oppression in what they call Babylon (basically any place where whites oppress the African diaspora is referred to as Babylon). They also relied on the gathering of Africans repatriating back to their homeland, Mama Africa. There are several mansions of Rastafarianism, the most popular being Nyabinghi, Bobo Ashanti, and the Twelve Tribes of Israel. Although they each held different beliefs and viewpoints, they share common views in rejecting racism and oppression while promoting Black consciousness. Even in the present day, the differences are found in the sounds of reggae music. We can identify which mansion each Rastafarian-reggae artist associate themselves with based on the musical context and sometimes even by the energy behind it. Marcus Garvey's principles ignited the Rastafari movement, and they believed Haile Selassie, Emperor of Ethiopia (1930-1941), was the returned Jesus or the Black messiah.

My Aunty Lark and other family members shared their experiences in Jamaica with Rastas in the community, and additionally I have had my own experiences. Rastas are commonly about, and they have their separate communities like Maroons throughout the island, although many intergrate with the everyday-Jamaican people. When my relatives encountered a Rasta while growing up in Jamaica, they recounted the safety and assurance they always felt. I personally observe Rastas to be non-violent soldiers of Jah (God), with their most potent weapon being their Soul poured into reggae music, a tool. Their Maroon counterparts centuries prior also recognized non-violent methods; however, perhaps because of living in different times, they were clear in their intent to battle to protect their peace if necessary. Rastafarianism significantly influenced reggae's music development and is responsible for further driving the social, racial, and political consciousness in Jamaica through music.

Fearless

What we just uncovered is a rudimentary background to understand the basics. I implore those intrigued by the vibe or energy of the Jamaican people to join the growing interest in Jamaica's history, especially with the many different groups sharing the island. I have compiled a list of sources at the end of this book to reference for further research. This background solidifies my belief that Jamaicans are indeed the most fearless set of people on earth, and we will go further into depth. I often hear Jamaicans say it's not the land itself that gives the island its reputation; it's the people. This idea gives way to our motto, "Out of Many, One People," and additionally, "One Love," that we continue to live by, before and after the island officials severed ties with Europe and gained independence from England on August 6, 1962.

In the chapters following, I hypothesize why Jamaicans collectively can thrive happily, with a firm mental and spiritual stance in the 21st century, even while the world around them battles spiritual fights already fought and conquered by them centuries ago. I want to end Part One with the following quote to sit on by a prominent Jamaican filmmaker, with French ties:

"And where does this eternal feeling of optimism come from? I guess, maybe, because Jamaicans really do believe in freedom. They really do believe in intellectual freedom, political freedom, and I think that gives inaugural spiritual freedom. How many countries really, really believe in freedom? They really have freedom as their ideals. As opposed to nationalism, as opposed to religion, or as opposed to race, or money, or whatever, whatever obsession it is, you know?" - Peter Henzell, Director of *The Harder They Come*

PART TWO

The [R]Evolutionary Mindset Of Jamaicans Explained

As I speak of Jamaican society today, I speak of the favorable and unfavorable I have witnessed. I highlight both aspects to cultivate unity amongst myself and readers from all backgrounds. I shed light on the good and bad so we can collectively learn and appreciate each other's strengths and teach each other how to rise from weaknesses.

In Jamaica, there exists classism, colorism, and homophobia. The disparities within social classes are quite noticeable. Extreme cases of colorism exist with evidence of the popular bleaching method that results in lighter skin tones. Interestingly, bleaching is more prevalent in impoverished communities, as a lighter color is still equated to beauty and power. Homosexuality is an ever-controversial topic that moves particular Jamaican musicians to address homophobia in their music. These issues continue to taint the paradise that has earned its "everything irie" reputation through centuries of fighting for peace and its current relaxed way of life. However, there is one ism that does not exist on the island, and its racism. In the same sense that Jamaica's cons more hurt than help the "everything irie" reputation with this behavior, it's strengthened by the pros, such as racism's non-existence. The omission certainly is a contributing factor as to why Jamaicans abroad continue to go back home and retire their lives after making enough of a fortune, why tourism continues to increase, and why investments continue to expand throughout the island from foreign investors. It essentially leads back to the "vibe."

I interviewed my grandpa, John Rose, whose mom was of Indian descent and his dad was of African descent, about his life in Jamaica. As I uncovered his childhood, I inquired about his views on Jamaica's current state after retiring in Buffalo, New York. He shared he did not know racism until he came to America. He did not know or understand the word "nigger" until he came to America. Before migrating, he stated that he thought the word was the name of an animal. The validity of his opinion on racism strengthens his stark views on the current state of affairs in Jamaica. He is not in favor of the Jamaican political system and thinks the island needs Britain's guidance. He is very adamant about his views because he believes the island was once free of crime, and there was an abundance of opportunities when England was in control. I asked him to elaborate on his views while reminding myself he and I are of different generations. While I did not oppose him during the interview, I maintained my beliefs. I believe the country deserves to the chance to master autonomy since its' "peaceful" history, according to my grandpa, is one of control by another country.

My great-grandmother, Stagee, who died in 1996, was a white woman. The mention of her name sparks loving memories and stories that leave my relatives in tears and lasting disbelief of her absence, still to this day. During conversations about Stagee, I watched her video recordings where she seemed to float through the room angelically. Hearing stories of Stagee, observing her in the recordings, and having faint memories of meeting her in Jamaica as a child, it became apparent how my aunts, uncles, grandma, and mother maintained their loving disposition. Each one of my relatives had their favorite memories they shared with me. It is honestly the one thing I see them all agree on. As they gave their accounts of Stagee, I noticed not one of them mentioned her race. I introduced the topic of skin color later in my life after noticing myself that she was very light, which was lovingly dismissed with looks of shock and laughs. Skin color and ethnicity were not a factor amongst my family, and as a result, my mom passed those sentiments on to myself and my siblings. Even though she was clearly white, for some reason, I never once thought about why she was white and everyone else was black. It turns out that she was not my biological greatgrandmother, she married my greatgrandfather and took care of his children and grandchildren. I am still doing more research on her background.

Evelyn "Ema" Matalon was a beloved Jewish-Jamaican well-known for her positive and kind spirit throughout her life, touching lives of all backgrounds. In an interview, she said she never knew what antisemitism was, another form of prejudice, until she went to America, even while being the only Jewish girl going to St. Andrews High School. "Everybody was just…together."[88]

This text focuses on how the Jamaican people possibly developed some of their current mindsets to the fearless stage today they seem to have collectively built together. They continue to learn and teach each other as centuries go and new generations come. With today's political climate and emotions being swayed to extremes, it's more important than ever to learn how to exercise autonomy, emotional intelligence and maintain inner peace, happiness, and determination despite one's circumstances. Jamaicans have collectively held their independence and their freedom to coexist as humans together, despite race differences.

Fearless

For most of this storyline, I follow the mindset of the Maroons. In my bold and calculated opinion, they were the first set of people on the island to display a mastery of resilience and resistance from oppressors in worse environmental circumstances than we see today. We can learn something from a group who still, today, upholds their resilient and progressive community in the secluded mountains of St. Elizabeth. They have shown no sign of conforming as they have even started their own currency in July of 2019.

So here begins the transcendence of the Jamaican Soul. The following stages reflect how the Soul magnifies in a substantial energy force and translates outwards into a permanent state of fearlessness. This endless glow began with the Maroons. Still operating without the Jamaican government's interference, they dominated these stages in a way so profound, it leaves those who encounter the story energized.

CHAPTER ONE

The Rebellion

Fighting For Justice Is The Foundation For A Better World

♪ *Bob Marley - Get Up Stand Up*
♪ *Peter Tosh – Equal Rights*

We need to continuously fight for equal rights for all. Jamaica, the crown colony for England, has always been a masterpiece in progress cultivated by various people that arrived from all over the world. Before Columbus and the Spanish arrived, there were the Taínos from South & Central America, with their ancestors; the Ostionan/Meillacan. Then, Africans, Jews, Indians, Chinese, Germans, and Middle Easterners followed. With every wave of a new group that arrived on the island of Jamaica, I noticed two prominent factors in my research. There is clear evidence that while battling European ideals, each group made sure to protect their original customs throughout time. Second, groups fused their traditions with other groups that came in as enslaved peoples or indentured servants.

When the Taínos and Africans decided to ascend to the mountains and start a new life free of European rule, one can only imagine their thought process as they prepared for their new life. A popular claim regarding Jamaicans' origin was that the island was populated with rebels coming from different countries. My research shows this claim is weak. As we have discovered, Jamaica was a compilation of other peoples forced into slavery either in their homeland or taken from their land. The island was also comprised of people brought from their homeland with promises for a better life or migrated to Jamaica to seek refuge from religious persecution. Everyone that migrated to Jamaica was not a captive or a so-called rebel. The tales of Jamaicans all being born rebels are misconstrued. These new peoples that were brought to Jamaica, besides the Taínos, weren't rebels but instead were regular people that fearlessly resisted oppressive and demeaning circumstances.

Enslaved peoples of Jamaica came from different backgrounds but held the commonality of fighting, in different ways, for their freedom. In the fields of a sugar, banana, or rice planation, the work was laborious, harsh and often dangerous, in addition to the threat of the lives of the enslaved people by violent overseers. Terror was normalized. I believe they recognized the resilience and determination in each other and honored the steps they had already taken toward liberty. This recognition allowed them to put their differences aside and work together to continue their pursuit of freedom. Based on my findings, I believe they worked together as a unit to develop more efficient methods to obtain independence. The Maroons' storyline is best to use when dissecting the spirituality of Jamaicans. To this day, they have achieved what most-Africans outside of Africa have not achieved, a fully functional society free of European rule.

The Taínos and Africans made up the beginning of the rebellious Maroons in the mountains, but another set of enslaved Africans came to join them after the British took over in 1655; they were known as the Coromantee. As mentioned before, the British took most of their enslaved

Africans from The Gold Coast, specifically where the Akan culture of West Africa populated. This region is modern-day Ghana. It was the preferred region to take enslaved Africans from because they were known to be the hardest workers, and as a result, they became the predominant African culture in Jamaica. One colonial historian wrote that the Coromantee were "hardy, laborious, and manageable under mild and just treatment," but warned that they were "fierce, violent, and revengeful under injury and provocation." The New Yorker describes the awe amongst the colonists in the Americas. "For much of the eighteenth century, Jamaica was the most profitable British colony and the largest importer of enslaved Africans, and Johnson once described it as a place of great wealth and dreadful wickedness, a den of tyrants, and a dungeon of slaves. He wasn't the only Englishman paying close attention to rebellion in the Caribbean: abolitionists and slavers alike read the papers anxiously for news of slave revolts, taking stock of where the rebels came from, how adroitly they planned their attacks, how quickly revolts were suppressed, and how soon they broke out again."

The Akan people brought their fearless spirit across the Atlantic into the Caribbean. As a result, their energy rested amongst the other ethnic groups around them, including their fellow Africans from various tribes. "Among the Maroons—and among the people brought to Jamaica as slaves in general—Akan cultural influences predominated," Leanna Prendergast wrote in her *Maroon Culture & How It Came About* article.[17] Once a people who dominated tribal wars, the Akan culture faced a fight larger than what they were accustomed to back home in Africa. All the African peoples had to learn to put aside their differences brewing from back home to obtain the common goal of freedom. This unified goal lessened the intertribal conflict. In a sense, there was no time for it because their enslavement brought on a new oppressor.

The Coromantee enslaved Africans brought militant skills that afforded them victories and a fearsome reputation amongst both Africans and Non-Africans. "Eventually, the Coromantee became so feared that colonists in Jamaica proposed banning their importation," Casey Sep wrote in her article for the New Yorker. This was before colonists decided to separate the enslaved throughout the island to gain better control of the uprisings. Some notable people of Akan descent include Queen Nanny, Harriett Tubman, Nat Turner, Marcus Garvey, and Colin Kaepernick. It almost seems as if the rebellious or resistant energy is hereditary. Marcus Garvey was a Jamaican-born Black nationalist that sought to encourage African pride by connecting and unifying the African diaspora with their roots. Harriet Tubman was an American abolitionist known to have saved and brought over 300 enslaved people to freedom in the North through the underground railroad without losing a single passenger on her dangerous travels from the South, amongst other courageous battles. Nat Turner was an American preacher famous for having a successful slave rebellion in Virginia that ignited fear amongst the whites so much, it forced them to make harsher laws on the Blacks. Colin Kaepernick is an NFL player who famously kneeled at an NFL game in 2016 during the Pledge of Allegiance. His action took a stance against the racial injustice still exploding in America. Kaepernick continues to hold his stance. The mother of Bob Marley's paternal great-grandfather was also said to have been a descendant of the Akan. Akan people arrived as early as 1676 in Virginia, about 5,000 compared to the nearly 500,000 in Jamaica.[26] The connection of the fearless and resilient characteristics amongst the Akan culture throughout generations, no matter the location, is evident.

The entire social climate of Jamaica changed as the attitudes of the enslaved arriving on the island had an influence on their new environment.

CHAPTER TWO

Acceptance

Making The Best Out Of Reality

♪ *Everton Blender – Lift up Your Head*

♪ *Popcaan – Everything Nice*

There is a more Mystical and Powerful Force beyond what human beings can see, that exists in this world. The many different African tribes lived among each other in unity. They learned to do this because now there was no other choice for survival. These Africans reached a new level of consciousness collectively. The recognition of their past acts of courage afforded them a new level of both respect and awareness that led to a new level of power, and mental and spiritual strength. The Maroons, having fought their battles on the lands they were brought from, were ultimately brought together into the mountains because of one common trait: fearlessness. At sea level, Africans raised nonstop havoc to obtain some balance in their society, with the same characteristic of bravery working on their behalf.

The conversations amongst these new groups of Africans living together on the island, heavily influenced by the Coromantee in areas they populated, were more advanced than they had been before. They learned to respect each other's way of life and learn to communicate in order to live and survive together. Although the language from the Coromantee eventually became the dominant language, Africans used body language to communicate before developing their language, as Pendergrass describes in her article:

"Many of the slaves did not speak the same language as other slaves that joined them throughout the years. Many of the slaves brought over to the Americas came from different parts of Africa, and therefore, were unable to communicate by verbal means with other slaves. Instead, they often used body language to communicate with hand gestures and various physical actions. As time passed on, verbal communication improved among the slaves because they learned to communicate using their own language, they invented using variations of their previous language and that of the people who owned them. According to English historian Bryan Edwards, 'they [Maroons] are in general ignorant of our language.'"

Their language was a mix between African dialects, Spanish, and broken English. Many of the words still used to say are derived from Akan and Igbo words. Their creation of a collective language shows how they elevated their consciousness to a "we are one" mindset, which opened new ways of dealing with their oppressor. Today, this militant language in tone and speech has evolved into what we now know as Jamaican Patois.

Their focus was to restore the energy of peace, confidence, and love with their new way of life. This energy is what they were most accustomed to for family and tribal survival while in Africa. Their collective focus reminded them of their true nature and reached a level of mental restoration on a new, strange land together. While the energy could not be physically touched, this spiritual energy still rested inside of them.

CHAPTER THREE

Love and Sound

Love And Sound As Catalysts For Evolution

♪ *Burning Spear – House of Reggae*
♪ *Bob Marley – Three Little Birds*

It may seem, at first, that it is easier to hate and be hated than it is to love and be loved. The awareness of the power of sound can be recognized in something as powerful, and accessible, as Mother Nature. At a certain point during their enslavement, the Jamaicans achieved unity on the island. They also wanted harmony blended with happiness and love. They believed this spiritual mix was a foundation to being triumphant over their enemy. They began to focus on the power of love and the healing it could provide. As they aligned their actions to their desired life, they found an elevated level of consciousness through sound and dance.

The most successful rebels on the island, the Maroons, were one group we see mentally advanced to a new way of being by choosing to live in unity with their cultural differences. There existed a unified belief that a new way of being was necessary for evolution into total freedom. They accepted their current mindset because the alternative could have produced negative vibrations and mentally send them on journeys away from their original beliefs, customs, and dreams. That strong belief in qualities mirroring God, believing in One Source, still exist in Jamaica today.

Other links between the culture of the Jamaicans and their African forebears include their music and instruments used. In the article, *African Music in 17th Century Jamaica*, Richard Rath explains how an English physician, Hans Sloane of the Royal Society, discovered the similarity between the music played and instruments used by Jamaica's enslaved people, and the sounds of African music. He attended a festival held by the enslaved Africans and found the music and instruments to be unfamiliar to the Europeans, described as sounding like African music. He took a sketch of the instruments they used and found the way they were made was similar to how the Africans made their instruments. Among these included the central African lute, and also the eight-stringed harp, a Coromantee instrument. Instruments were often wound with fiber in the Gold Coast style. The style of the dances, including the style of movements done by the Jamaicans, were also very similar to that of the Coromantee."[17]

As African tribes adopted each other's languages, diet, and sports, sound and music became even stronger unifying forces. Sound and dance were particularly important because they were used as tools for unity, and provided an energy boost in the fight against the British.

I visited Accompong in St. Elizabeth, one of four existing Maroon communities in Jamaica, to learn more about Maroon history. It is located very high up in the hills of St. Elizabeth, bordering the hills of Trelawny. It took my group of cousins and friends at least an hour to get from the main road and up the rocky and thin roads to reach the Accompong community from where my maternal side of the family comes from in the Black River area. The rough drive was worth it after being welcomed by the very friendly, prideful and adroit Maroon people. There I learned the Maroons living closer to sea level would use an abeng, a cow horn, that made distintive sounds that sent signals to Maroons living in the nearby mountains, especially if and when the British were coming. This reminded me of Paul Revere's famous line said to have been pivotal in the American Revolution, "The British are coming!" Sound was the most valuable tool for the Maroons. The reverence for sound was evident in various areas of Jamaican society. For example, the bass had a profound effect on Jamaican culture, so much so, both the government and the church tried to have it banned. These powerful systems viewed the instrument as a threat. "It was in this drumming which the authorities and the missionaries tried unsuccessfully to eradicate by legislation and persuasion, respectively, which retained and transmitted important and distinctive elements of African/folk culture into the period after Emancipation."[20] Today, Jamaicans still use sound as a tool to fight Black oppression, most notably with reggae music.

The government successfully passed laws criminalizing things like Obeah (simarly to what we know as *voodoo*), forbidding enslaved Africans from possessing guns, and even preventing Blacks from gathering, other major tools used in fighting for their freedom.[94] Still, the power of drum and bass was sustained. The sound of the drum and bass brought people together in a way that no system could break.

CHAPTER FOUR

Dance

Dance Is A Powerful Force For Connection

♪ *Alton Ellis – Rock Steady*
♪ *Marcia Griffiths – Electric Boogie*

D*ancing is a tool for strength and unity.* As the sound became a vital component of how Jamaicans communicated with each other and focused on their freedom, dance and movement were incorporated as an additional tool for unity and battle. Dancing remained part of the Maroon culture. They regularly practiced the Kromanti dance, a dance performed during religious ceremonies with traditions brought from the Gold coast. It is characterized by complex, rapid and rhythmic movements centered around possession. Despite the Maroons' conversion to Christianity, resulting in the loss of some of the religious aspects of the dance, Maroons still use it as a tool for spiritual protection. These ceremonies started after nightfall and lasted until the next morning. Different from the contemporary Jamaican dancing, although an influence, the style was marked by forceful movements of the body. The style provoked the Souls to be possessed by ancestral spirits, causing the body to jerk in distinctive styles. "The person going into myal (spiritual possession and dancing) begins to execute a very distinctive dance motion, a sort of jerky, spinning movement in which one leg is crossed over the other in a rapid backward kick. His legs begin to quiver rhythmically, and as he bounds back and forth in this circular motion, his eyes are directed upward in a blank stare. This continues for some time, and as the state of possession stabilizes, the individual, still in motion, expels a succession of piercing screams. In a matter of time, the spirit will 'cool down', but before this occurs it is dangerous to approach the person in possession."[97]

The Taínos had their style of dance called Areito. "Some dances were done by just women or men, but many included both genders dancing together. These joint dances often occur on special occasions, like that of a cacique's marriage. Dancers also traditionally drank a great deal of alcohol during these performances." It seems the Taíno dance style was rather conservative compared to the Maroons. However, both styles were appreciated as they both hold its influences in the way Jamaicans dance with each other today. Historian and author Edward Brathwaite shared a statement from a Moravian missionary, John Becker from 1812, "...[but] scarcely was our worship closed, before the heathen negroes on the estate began to beat their drums to dance and to sing, in the most outrageous manner. The noise lasted all night and prevented us from falling asleep. After breakfast, I went down and begged the negroes to desist, but their answer was: 'What, Massa, are we not going to dance and make merry at Christmas? We always did so.'"[20]

This account brought a smile to my face because Christmas time is still filled with lively celebrations in Jamaica. When I looked at the period of when Brathwaite detailed these happenings, it was a few decades after a peace treaty was forced upon the Maroons by the British in 1739. "The exploitative terms of the peace treaties mask reality: it was the British who sued for peace while many Maroons may have been war-weary, they did not submit as defeated people...many of the colonists were very much aware of this and came to rely on the Maroons for protection a mutual recognition of the benefits of an alliance emerged." [23] Enslaved Africans were aware of the effect their dancing and celebrating as one unit had on slave owners. The slave owners became nervous and afraid. Dancing was an act deeper than socializing and celebrating life; it was a natural complementary component of power to add with sound.

I like to think the drums specifically made dancing more potent as a tool in the fight against oppression. Kumina is a Jamaican religion and practice that incorporates music, dance, and ceremonies developed from beliefs brought from West Central Africa, specifically the Congo area, after abolishing slavery. It is known as a drumming style that greatly influenced the Rastafarians who incorporate drumming into their spiritual healing and chanting, counseling and other spiritual structures, very similar to the practices of the Maroons who came about nearly three centuries before them. As a dancer myself, I noticed the presence of the bass forces us to lock in our movements as we dance for better synchronicity. We must end one move before eventually moving onto the next one for precision. And it seems as the dancing progresses in vibrations along with the music, the air and products of its environment, as a result, become vibrant. To say dance increased the vibrations of the atmosphere sounds plausible. The Jamaicans eventually realized it was a power that reignited them collectively when in action. It made them feel good. It was joy and fearlessness inward expressed outwardly.

In the following chapters, we will see how Jamaicans used the energy from the expressed vibrations to advance spiritually.

CHAPTER FIVE

Only the Best

Energy Is The Most Valuable Currency In The World

♪ *Jah9 – In the Spirit*
♪ *Vybz Kartel – Highest Level*

We must remove ourselves from toxic environments if we want to advance passed familiar levels. Here I begin to dissect Jamaican spirituality deeper.

We start to notice the psychological shift demonstrated through action. We will see how these mental shifts change the discourse of how Jamaicans, or Africans in Jamaica, would forever respond to circumstances that did not and do not align with their desired future.

As previously examined, sound and dance elements were a regular part of the Jamaican culture. The positive vibrations produced from their music-making and dancing led them to create more space for peace and clarity and increased their capacity to build on other survival skills. They were mentally preparing to embark on a new skill that complimented their original goal of emancipating themselves from physical slavery.

The Maroons became very familiar with their land, from the ground level to the mountaintop. They often left the mountains to raid plantations and free other enslaved people, aside from escaping on their own into the

Fearless

mountains to join the Maroons. "Slaves escaped singly, in groups, or by the hundreds in bloody rebellions."[74] They had the stamina and physical skills because they navigated the difficult terrains also in their home country. The Taínos were already familiar with their land before the Spanish came, and the Africans who came under Spanish rule became acquainted with the terrains quickly. The Africans from the Coromantee region in West Africa, brought their militant skills with them across the Atlantic.

Many various Maroon towns existed. To the best of my ability, I have created a timeline from multiple sources of the towns' inceptions and end-life, whether the town diminished on its own or if it was destroyed. Today four of them are still standing.

After the Spanish colonists fled Jamaica upon British arrival in 1655, there were about four maroon groups in existence. One group was under the leadership of the aforementioned Juan de Bolas, without any exact name given to the group, and the people resided in the mountains of the St. Catherine area. There were additional groups, each without a known name, that lived in the Porus area of Manchester and another in the Blue Mountains. The fourth group was the Karmahaly Maroons, established by one of Jamaica's first Maroon leaders in the Cockpit Country, present-day Accompong-Maroon Town, the aforementioned Juan de Serras. The Karmahaly Maroons were the only group known to have survived any opposing British forces.[14]

All groups were loyal to the Spanish except de Bolas, who eventually supported the British after it was clear they would defeat the Spanish. De Bolas' groups of Maroons were the first to have a peace treaty signed with the British in 1663, allowing them to live on the land with the same terms as British colonists.[118] De Bolas and his men aided the British in raids that helped to end the Spanish rule. However, when the British assigned de Bolas to search for de Serras and his Karmahaly Maroons, de Serra's men ambushed de Bolas, killed him, and retreated into the Blue Mountains away from angered British governors. They were most likely the ancestors of tday's Windward Maroons. They were established around 1673 when a surge of uprisings began after the Akan started to arrive from the Gold Coast, including the famous "siblings" from the Ashanti tribe: Nanny, Quao, Cudjoe, Accompong, Johnny, and Cuffy.

The Windward Maroons, considered apart from the Maroons on the west side of Jamaica, had three villages that appeared as Nanny Town around 1720, named after its' leader, Queen Nanny. After it was destroyed in 1734, the Windward Maroons split into two different parts of the Blue Mountains, Crawford Town led by Quao and Nanny Town led by Queen Nanny. The First Maroon War, which lasted from 1728-1739, first started against the Windwards, who the British considered less organized. In 1734, Nanny Town was destroyed. After the peace treaty was signed in 1739, which Nanny disagreed with, her supporters followed her over to Moore Town in the Blue Mountains that developed in 1740 where they were promised land from Trelawny; a British governor who surrendered in the fight against the Jamaican Maroons in her brother's [Cudjoe's] Town.

Crawford's Town was destroyed in 1754 after a dispute between Quao and another colonel that the British appointed. As a result, the supporters of Quao went to join his other supporters who had already established Scott's Hall in 1749, which still exists today. Between 1754 and 1760, Charles Town was founded after the treaty was signed, and a portion of the Maroons from Crawford's Town migrated there. Charles Town still stands today. Queen Nanny's successors lost control of Moore Town, although it does still stand today.

The Leeward Maroons were established about 1690 after several slave rebellions led by Cudjoe & his father, Naquan, a chief from the Akan people, brought a number of runaways and rebels together in the Clarendon area. The Leeward Maroons turned into Cudjoe's Town, being so nonperishable in The First Maroon War where the governor of Jamaica at the time, Governor Trelawny, offered a peace treaty to Cudjoe with the help of a neutral middleman named John Guthrie in 1739. Cudjoe's town was renamed Trelawny Town after the governor. Trelawny Town was eventually auctioned off after the Maroons lost the Second Maroon War lasting from 1795-1796. Colonel George Walpole promised the Trelawny Maroons non-deportation if they laid down their arms. However, the governor at the time, Alexander Lindsay, managed to reverse the promise, resulting in the deportation of most of the Leeward Maroons to Nova Scotia. After the deportation, Walpole retired from his post and returned to England in protest against the Britith government in Jamaica acting poorly against the Maroons. Some of the Leeward Maroons remained and either disbursed to the free Black community or resettled to nearby Accompong. Today, Trelawny Town is now known as Maroon Town and the group is named the Flagstaff Maroons. The town has been resurging over the years and they are opened for tours to support the development of their community, similar to the others.

At Accompong, the famous 1739 peace treaty was officially signed, specifically at a mango tree existing there ever since, called the Kindah Tree. I had the pleasure of visiting the landmark during my trip to Accompong. Accompong was a part of the land granted in the peace treaty to the Leeward Maroons in the Cockpit Country, and Accompong continued to lead until his death. They have a progressive community consisting of a primary school, a church, and just recently, their first bank with their own currency, as previously mentioned.

The British colonial authorities abolished the role of the superintendent in the 1850s, where a British official would also govern the Maroon terriotory. It is important to note the Maroons' involvement in helping the British with rebellions on the island occurred only after the peace treaty, when the British started assigning superintendents to each Maroon community in 1740.

Although Moore Town stayed neutral in the Second Maroon War like the rest of the Windward Maroons, they aided the British in winning many slave rebellions, including most famously Tacky's Revolt (1760), The Baptist War (1831-32), and The Morant Bay Rebellion (1865). Charles Town also helped with The Baptist War and, along with Scott's Hall Maroons, the capture of Three Fingered Jack in 1781, the leader of a group of runaway enslaved people that formed communities in the Blue Mountains in the late 1770s.

I soon realized there were plenty of runaway enslaved Africans, aside from the Maroons, that the country has recognized with monuments erected throughout the island. One source I discovered states that Jamaica's government continues to fight the Maroons when it comes to their autonomy. When I visited Accompong, I learned there had been recent disputes, albeit peaceful, over the newly built Bank of Accompong and the Bank of Jamaica wanting it to be under their jurisdiction. Another community started by the runaway enslaved African Cuffee, named after him in 1798 in the Cockpit Country, whose community managed to thrive amongst British and Maroon forces. Members of his community joined the Me No Sen We No Come community in the cockpit country before its abandonment in the 1850s when slavery was abolished. Both the Cockpit Country dividing St. Elizabeth and Trelawny, and the Blue Mountains that take up most of Portland and borders St. Thomas and St. Mary, were mountainous areas the Maroons and hundreds of other runaway enslaved Africans went for refugee. Accompong often failed in capturing runaway enslaved Africans, some of whom started communities like Cuffee and his supporters did, or the Me No Sen We No Come community in the Cockpit Country, but they tried. Consider the following detailed runaway description from a slave owner, John Tharp, who gave his account of the infamous Cuffee and his gang on March 26, 1786. "Cuffee is a desperate villain and the leader of a gang; they are all in a gang and will probably become troublesome to that neighborhood." At the time of his official escape, he was under the ownership of James McGhie.

Jamaicans started to create their own society and began preparation for the inevitable as well. Remembering reality allowed them to maintain a particular attitude, no matter the vibe of the environment. They knew the dream of freedom would not be possible to maintain if they didn't protect it with their energy. They anticipated those who did not wish them freedom would attempt to disrupt it, so they became increasingly prepared, mentally and physically, to defend themselves.

CHAPTER SIX

War

Poor Treatment Can Warrant War

♪ *Bob Marley – War*

♪ *Capleton – Who Dem?*

*P*hysical war is necessary if the refusal from oppressors to exercise their conscience affects human life. The British made attempts to retrieve enslaved Africans to regain control. They were not as familiar with the mountainous terrain as the Maroons, which made their attempts difficult. The Maroons used weaknesses of theirs like this as an advantage. It took the British a while to reach the Maroons, and they were ill-prepared for the enslaved people's awareness. The Jamaicans created traps and camouflaged themselves to launch sudden attacks. It is believed they were the first to utilize guerrilla warfare. When a Maroon leader named Lubolo served as a colonel to the British governor was killed by other Maroons in 1663, the British lost hope in British-Maroon relations. The British, who once had help from the Maroons when taking Jamaica from the Spanish, grew frustrated about their relationship with them. Tensions remained high between the two groups until about 1720, before the Maroons decided to take the offensive position. The Maroons raided plantations amongst the estates neighboring the mountains. From 1729 to 1739, a state of open warfare existed between the British and the Maroons.[115] The British would attempt to go up these mountains, repeatedly, to try and capture the Maroons. Repeatedly, the Maroons resisted.

"The men are forced to march up the currents of rivers over steep mountains and precipices without a track, through such thick woods that they are obliged to cut their way almost every step ... the underwood's being always full of saps and new shoots, exceedingly tough and bushy, twisted and entangled in a strange manner: add to this that they frequently meet with torrents caused by heavy piercing rains that often fall in the woods and against which tents are no shelter. In short, nothing can be done in strict conformity to the usual military preparations and according to a regular manner, bush-fighting as they call it being a thing peculiar by itself."[74]

One thing is for certain there were bloody encounters. Still, there was never any intent to kill the oppressors when interactions occurred in the mountains immediately, and it showed amongst the Maroons' actions. An attack was launched when their freedom was threatened. Times were changing, and enslaved Africans could negotiate their release with their oppressors. One might say this was an upgrade from being kidnapped. At some point, the British and Maroons must have had a conversation to address the repeated attempts to destroy the Maroons' freedom. Researching my Jamaican roots has been liberating and, at times, emotionally heavy. So, in my effort to step out of the emotional heaviness while still honoring my ancestors, I'd like to give my theatrical account of how the conversations between the British and Maroons could have occurred.

Envision the soldiers, planters, colonists, slave owners marching uncomfortably up the mountains to confront and capture runaway enslaved people, not understanding these self-proclaimed freedmen had enough physical and mental power to delay their aggression and arouse fear.

British: Hey guys, you gotta come back down. You're not allowed to be up here without us.

Maroons: Ehhhhhh, with all due respect sir (or not), we're not going back down. This is now our home, and we want to be free. We deserve to be free. This was promised to us by our Maker. You can't take that away.

British: Actually, we own you, and you guys have to come back down because we said so.

Maroons: Own us? You stole us. We're not going back down. And if you can't deal with that, then we're going to have to fight to see what happens next.

Perhaps the conversations were as simple as this? Or not.

Of course, no one knows precisely how these non-physical interactions played out. But there was a constant yearning to negotiate with Maroon leaders to subdue the number of revolts and attacks on the island. The enslaved Africans' behavior in Jamaica between 1655 (when the British arrived and even before) sent shockwaves to Europe and the American colonists and started to change the overall attitudes towards slavery. "The whole Island remained in great Terror and Consternation for some time," a British squadron commander observed. The enslaved Jamaicans often attacked and then dispersed, frustrating the militia's attempts to track them and stop them from harassing estates near the edges of the forest, stealing supplies or damaging property. The colonists [in an attempt to combat the Maroons] would sometimes burn their crops to try to starve the rebels out of the woods, but struggled to supply enough troops to pursue many separate insurrections. This problem grew worse as the conflict dragged on and members of the militia deserted."[94]

I believe the Maroons consciously and powerfully gave their oppressors a chance to choose peace regarding their treatment towards the Maroons. They gave the British the power to choose peace which is something the British never once offered the Maroons, only under their standards of freedom. At this point in consciousness, Maroons knew they made the utmost attempts to avoid physical battle. "Edward argues that the primary cause of the first Maroon war was that the white planters and the militia members were becoming more aggressive towards the Maroons," Harris sub quotes from Bryan Edward's, *The Proceedings of the Governor and Assembly of Jamaica, in Regard to the Maroon Negroes*.[12] Since the slave owners kept denying their freedom, the Maroons had the right to fight for and protect their liberty at all costs, powerfully so. A Colonel Cornwallis from England who was sent to Jamaica along with other troops in the hope of defeating the Maroons described their hardships and frustrations after arriving on the island: "I'm sure there is not an officer here but with Pleasure would go to the most desperate siege rather than Stay in this damned unwholesome place for then one should have a chance to gain some credit or die honorably, here no Reputation to be gained & no service to be done."[74]

In addition to calling Mother England for aid against the Maroons, the British colonists even tried unsuccessfully to enlist their enslaved Africans and others of non-African descent to fight against the Maroons. All routes were being tested. This occurred during the 1730s at the time of open warfare between the Maroons and the British. By the 1730s, mixed wars were happening in Jamaica, with Africans fighting on both sides. This highlights centuries of Jamaicans and British working together. The British could not beat the Maroons on their own. We start to see, in earlier stages of the enslavement of Africans, a change in humanity in Jamaica due to these revolts.

CHAPTER SEVEN

The Power of Consciousness

The Silent Killer

♪ *Luciano – It's Me Again Jah*

♪ *Turbulence – Notorious*

*K*nowing what's right, and sticking to what's right, despite fear, triumphs in the long run. In this chapter, I start to use the term *God* heavier. We can replace the word with the Ultimate Power in our life that signifies Love. This Supreme Power could be the Self. More eye-opening than the fear rested among Europeans was the Africans' ability to endure oppressive cicumstances and still prevail. Europeans in Jamaica and other settlements carried a contagious mentality that anyone of non-European descent was less than human. In the 18th century, Jamaicans psychologically proved they were mentally more robust and that this fight was so much more than skin color or ethnic origin. The courageous step to fight back revealed a more considerable weakness amongst the British: fear. Fear was something the Maroons recognized as the bigger enemy when they saw how Europeans reacted to their love and respect for music and dancing. Europeans showed fear of harmless acts by trying to ban certain instruments and dancing on the island. With this realization, the Maroons' focus was to defeat fear. They were able to defeat it enough to create a powerful air in Jamaica building on itself ever since. They realized the conflict was no longer between them and any other human being; it was between Self and fear. And if they could defeat fear, then they could conquer any system operating from fear too. The battle against fear set the mentality for Jamaicans forever.

Racism developed in the United States in the colonial era. Before there was a label that described the ill-treatment and attitudes whites gave Blacks, Jamaicans eliminated that by immediately imposing an attitude in response to Europeans and their wrongdoings, and being able to maintain it throughout centuries. Because of their attitudinal approach regarding fear, the word racism never existed in Jamaica. Jamaicans achieved a high level of knowledge on the power they had and used consciousness as their weapon. They understood we are all human beings with nearly the same body makeup, with color being one of the few things that make us different. Jamaicans understood we are all equal, which was enough reason to fight for one's freedom.

This is the most critical psychological shift we, as humans, currently have reached as a group. Yet, racism is still prevalent worldwide, which means another shift is crucial in order to further influence environments still stuck in time. We have seen pivotal movements in America like the Million Man March movement and, more recently, the Black Lives Matter movement. The people behind these actions of recent times and Jamaicans from the past and now all understand that belief in Self makes one unstoppable in achieving what God says each human can have and achieve.

War was not the Jamaican's first option. If that were so, they would have initiated it when they first arrived on the island. Eventually, they had no choice but to engage in it to protect themselves. There is an extensive history of enslaved Africans believing in their freedom and themselves that led to uprisings until 1831, leading to the final abolition of slavery in 1834-1838 in Jamaica.[115] Tacky's Rebellion in 1760 was led by an Akan leader known as Tacky, who was once an Asante chief on the Gold Coast before being sold to Jamaica. He led this rebellion, killing over 60 white people, before being shot by a Maroon. The uprisings lasted for months, igniting other revolutions.

When I visited Accompong, I learned Maroons are still divided regarding religion and spirituality. Their first church that is still standing is the Church of Accompong. They believed in Christianity and still practice traditions brought from West, and Central Africa called Kumfu, where a supreme deity rules the cosmos but doesn't want human contact, so instead, spirits or *duppies* communicate with them to navigate through the world's obstacles. The actual matter of these spirits is known as Obeah. Obeah is said to have come from West Africa, which aligns with that region primarily influencing Maroons' customs. It is similar to a more familiar term, voodoo, practiced in places like Haiti and New Orleans, although each of these regions has distinct ways of practicing. The Jamaican Maroons do not worship gods. Instead, the focus is on spiritual and physical healing through ancestors. "…Europeans in Jamaican slave society were unable to conceive of the possibility that the slaves did not wish to be christened because they had their own alternative to Christianity…. 'They find no change produced in them [by christening] except the alteration of their name.'"[20] Obeah was used as a tool and was not looked at as the ultimate power to worship, as was the case with Queen Nanny, one of Cudjoe's four siblings who led the Maroons. She is said to have to use Obeah as a tool to help in the fight against Europeans. It is said she could catch bullets and launch them back at her enemies, although we don't know how true this is. The mysticism of Obeah, however, was so influential that Florence Nightingale, the founder of modern-day nursing, used the blueprints from Nanny and other Jamaican doctors, such as Grace Donne (Simon Taylor's main lover, the richest sugar planter in Jamaican history) and Cubah Wallis (William Cornwallis mistress who also treated Prince William Henry). These blueprints included what was perceived as magic and witchcraft but was really the usage of traditional home remedies with natural plants and herbs and exercising good hygiene.[98] The influence and power of Jamaican women is discussed further in later chapters. Also, a Senegambian named Boukman, who moved to Haiti from Jamaica, is one of the figures credited for igniting the Haitian Revolution in 1791 with the Vodou ceremony. The Maroons and other African freedom fighters likely influenced Boukman in Jamaica.

Obeah was said to have been successfully used as a tool in the Windward Maroon's decision to stay neutral in The Second Maroon War. They avoided deportation to Nova Scotia because of it, which was the fate of many Leeward Maroons. The British asked for the Windward Maroon's help against the Leewards, but an Obeahman is said to have strongly advised them not to go as they would be deported. The Windward Maroons listened to the Obeah man and did not join the British. Soon after, reports emerged that they would have indeed shared the same fate as the Leewards. About 600 of the Leeward Maroons were deported to Nova Scotia in 1796, where they lasted until 1800, and then many returned to Sierra Leone.

In Jamaica, it was evident that whites aided some revolts. As there was a force to achieve freedom from slavery by enslaved Africans, it was also reciprocated by whites who were anti-slavery, although the power was not strong collectively among whites. William Wilberforce, the co-founder, and leader of the Committee for the Abolition of the Slave Trade submitted many bills for abolishing the slave trade. His perseverance eventually led to the 1808 abolition of the British Trans- Atlantic Trade from Africa. William Knibb was a Baptist missionary who came to Jamaica in 1825 to spread Christianity amongst the enslaved population and faced significant opposition from fellow whites. He received blame for one of the most destructive slave rebellions in the Americas, the Sam Sharpe Rebellion known as The Baptist War. Over 200 plantations were destroyed, and the atrocities were so dismal that the British eventually drafted their first version of the Emancipation Act of 1833. This type of dynamic force between Black and white was a force for advocates of slavery to reckon with.

Giving people a choice for peace and freedom is a Godly act. When the Maroons offered this choice to their oppressors in their conquest for freedom, they were touching dimensions that scared the Europeans into retreating and developing a peace treaty. Jamaicans relied on their belief in God, which was their inner power to fight for peace and freedom. In their reliance, they were reversing the curse that began when humanity created the slavery system.

CHAPTER EIGHT

Peace

Peace Without Racism, The Possibilities

♪ *Cocoa Tea – Sweet Life*

♪ *Protoje – Like Royalty (ft. Popcaan)*

Jamaicans know love and harmony amongst different races in any one country is possible. This new plateau has permanently shifted them into a new dimension from many places in the world still fighting racism. In the previous chapter, we looked at how the psychological shift in the enslaved influenced the Europeans' outlook on slavery. The rebellions that occurred all over the Americas eventually led to the universal will of abolishing slavery. As I proceed through my Jamaican heritage, I pose questions for all of us to consider. Would the Europeans have adopted an elevated level of awareness to co-exist with free Africans without a physical battle with the Africans? As inequality issues persist today, does the African diaspora need to adopt the same energy their ancestors did centuries ago to solve present-day challenges? Does the African diaspora need to familiarize themselves with their roots and history to understand what has or has not worked in the fight for freedom and equality? Taking on another perspective, can the European diaspora, whose wealth is built primarily from Africans' enslavement, increase their contribution to the improvement of urban environments where the African diaspora is seriously in need? How much effort will it take from either side to understand their roots and place in slavery, what steps need to be taken to make America, and all countries where racism is rooted, a place all people would be proud to represent?

I grapple with those perspectives as I regularly reflect on my experiences while growing up and living in America. There is a difference in energy between my homeland and that of my parents. Without the frequent trips as a child, teenager, and adult, I would not have known energy in the form of power was so vital. It is the most essential and valuable currency in this universe. There is a profound sense of confidence I feel amongst Jamaicans of the African and non-African diaspora.

The resistance from particular African groups caused Europeans to focus heavily on catching and controlling rebels, specifically the unstoppable Maroons. "For Edwards and other planters, their political control of the Maroons provided an alternative model to abolition, letting them worry about the 'Tackeys among us,' that is, specific rebellious slaves, rather than the institution of slavery."[94] Suppose one read this from Bryan Edward's perspective, author of *The History of the West Indies (1793)*. In this case, it seems to him that having political control was going to be a successful alternative to abolition in the time it was advocated for. He was so power-hungry; he did not recognize that suing the Maroons to sign the peace treaty was the beginning of all African people in Jamaica reclaiming their freedom. The rebellions initiated by the Akan were rampant and intimidating enough to have colonists urge for their importation into Jamaica banned. After 1765 when a bill was proposed to prevent the importation of Coromantees, Edward Long, an anti-Coromantee writer, stated in disappointment of its rejection: "Such a bill, if passed into law would have struck at very root of evil. No more Coromantins would have been brought to infest this country, but instead of their savage race, the island would have been supplied with Blacks of a more docile tractable disposition and better inclined to peace and agriculture."[105] We can safely assume that the Maroon wars lasting from about 1690 to 1832 changed the course of history and paved the way for ultimate freedom for Africans in Jamaica.

The war's loss led to a peace treaty between the British and Maroons in 1739, but the conditions included Maroons agreeing to catch other runaway enslaved Africans to keep the autonomy. Although this did not stop the Maroons from secretly helping runaway enslaved Africans, we can rightfully wonder why they agreed to do such a thing. At the same time, it's interesting to think what would've happened if they decided to disagree with the treaty and continue their attacks to avoid helping to catch their own. Would other Africans have assisted in the fight as well? Did they consider the risks? Or was it something they only agreed to predominantly do on paper? We see instances in Tacky's War where it was the Maroons that killed him. It is worth mentioning that Tacky was known to sell Ashanti slaves to the Europeans. Tacky suffered the same fate by being sold to a rival army, subsequently leading to his death. Perhaps he was still seen as an enemy amongst his own, but then there are cases that are not so. Ultimately, Samuel Sharpe, who led the Baptist Army and now graces Jamaica's $50 bill, wanted to peacefully fight for more freedom and a better wage. Britain, with the help of the Maroons, defeated Sharpe and his army. The Maroon involvement in these battles continue to be of debate. These wars, however, had shed more light on the brutal working conditions on plantations and accelerated emancipating enslaved people from slavery. The enslaved eventually were able to take a lot of their power back after the abolition of slavery in Jamaica in 1834-1838 and with independence from the UK in 1962, though there is still political jurisdictions Jamaica needs to strengthen their stance in so they may part and be completely independent.

Before moving into Part 3, I would like to summarize my thoughts on this book's previous sections. Beginning with the Maroons' evolution, Jamaicans have lightly tapped into the fifth dimension with their ability to overcome fear and live free at any cost. Why do I use the term *lightly?* Because the issues of poverty and crime have attempted to interfere with Jamaican's complete ascension. Even though this weakness exists, Jamaica has capitalized on its' strength to walk confidently in our ancestors' purpose. Jamaica can continue to evolve as a collective between Jamaican leaders, Jamaicans at home and Jamaicans abroad. We are at a point where we don't need to fight in the ways we once did before because we have evolved into increasingly conscientious human beings. We can learn to stay at an elevated level of awareness by studying the Akan people's evolution throughout their journey from Africa to Jamaica, especially with their influence on the Maroon development and other slave rebellions across the Americas. We can learn new ways of being and doing from history so we do not repeat the same mistakes.

Although I believe Jamaicans have lightly tapped into the fifth dimension with their ability to overcome fear against their past oppresors, I observe the island still struggles with familiar issues stretching back to the homelands before European rule. These issues prevent Jamaicans from collectively ascending permanently into the fifth dimension and beyond, where total awareness and peace feels more reachable; poverty and crime at the utmost need attention. I do believe, with the right leaders capable of building on Jamaica's weaknesses and capitalizing on her strengths, like any othr nation, that she can officially be locked into the fifth dimension here on earth; a spiritual realm that tourists can feel a difference in when they visit the island. It's going to take a collective effort between Jamaican leaders, Jamaicans at home, and Jamaicans abroad, all walking confidently for the purpose our ancestors courageously fought and upkept for us.

I invite us to use our conscience, which transcends color, ethnicity, race, and nationality. We are all connected. When we use our conscience, we are choosing what is right. When we choose what is right and just, we are choosing love and peace for ourselves. When we choose love and peace for ourselves, we choose love and peace for those around us. It is our natural state to live in peace and acceptance. Our inward peace influences our environment. The change starts within, and our courage to change, to choose what is right, affects our environment. Peace and justice that have been fought for up to this very moment have allowed me to write this book freely as a young, Black woman.

Our evolution to overcome fear and racism and move entirely into love and acceptance will affect generations to come. While our dance may not look exactly alike, the point is that we do not stop dancing. Our music may not sound alike; the matter is that we do not stop singing. Sound and dance provide the vibrations that bind us together over troubled waters. As Bob Marley would say, "One Love."

PART THREE

Recurring Behavioral Patterns That Have Traveled Through Generations To Present-Day Jamaica

While this book highlights the strengths of Jamaicans, there are many relatable and similar cultures. The Maroons were present in French Guiana & Surinam, Haiti, Dominica, Cuba, Louisiana, Florida, Dominican Republic, Puerto Rico, Brazil, Colombia, Ecuador, Nova Scotia, Panama, Guatemala, St. Vincent, St. Lucia, Honduras, North Carolina, Mexico, Nicaragua, Belize, and Virginia, so this storyline may be consistent with the energy in an environment familiar to you. Aside from this, there was a resistance that occurred in every place Africans were enslaved. It is my hope that by the end of the book, people will be moved to trace their roots, to discover their strengths and weaknesses; honoring where we all come from. For this project, the big question for me based on my experience with my family primarily, in addition to traveling back and forth to Jamaica, is why are Jamaicans collectively so strong?

Throughout my research and travels to the island, I observe Jamaicans maintaining a strong a sense of pride, unity, hard work, and they cherish competition. They regularly celebrate life, through music and dance, for no other reason than to acknowledge their existence and its temporariness. Nearly all island parish bars are filled with loud speakers booming different sounds of different genres at times. Reggae music can always be heard at any time of the day throughout the country, at the airport, on the highway, at the restaurants, at the beach, on the streets. I knew all these factors were connected to something extraordinary. To maintain the fearlessness, we now see music, dancing, and public celebrations have been the constants of Jamaican culture throughout generations.

If music and dancing had been banned in Jamaica, what would society be like now? I imagine not as celebratory and vibrant. Yes, societal issues currently exist, but their togetherness eliminates many non-progressive judgments and quarrels. Could we reasonably apply this workable formula in other areas of the world where similar issues persist today? If we promoted the party culture more along with the most basic and moralistic principles, would it be so bad for our Westernized-dominated societies today?

CHAPTER NINE

The Rebellion

Jamaicans Don't Wait To Take Initiative

♪ *Mavado – Messiah*

♪ *Chronixx - Odd Ras*

Jamaicans don't wait to take initiative. The fight for freedom extends back to the beginning of the first human beings living in Jamaica on record, the Taínos. Africans shortly joined them in the mountains. Since then, the determination for freedom never relinquished; the energy only heightened and multiplied. This determination is best proven and demonstrated by the Maroons' actions that defeated colonists in Jamaica, and other places throughout the Americas. They were relentless in their fight for freedom and inhabited swamps, mountains, and complex areas hard to access by the Europeans. Colonial governments were forced to initiate or sign treaties for the Maroons that secured their autonomy for their operations to continue peacefully. "But it is only in two areas, Jamaica and the Guianas, that the descendants of Maroons have continued as separate and distinct communities into the present. In Jamaica, descendants of the 17th and 18th century Maroons still live on the land their ancestors defended, ever conscious of their past as guerrilla fighters whom the British could not defeat."[74]

Fearless

Women lead. The matriarchy line is respected in Jamaica. We will find several examples of women in power throughout this book. Although her brother Cudjoe was the leader of the Western Maroons and, her brother, Quao, was considered the Eastern Maroons leader, Nanny was the driving force behind the rebellions initiated by her brothers.

Queen Nanny is a Jamaican hero born into the Ashanti tribe of Akan, present-day Ghana. She freed over 1000 enslaved Africans and helped them to resettle into the Maroon community.[99] The Queen was reputable for her Obeah powers and always left one of her enemies unharmed in battle so they could live to retell the story. There are many myths about her. She served as both a physical and spiritual leader and had a comprehensive knowledge of herbs and other traditional healing practices from Africa. Before visiting Accompong, I was under the impression that Queen Nanny died in the war; this is based on internet findings. In Accompong, I learned Queen Nanny was never killed but died of old age. Her face graces Jamaica's $500 bill today, almost equivalent to the $5 bill (due to volatility, Jamaican currency changes quickly). There is a monument of the Queen in Moore Town, Jamaica, formerly known as New Nanny Town.

Like Nanny took the lead in the past, her stories are reminiscent of Jamaican women I have come to know so well today. The initiative I see Jamaican women take is most evident in their household and workplace. Their attitude is often described as stern and serious, yet always loving or caring. It is common to have women as spiritual leaders of their household, which is in accordance for a country known for having the most churches per square mile in the world. Regardless of their financial or other circumstances, women manage most of the affairs. They bring order inside and outside of the home. Having Queen Nanny on one of Jamaica's most circulated bills is very representative of the women in Jamaica who assume leadership for their family and everyday environments, just as the Queen did for her brothers and the Maroons.

Akan culture is one of Africa's traditional matrilineal cultures, where descendants are traced through the mother's ancestral line. In reggae music, it is common to hear the adoration of women in songs by some of the island's notable artists. In dance, women take the lead. Although the Jamaican male often expresses his existence through pure confidence and ego, they have undeniable respect for a woman's spiritual position in their lives, especially grandmothers and mothers.

This matrifocal spirit was a new paradigm for Europeans. In a personalized letter from a German woman in Jamaica to her cousin in Germany, she writes, "the white women of Europe are not worth much here; instead of working, they become overly fond of luxury and spend about 12,00 ecus of their husbands' money per year. Therefore, those who do not wish to spend so much on a white woman prefer to buy a Black woman from Africa. Aren't there as many members of the human race as are European women? And of what importance is the color of their skin?."[35] This letter paints a detailed picture of the attitudes and angsts that rested on the island. This letter is dated December of 1778.

Returning to Jamaica to build or add on to a home is a part of one's life goals for many Jamaicans. It is common to see Jamaicans go abroad, mainly to the U.S. and the U.K., to build a strong financial foundation, only to return to Jamaica to build homes for themselves or their family. To this day, it is common for Jamaicans to work multiple jobs, which has afforded many the ability to acquire real estate in Jamaica and other countries. It is important to note here that acquiring land has become somewhat of a sport for Jamaicans, and always the most essential and valuable asset to secure. I witnessed my father, my maternal grandmother, and many relatives take this similar path. My dad established a financial foundation in the U.S. and then went back to Jamaica to build a home from scratch for his family, where his childhood home (or more like a shack) once stood decades before. I spent many summers, school vacations, and overall downtime there, and at my maternal grandmother's house.

I found an 18th-century document detailing the actions of runaway enslaved Africans in Jamaica. The detailed descriptions of how certain enslaved Africans lived give us an idea of how horrid the conditions were for enslaved Africans on plantations. A slave owner, who described his runaway as a 'negro boy who loves to play his fiddle', repeated the young boy's claims to someone else in his written search for him. He would "rather cut his own throat sooner than return to his Master."[16] This freedom or death attitude is reminiscent of what exists today in Jamaica and mirrors a popular Igbo characteristic of resisting (reading the young boy's claims instantly reverted my mind to things my mom say when she absolutely refuses to do something, "me radda [rather] dead than"…)! I equate the modern-day First World entities, the USA and the U.K., to the white supremacy Africans were running away from in Jamaica. Even if it's not in the most literal way as it once was during slavery, Jamaicans, in a sense, are still running away to a better life.

We continue to create our own language. In the first section, when we detailed the Jamaican Maroons' journey, it was noted that the language of the Akan eventually dominated other languages from Africa that made it to Jamaica. In Jamaica, the Akan language became a mix of African languages, with Spanish and English influences.[17] Aside from the Maroons adapting to the Akan language, I found no evidence of other Africans being forced to adopt the Akan language and dismiss their tribal ways of communicating. I believe the other Africans felt compelled to adopt some of the Akan language, when necessary, as they were often the dominant group. Perhaps this adoption of the language was an attempt to learn of the Akan's militant ways, although we cannot say this trait was sought after by all who wanted freedom. Maybe the various tribes thought adopting the Akan language would contribute to unity versus spending time learning everyone's language respectfully. We can assume time was not on their side, and getting to the goal of freedom superceded all other plights. As far as language goes today in Jamaica, while it's still influenced mainly by Akan culture, with heavy traces of the Igbo language as well, they create their own language regularly. One would think with language regularly changing that communication would be confusing. However, as a testament to Jamaicans' unity, when a new word or saying is created, it travels throughout the culture quite rapidly. We will hear expressions initiated amongst the younger generations, like "Ya mon (no problem)," "Dead with laugh (dying with laughter)," "Y pree (what's up)," "Everything irie (everything's fine)," "Wah gwaan (what's up)," "Big man ting (serious business)," "Nyam (eat)," "Blouse and skirt (appropriate slang when expressing suprise)," "More fiya (more fire)," "Raggamuffin (poorly/roughly dressed)," "Gyalis (player)," "bless up," "Earthstrong (birthday)," "soon come (I'm coming)," "My yute (homie)," "Bun (cheat on)" or "big up (respect)," amongst a long list of other idioms that develop powerful meanings and become a part of the everyday language.

CHAPTER TEN

Acceptance

Jamaicans Make The Best Of Their Circumstances, So They Can Advance Closer To Their End Goals

♪ *Damian Marley – Living It Up*

♪ *Koffee - Toast*

Jamaicans make the best of their circumstances, so they can advance closer to their end goals. The following is a descriptive scene of Jamaica's community during the late 19th century in Kingston town. "On landing in Kingston, new arrivals in the 1890s often encountered a full harbor and a vibrant market scene. Laborers in distinctive Jippi-Jappa hats, businessmen in morning coats, and East Indians in dhotis, all haggling over prices. Finely dressed women abounded. Single and double horse-drawn traps recruited passengers while mule-drawn tramcars offered alternate means of transportation. Even though they had to jump over open drains, there was electricity and potable piped water. The city was booming, there was a good reason to believe that a pedlar [another word for a 'legal hustler'] would do well."[56]

From Jamaica's earliest years of being inhabited, Taínos and Africans showed early stages of accepting each other's traditions and customs by proving they could coexist to survive and conquer the mountains together. The social climate of Jamaica today possesses a spirit of togetherness. Jamaicans, like many people, want to gain a life of total wellness emotionally, physically, and financially. These individual feats make the collective stronger.

When Africans came to inhabit the island, they recognized their environment and physical reality. However, to live and survive in the new environment, they used their available and intangible tools; their memories of their tribal traditions and customs, and new knowledge resulting from their growing engagement to traditions and customs from other cultures. Today, in many Westernized environments, it seems crucial African elements of togetherness, acceptance, and merely honoring customs have been ignored and seldom recognized.[20]

The customs of the people contribute to the unique energy in Jamaica. I recall watching a Rasta respond to a curious wanderer's question about Jamaica's special vibe, the wanderer continued his inquiry with, "What makes the island so special?" The Rasta responded mysteriously with a smirk and said, "it's not the island; it's the people." The Rasta's bright smile and confidence have remained in my memory. I have relied on these experiences to add to my thoughts and research in creating this book.

Today in Jamaica, there is an estimated 2.5 million Blacks, 5,200 Chinese, 20,000 East Indians, 4,300 whites, 162,718 mixed race, and 1,900 'other' ethnicities that may include the Irish, Lebanese; and 17,500 people were unreported. It is said that well over 400,000 Jamaicans are also descendants of Jews, although they may no longer practice Judaism.[58] When researching famous Jamaicans and their ethnic backgrounds, most peoples were mixed with so many ethnicities that it was hard for me to create conciseness, so I am noting only a few examples. Regardless of where one comes from, it is apparent everyone identifies themselves as Jamaican without explanation. This is the confidence I take great pride in as a Jamaican. This pride in their country has made it easy for Jamaicans to teach and share with others their music, dance, and spiritual/religious practices from their ethnic traditions.[24]

The colorful population of Jamaica is becoming increasingly evident to the world. Chris Blackwell and Sean Paul (also of Chinese descent) are two famous descendants of Jews. Some famous Chinese-Jamaicans are the NFL player Patrick Chung, Jamaican politician and Miss World 1993 Lisa Hanna, supermodel Naomi Campbell, supermodel Tyson Beckford, and reggae singers Tami & Tessanne Chin. Some notable people of Lebanese descent are Edward Seaga, the longest-serving member of the parliament and a former Prime Minister of Jamaica; Lisa Hanna is also of Lebanese descent. Some notable figures of East Indian descent: dancehall legend Super Cat, international superstar Diana King, Miss Jamaica Universe 2010 Yendi Phillips, R&B singer Justine Skye, and the recent Miss World 2019 Toni-Ann Singh. Alexander Bustamante, Jamaica's first prime minister, and the beloved Bob Marley are both of Irish descent. Colin Powell, the 65th Secretary of State to the US, was of Scottish descent. I realized many also all fall under the mixed category, such as Sean Paul and Liswa Hanna, considering their other contributing ethnicities. It is popular to integrate with other cultures on the island. Given the amount of older or now deceased mixed Jamaicans we know of today, it's been popular for quite a while.

Jamaican culture is a vibrant expression of the many enthusiastic people that make up the country. The island inspires writers, artists, dancers, musicians, and creators of all talents to explore the rich beauty in the painful ache of the past to the present. And they have settled themselves all over the world.

Jamaican cuisine is a culmination of cultural variants accepted by Jamaican masses over time. Certain foods have become staples of Jamaican cuisine. Some of the foods contributed to the Jamaican cuisine by the Taínos were cassava, sweet potatoes, corn, ginger, pumpkin, cashew, callaloo, guava, papayas, and various seafood. Bammy, made from cassava, is a popular complimentary type-of-bread commonly used with fish or chicken; its long-refrigerated life also gives life to its popularity (and was especially so for the colonial masters in slavery days). Seafood was a big part of the daily diet with popular dishes that still are popular today like parrot fish, groupers, lobster, crab and shark; and the popular Jamaican custom of making soup on Saturdays is traced back to the Taínos who believed in "Out of Many, One Pot," although Africans brought with them the tradition as well. The soup is still a mix of vegetables, meat, and/or seafood customary to the Taínos. Africans made thicker soups with beans and peas. Jamaican soup today is a combination of both legumes, vegetables, seafood, and meat.

Original African dishes are indicative of their resourcefulness. Using what they had, Africans created dishes using yams (fufu), okra, cocoa, and interestingly, ackee. Ackee is a fruit that can be poisonous if it is not ripe and the pink membrane and seed is not removed before cooking; it is so potentially deadly that it is regarded as poison in nations such as Haiti. Jamaica's national dish, a mix of ackee & saltfish, as well as the mix of mackerel and banana known as *rundown*, are just two examples of a generational cooking tradition of combining different foods.[30] Africans introduced the style of marinating meat and using cooking pits. One of the myths behind why Jamaicans run so fast is their widespread consumption of yams. It is quite common to find this in soups or as sides or substitutes for grains to compliment a dish. The yam was also the most important crop for the Akan & Igbo tribes in Africa. They both still have an annual yam festival celebrated to thank gods for their ham harvest. Yam is pretty important. Diet and food preparation was quickly adopted by others who migrated to the island from other countries.[20]

Jerking, one of the most popular styles of Jamaican cooking, can be traced back further than the Maroons. The Taínos and their ancestors most likely invented the technique of barbequing, which is similar to jerking, just with different spices. They used Barbacoa, a wooden grate on four sticks, to slowly roast meat and fish over slow fires. Africans would use their creative skills and add other herbs, such as the famous scotch bonnet pepper from West Africa.[31] The Akan introduced the style of jerking by roasting meats like pork over coal and branches. Today, Boston Beach in the parish of Portland, an area in the Blue Mountains where the Akan once heavily populated, is a popular tourist destination for their famous jerk pork, chicken and seafood; with yam, bread, festival or breadfruit typical for accompaniment.

The Spanish introduced fruit trees such as coconut, banana, plantain, ginger, lemon, lime, and tamarind. They also brought over cattle, goats, horses, pimento, and sugar cane to the island. Oxtail, cow foot, stewed peas, all popular Jamaican dishes, and most beans and pea dishes are Spanish influenced. Frying, cooking and baking methods such as soaking fruits in wine for celebratory cakes were also introduced by the Spanish. The popular escovitch fish and gizzard pastry originated in Spain.

The British introduced several Jamaican staples today, including molasses, breadfruit, black pepper, and coffee.[31] Coffee came to Jamaica in 1728 when Sir Nicholas Lawes, Governor of Jamaica, imported Arabica seedlings from Martinique. The breadfruit was brought to Jamaica in 1793 by Captain Bligh from Tahiti.[32] Portland became a new home for both the coffee and breadfruit crop. Coffee is now one of Jamaica's most significant exports, in addition to bauxite, cane sugar, yams, and alcoholic beverages. The molasses contributed to Jamaica's development of reputable rums and produced most of the world's dark rums. Britain's love for sweets is also evident in other well-known Jamaican pastries, like the Easter bun, Jamaican drops, Christmas/rum cakes, grater cakes, and puddings. It is also said that the beef patty originated from the British's Cornish pastry, consisting of meat and potato in it.[31]

The Scottish were have said to influence Jamaica's love for porridge.

The Chinese are known for their style of stir-fried, deep-fried, and steamed cooking technique, having a 'sweet and sour' influence on the island. They also brought pak choi, another popular staple in Jamaica for farmers.

East Indians are responsible for everything involving curry, from seafood & meat to vegetables & fruits. They introduced rice, which is now an essential part of Jamaican cooking, often the complimentary choice with a chosen meat (often oxtail, curry chicken, curry goat, jerk chicken, stew chicken fried chicken).[24] The East Indian mango is a famous mango on the island, and they also brought over the Julie and Bombay mangoes.

The Lebanese brought traditional foods that became a part of Jamaican cuisine, such as Syrian bread, hummus, and stuffed grape leaves.

Rastafarians introduced us to I-tal food, which is a vegetarian delicacy. Rastas believe we should eat what's natural from the earth. Their plant-based attitudes were directly Hindu-influenced, as the religion's founder, Leonard Howell, was fascinated by Hindu practices. Being the strictest of the Rastafari mansions, Nyabinghi is the only mansion that requires that Rastas eat only I-tal food. Their main dish is of Jamaican influence, but without salt fish. Their dislike of meat and seafood is strong, even with saltfish being apart from the national dish. I recall listening to Chronixx on speed one experience, "Dah Fish Deh come a far way, dem bring him from Norway, hey, a couldn't Rasta dem a try fi trick, cause Dat cyah be me national dish." It is seafood that comes from the Norway area and was imported to Jamaica from Nova Scotia in the 18th century. It is safe to assume this was most likely around the time Maroons were deported to Nova Scotia in the last 18th century, geographically close to the Newfoundland area.

The community structure of Jamaica is notably influenced by the multiple cultures that moved there. The Taínos survived in the wilderness and shared their knowledge of medicine and plants with Africans, who would later join them to form the mountains' Maroons. The enslaved people had no choice but to adapt to one another and create a new society. They made new traditions for courtship marriage and childrearing. However, with 300 years of colonization, the British had an enormous impact on Jamaica. Jamaica's government, the judicial system, military, police and education are modeled after the British system. Schools and most churches are British-influenced.[24] While the British established

Jamaican society's formal structure, Black Jamaicans created a large portion of the ancestral feel of the culture; through spirituality, art, music, food, style of dress, social relationships, family structure, and language.[24]

The Jamaican Jewish community was established after their arrival under Spanish colonization, although they did not receive voting rights until 1831. By 1849, eight of the forty-seven members of the colonial assembly were Jewish. That year, the Jamaican Assembly became the first modern political body to shut down shops and celebrate the Jewish holy day, Yom Kippur, which is still celebrated.[26][65] Jamaican Jews, Joshua and Jacob Decordova started the first news publications on the island, the Jamaican Gleaner, that still operates today. Although they have been small in number, they have had a notable influence on economics, politics, and commercial life.

The Irish were familiar with British rule before arriving in Jamaica, as they only gained their independence 25 years shy away from Jamaica's gain in 1962. It seems they were known for their love of laughter, spirits, women, and pastimes like horse-racing. Simultaneously, some were known for bad habits that included excessive drinking.[54] Drinking is apart of everyday life in Jamaica for many. The Jamaican Constabulary Force is modeled after the Royal Irish Constabulary, evident with the red stripe on the pants leg.[54] This could perhaps have influenced the famous Jamaican Red Stripe beer. Digicel, one of Jamaica's (and the Caribbean's) leading mobile phone network carriers, is owned by an Irish billionaire. The Irish priests and nuns taught in Catholic schools across the island. A proud Irish writer wrote of her surprising discovery of the Irish-Jamaican history, and in that piece, she mentioned that "they landed in Kingston wearing their best clothes and temperance medals."[29] They laid their roots and contributed to Jamaica's evolving island and motto, 'out of many, one people.

It seems as if the German population we first discussed in part one phased out over time, but German towns still exist throughout the island. Seaford Town, the most famous German Town, often used interchangeably, still exists in Westmoreland. Today we will see descendants with distinctive blue eyes and long nose features. Other existing towns with German descendants include German Town in Trelawny, Alexandria, Christiana, Brown's Town, Stewart Town, and Ulster Spring. There are various videos online of a small number of German descendants speaking about their heritage confidently. Manhertz Gap, Charlotten-burgh, Mount Holstein, Bremen Valley, New Brunswick, and Hessen Castle are all towns in Jamaica that are German-influenced.[35] I am eager to see the German population revive and their evolution progress on the island. I believe there is more to the German-Jamaican story.

The Chinese influenced Jamaicans with their values, such as the importance of hard work, the extended family, and education.[24] The Chinese started their businesses when the sugar and banana industries crumbled. Some Chinese-Jamaican families own supermarkets and restaurant chains, such as SuperPlus and Island Grille. Currently, they also control the NCB bank in Jamaica. Eventually, in the 1940s, the Chinese-Jamaican descendants began to speak out against their families' desires of marrying into their culture and begin embracing other aspects of the Jamaican culture.[55] This is evident with the many Chinese persons mixed with other ethnic groups there today.

East Indians made contributions to Jamaican society as artisans, jewelers, merchants, fishermen, manufacturers, barbers, and shopkeepers. The descendants have also largely influenced medicine, farming, politics, and horse-racing.[57] A lack of ships available during World War I severely limited the ability of second-generation Indians on the island to return home. The Indian government also grew unfavorable of repatriation of Indians who served as indentured servants, as they often returned home in poor conditions, and therefore became burdens. Over time the social caste system became less of an issue among the Indian community, and arranged marriages were no longer common. In everyday life, Indians often tended their gardens and filled their evenings with storytelling, singing, ganja smoking, and drinking. Their contribution towards Jamaica's upbeat, positive spirit is evident in their celebration of Diwali, where they value the victory of good over evil. It is common to find African-Jamaicans alongside their Indian-Jamaican brothers and sisters for Indian cultural festivals like Diwali.[57] Many Indians have also intermixed with the other ethnic groups on the island.

Also coming from Asia were the Lebanese, giants of retail, tourism, and manufacturing.[33] The first set of Lebanese to arrive on the island seemed to have moved there intentionally. They were looking for better environments to live in to run from civil wars and downturns within the economy, and better territories to migrate to than America with their civil war between the north and the south just concluding. British represented freedom to the Lebanese, so they sought to live in any British-owned country for protection.[56] Many of these Lebanese people remained in Jamaica after their servitude ended. Sometimes they even returned to Jamaica after going back home to get married. Because World War II limited the second generation of Lebanese from returning home to marry, Lebanese became heavily immersed in the Jamaican way of life.

The Rastafari structure is patriarchal-dominated, where women are subordinate to men. Women have a lesser role in the movement, and as a result, abortion and contraception are forbidden.[63] In general, they believe materialism and bills take away time, therefore take away from our life. They believe the material and the spiritual world should not be divided.[41] As a result of these ways of life, we'll see Rastas having their communities in Jamaica, generally separated from society like the Maroons in the mountains. Many Rastafarians are integrated into regular society, however. Rastas practice levity with strict attention to prayers and meditation, loving behaviors towards others, and a natural lifestyle, most notable with their signature Ital food and the wearing of dreadlocks. "Rastas respect nature as a manifestation of Jah and sees it as a vast source of knowledge. Furthermore, Rastas understand ancient African warriors wore their hair in dreadlocks. So their hair brings them even closer to their roots and is an expression of their unique identity."[41] Fire is a crucial element of the culture, and its symbolism is known to purify and eliminate misunderstandings. The Rastafarians' teachings aids in liberating the minds of the impoverished Jamaicans, having an undoubtedly profound effect on Africans' consciousness, especially.[42] I believe the Jamaican government seems to appreciate Rastafarians more as they continue to work towards a crime-ridden society: increasingly voicing support of the community over the decades following tension between the two in the 50s and 60s, paying respects to Rastas who have made lasting impacts in Jamaica and the world, and often collaborating with musicians and other people of fame or nobility in the ever-pursuit of balance on the island, both of and outside of the Rastafarian culture. The term *I & I* is used instead of 'you' or 'me' to symbolize God's overall awareness of oneself and others alike. They don't consider themselves special brethren, and they believe guidance only comes from God, not a human being.

There are several private and public hospitals in Jamaica, including a university hospital, a pediatric hospital, and various health centers and clinics throughout the island. The National Health Fund subsidizes some prescription drugs used in the treatment of chronic illnesses such as diabetes. Jamaicans believe their healthcare system needs significant improvement as hospitals often face scrutiny. Regularly the media shares sad stories with the public, like that of Jodi-Ann Fearon, a pregnant woman who died after being turned away from a hospital. There are hundreds, and possibly so, thousands of which we never hear about. On the other end of the spectrum are groups of people like certain Rastafarians who do not utilize human-made medical remedies and don't believe in doctors. As a result, they tend to avoid the healthcare system and stick to herbal doctors. There is robust generational respect for natural remedies in Jamaica. Even in recent times, with the emergence of Covid-19, a Jamaican therapist in Florida successfully cured himself with Jamaican natural remedies. "Respiratory therapist at Brooklyn's Maimonides Medical Center got infected with the coronavirus — but was able to fight it off and eagerly returned to the front line," using turmeric, garlic and ginger.[100] Raeburn Fairweather was featured in a New York Post where they lauded him for his ability to take care of himself so he could return to taking care of his patients. This is a common practice with Jamaicans at home and abroad.

There are two major political parties in Jamaica, the People's National Party (PNP), founded in 1938, and the Jamaica Labor Party (JLP), founded in 1943. Both have been alternating running offices since 1962 since Jamaica's first prime minister was elected, Sir Alexander Bustamante of the JLP. There have been nine prime ministers in the office since; Sir Donald Sangster (JLP), Hugh Shearer (JLP), Michael Manley(PNP), Edward Seaga (JLP), Michael Manley (PNP), P.J. Patterson (PNP), Portia Simpson-Miller (PNP), Bruce Golding (JLP), and Andrew Holness (JLP). Each party and leader deserves their respctive research, as each brought something distinctive to King's House (Jamaica's version of the White House) and progressive for Jamaica overall. Portia Simpson became Jamaica's first woman to be elected as Prime Minister and was once ranked by Time Magazine as the '100 Most Influential Persons in the World' in 2012. Both parties have demonstrated their commitment to Jamaica's development and improved the island's inhabitants' quality of life. "We are Jamaicans, strong, resourceful, resilient; and when this is all over, we will be stronger than ever. Nuff love, nuff respect, and one love still" was said by the current prime minister in response to the pandemic of Covid-19. Andrew Holness is currently Jamaica's Prime Minister who recently won the 2020 election, serving in office for a third term. He was the first prime minister to be born after Jamaica gained independence in 1962 and has been lauded for his progress with Jamaica's development with such a short time in office, though Covid-19 has brought on more tumultuous times for Jamaicans. There are various branches of ministries in the government, and they serve multiple purposes falling under Jamaica's pertinent societal needs. It is a 3-part parliamentary democracy under the legislative branch modeled off the Westminster System. It consists of a Governor-General, a Senate (the Upper House) consisting of 21 Members of Parliaments appointed by the Governor-General, and the House of Representatives (the Lower House) consisting of 63 Members of Parliament elected by the Jamaican people. The Members of Parliament are known as MPs who are responsible for the 63 constituencies spread out throughout Jamaica. The MPs under the Prime Minister's cabinet currently led by Andrew Holness of the JLP, as well as the MPs under the Leader of the Opposition cabinet currently led by Mark Golding, run for office every five years, dividing the political representation in each House.

Jamaican households are more matrifocal, and nuclear families are most popular, especially amongst the middle and upper classes. Mothers have a strong bond with their children, especially their sons.[34] Children are raised under strict ideals but with a lot of love and nurturing. Girls are giving household chores more than boys; however, it is common to find Jamaican men trained in cleaning and cooking from a young age under matrifocal influence.[34] Inheritance is typically allocated evenly and usually with land, the most common source of contention in families since it is often of most value. I find it to be accurate in areas such as the countryside, where families have owned the same land for generations, such as mine on botht he maternal and paternal side.

Men are affectionate towards their children, but the mother generally handles childrearing.[34] The father typically holds a stoic, respectful stance who the mother or grandmother can fall back on for child support. Grandmother, or *Granmas*, are highly revered. In the *Man Free* documentary, the importance of the *Granma* role is highlighted with a story of a community Granma who had been working at a place known as Boys Town since 1964.[99] She shared her reasoning behind the actions she had come to be respected for, "It doesn't matter who, it doesn't matter what color, it doesn't matter who the child is, since the child needs help, I am willing to do it... I feel they [the children] belong to me. I am their grandmother. I provide for them sometimes. I do everything for them. If their clothes need to wash, I can take them home to wash them. If they have no food, I'll supply it. And I pledged that as long as I can manage, as long as I have life, I will serve them." This is a very standard view of elders in Jamaica.

To me, the way Jamaicans raise their children is no different than how they treat each other. The same "disciplined" and militant attitude is exercised, although it may be on a more frequent scale with children. Parents are known to "exercise a kind of sovereignty over their children which never ceases during life, chastising them sometimes with much severity."[20] This is true for both my maternal and paternal side of the family and the case for most Jamaicans I know. It can be challenging to be raised by Jamaicans. However, I believe this intense directness contributes to the quick maturity amongst the younger Jamaicans. And over time, respect is returned. I read an observation from slavery days, "they are in general so attached to their families, that the young will work with cheerfulness to maintain the sickly and the weak, and they are much disposed to pay to age respect and veneration.[20] The ways of childrearing contribute to the respect that adults maintain for their parents. I have disagreements with my mother, and I speak my mind with passion at times, but disrespect is never an option with any of the elders.

To address more about the family unit, lower-class households tend to have a higher volume, including "children of previous relationships, children of poorer relatives, informally adopted children," and children of daughters who migrated to urban areas or abroad worked.[34]

These are basic common practices within the Jamaican culture, to help take care of others' kids and loved ones. In Jamaican households, food is used as a way to keep the family unit connected. For example, family members who come home and be welcomed with food on the table are heartfelt love languages between relatives.

Socially-accepted non-legal unions most commonly follow extra-residential relationships. The marriage unit tends to be the most popular amongst the middle and upper classes and tends to happen after having kids. "Divorce is rare, but extramarital relationships are common."[34] Jamaican weddings mostly resemble English and American weddings and consist of African influence with their inclusion of family and community in their wedding planning, French with the influence of gifting fruit/rum cake to guests, and Scottish influence of gift-giving from wedding guests. Miss Lou, who excellently recounted the Jamaican way of life through her Jamaican folklore, included the Jamaican wedding customs in her folkore. As Dr. Rebecca Tortello detailed from a piece by Miss Lou in the book, *A Tapestry of Jamaica: The Best of Skywritings*, "dress included the latest trends like satin and lace. Dinner included foods like mannish water, curry goat and rice, chicken and rice & peas, roast breadfruit, and roast yam as just a few examples do today."[53]

Freedom of religion in Jamaica is a law. Nearly every major religion is practiced in Jamaica, with their respected places of worship found throughout the island. Religious discrimination is outlawed except a colonial-era law that still criminalizes both Obeah and Myal, both practices that have a focus on the supernatural. Religion was not institutionalized in the Caribbean and Africa like it was in the western world.

Christians represent the largest religious group on the island, including most Protestants, followed by Roman Catholics and Jehovah's Witnesses. Protestantism has several denominations, including the most notable, Church of God, Adventism (Seventh-Day Adventist), Pentecostalism, and Baptism.

After Christians, Rastafarians represent the second-largest group, followed by Muslims, Buddhists, Hindus, Jews, and Bahá'ís. I imagine there will be a new set of statistics to cover the 2010-2020 decade soon. Here are the most recent breakdowns I could find comparing statistics from Britannica in 2008 [36] to _____ in 2011:[37]

(36) —> (37)

Church of God: 24% —> 21.2%

Seventh-Day Adventist: 12% —>12%

Pentecostal: 10% —> 11%

Baptist: 7% —> 6.7%

Anglican: 4% —> 2.8%

Other: 20% ——> 25%

Other also includes (but not limited to), approximately:

Roman Catholic: 2%

United Church: 2%

Methodist: 2%

Reform: 2%

Jehovah's Witnesses: 2% —-> 11,334 [49] (the year is unclear)

Moravian: 1%

Brethren: 1%

Rastafarians: 24,020 —-> [(25,000)[40] 1.1%

Bahá'is: 8,000 [38]

Muslims: 5,000

Hindus: 1,453

Jews: 350

Unstated: 6%

No religious affiliation: 21% —->21.3%

98% (International Religious Freedom Report, 2008). —> 100% [37]

I suspect the missing 2% entails Buddhists, Bahá'is, and Sikhs.

When Africans arrived in Jamaica, they brought with them their various spiritual practices and religions, each tribe with their traditions. Ultimately, with several different Africans on the island in the 18th century, they collectively formed the Obeah and Myal practices. "The Obeah man was a doctor, philosopher, as well as a priest. It was difficult to discern whether the Africans had any religious beliefs or practices since the only external signs were Obeah."[20] However, the Ashanti tribe from the Akan region, who were primarily sold by the Fante as captives and imported by the British to Jamaica, believed in a Supreme Being named Nyame. The Akan believed in one Supreme Being but also believed there were gods under the Supreme Being connected with humans. "The African negroes of the West Indies...whatever superstitious notions they may bring with them from their native country, agree in believing the existence of an omnipotent Being, who will reward or punish us in a future life for our good or evil actions."[20]

For Ashanti, the title of their Supreme Being, Nyame, was Nyankopon, which means an alone or great one. Like the Europeans did with African words they couldn't pronounce right, they made their version of the title and instead used Accompong. Overtime, Obeah became a practice associated with evil, and Myal became the practice that freed one from spells cast by the Obeah man or Obeah woman. As a result, Europeans generally built up fear against the Obeah practice, and the 1898 Obeah Act was established. Today, that fear still looms, and the practice is typically shunned upon. This is as evident in the music as it is in reality. Jamaican artists will site inefficiency in a prideful manner when Obeah threatens their spirit or what they tend to believe in. "Little can be said with confidence as to the religious beliefs of these people. The influence of the Koromantins seemed to have modified, if not entirely obliterated, whatever was introduced by other tribes, recognized, in a being called Accompong, the creator and preserver of mankind; to him praise, but never sacrifice, was offered...... The tutelary deities included the departed heads of families and the worship of such was almost the only one observed to any great extent by Africans or their descendants in Jamaica."[52]

In Jamaica, Obeah is an Afro-American religion that focuses on spiritual and healing practices, practiced mainly by the Akan people, although its origin is debated to have derived from the Igbo when researching the origins on my own. There are no gods that are worshiped, which makes Obeah a little different from other West-African-based religions, such as the more popularly known Santeria or Vodou. Myal is a variation of Obeah that focuses on the connection between spirits and humans but with a more complex process. Obeah and Myal practitioners became rivals but eventually joined forces to combat white oppression. Only Obeah continues to be practiced, although it is not popular.

Kumina is an Afro-Jamaican religion started in the late 18th century.[42] It was a rigorous dance that grew popular and eventually turned into a religion. It resulted from the tension between Obeah and Myal, and their mission was to expose and reveal hidden secrets of witchcraft and bad medicine.[41] What was common among these three religions, Obeah, Myal, and Kumina, is the consistent respect they all had for the ancestors, mainly because their ancestors' presence reminded enslaved Africans of their African roots and seemed to provide meaning and direction in life.[41] The law that prohibits Obeah has rarely been enforced since Jamaica's independence from Britain. The fear which was once present with the British eventually disappeared as the practice became more private and less collective, possibly even immersed into the culture overtime though no evidence can be found, leading to the lack of urgency or attention the Jamaican government has had on The Obeah Act or The Obeah Law since its independence. Although Obeahmen and Obeah-women still exist, they do not appear to be a primary concern for independent Jamaica compared to other issues that affect the island. However, I read several articles in the Jamaica Star, where police officers actively pursued those being accused of harming others through the Obeah practice. As of 2019, there have been actions taken within the Jamaican cabinet to have the Obeah Act repealed.[39]

Jamaica's first Muslims came from West Africa as Moors as early as the 16th century under Spanish rule. Indians also held regular weekend prayer meetings and special ceremonies to commemorate Hosay and Eid's

Islamic festivals. There are 11 mosques throughout the island, including the Al Mahdi Mosque, and festivals are still celebrated on the island, including The Ramadan Fast.[40]

European Jews escaped persecution in Europe in the 16th century and found freedom in Jamaica to practice their religion, at first, disguising themselves as Portuguese when the Spanish ruled. The Shaare Shalom Synagogue, first built in 1885, still stands today, and is now accompanied by the Chabad in Montego Bay that opened in 2014.

Roman Catholicism was introduced to Jamaica in 1504 when the first Spanish settlers arrived. This was the first type of Christianity presented to the island before being removed by the British in 1655 until 1837. Irish priests and nuns taught in Catholic schools throughout the island for generations. Germans practiced Roman Catholicism when they arrived under British rule, and their Sacred Heart Catholic Church is one of the oldest churches in Seaford Town. The British in 1655 replaced Roman Catholicism with Protestantism. Protestantism ultimately became associated with the anti-slavery movement, and it is most likely the reason Jamaica remains predominantly protestant today. In 1664, Anglicanism was introduced, and the Anglican St. Jago de la Vega Cathedral was erected in Spanish Town, the most senior place of continuous worship in the western hemisphere. George Liele, a once enslaved African from America, brought Baptists to Jamaica in 1783. The Baptist Wars of 1831 initiated by preacher Sam Sharpe ignited the British to abolish slavery in 1834. Methodism was introduced in 1789 by Dr. Thomas Coke from England.

Seventh-Day Adventists were introduced to Jamaica in 1890 when The Coming King book was sent to James Palmer, who passed it on to an eager upper-class white woman in Jamaica named Margaret Harrison, well-known for her care of the sick and the poor.[46] Today, Jamaica is known to hold one of the world's largest conferences for Seventh Day Adventists. Pentecostalism began in 1916 during World War I with Methodist Mother Russell's zeal for sharing the love of God.[43] Presbyterianism came around 1824 by Scottish reverend George Blyth.[45] The Church of God, which represents the largest group of Protestants, has about 111 various congregations, including the Moravian church, the United Church in Jamaica and the Cayman Islands, the Society of Friends (Quakers), the United Church of Christ, the Ethiopian Orthodox Tewahedo Church, and the Brethren Christian religious groups. They even have a Mormon congregation, the Church of Jesus Christ of Latter-day Saints, that was finally able to have some movement in the 1960s after two failed attempts in the 19th century.[48] Many early Christian opponents of slavery came from congregations such as Presbyterians, 'Methodists', Baptists, and Quakers, who were labeled nonconformists due to their disagreement with the Church of England's principles.[51] Today, there are more churches on the island than anywhere in the world.[47] In a way, Jamaicans have revolted against their oppressors with their nonconformity to the Church alongside the acceptance of other ideals and creation of their own practices.

I believe apart from the reason enslaved people warmly accepted Protestantism and its denominations was because of the energy behind the white missionaries. "The Blacks resented British missionaries' attempts to consider and promote themselves as leaders of the afro-Jamaican communities in all things religious, moral, and cultural. For one thing, most Blacks considered their morals, dancing, drumming, concubinage, the Christmas festival, and Sabbath-breaking as private concerns separate from their religion. Also, British missionary pastors discouraged baptizing or christening illegitimate children. The implication of these postures and arrangements was that 70 percent of the afro-Jamaican population was barred from British missionary or orthodox Baptist churches."[61] Missionaries weren't as present in the early years of slavery as they were in the last because the British were fearful of Africans using religion to counterattack their cruel treatment.[51] However, this was not as much the case for new emerging Christian denominations such as Baptism, Presbyterianism, and Methodism missionaries, as British missionaries from the past. "The only objective was a perverse desire to gain notoriety particularly in England, and make money by piggybacking on the slaves' relentless struggle for freedom."[61]

Not only did they accept certain protestant denominations, but Blacks also mixed their Myalism beliefs from West Africa with the new religious denominations Americans and British were bringing to the island, giving birth to Pocomania, meaning 'a little madness'. The Great Revival that lasted from 1857-1860 in America had an extraordinary influence on the entire Western World, including Jamaica, which emphasized on one's personal relationship with God, instead of relying solely on ministers. This new wave for the love of God started amongst the Moravians in St. Elizabeth in 1860 before spreading throughout the whole island.[60] It gave way to three various sects, Pukumina, Revivalism, and Revival Zion (Zion Movement).[64] "God was the topic of conversation everywhere - in the market-place and shops, amongst merchant planters and field-hands alike.

Although, as usual during authentic revivals, the whole town was in excitement, some were mocking and some praising God."[60] Pocomania also received criticism from some British. "No clapping of hands, no playing of musical instruments, no dancing and swaying of the body, no speaking in tongues, nor getting into the spirit," or wearing costly clothes were allowed; leading to the need for Africans to revive their faith.[61]

Shalman Scott poised a great question in his article detailing the rise of revivalism in Jamaica, "how do you separate an African from his/her drums, music and dancing, etc. — those cultural norms and patterns that characterize their way of life for millennia and long before the arrival of the European slave traders?"[61] He ends with reminding us how "the rise of revivalism in Jamaica served the loudest purpose and expressions of our ancestors' defiance to secular injustice and recognition that the long arc of their worship of God must bend towards an Afrocentric trajectory." Pocomania was the most prominent religion indigenous to Jamaica before Rastafarianism came in the early 20th century.

Indians and their descendants largely practice Hinduism. The Sanatan Hindu Temple and the Prema Satsangh Mandir are the only temples in Jamaica, the former being recognized by the government. Indians held regular weekend prayer meetings and special ceremonies to commemorate weddings and Hindu festivals such as Diwali.[57] There are two Dhammadipa Vihara monasteries Buddhists in Jamaica call home.[40] I wasn't able to find any statistics on Sikhism, but the presence is said to have been there.

Taoism, Chinese philosophy and religion, seems to be extinct on the island as many Chinese have turned into Christians. The Chinese temple,

Taoist Kuan-Kung Temple, has still been standing since its inception in 1897. It is no longer used for worship, but Chinese-Jamaicans still visit during important cultural celebrations. Its original organizers, the Chinese Benevolent Society in Jamaica, continues to manage it and focuses on dispute resolutions within the Chinese community.[50]

    Rastafari was the first Afro-Jamaican religion started in Jamaica in the 1930s; relatively speaking, not many decades have passed for such a strong following. Followers generally worship God, or Jah, a shortened form of Jahweh or Jehovah found in Psalms 68:4 in the King James Version of the Bible. They did not worship Jesus and instead looked at the Emperor of Ethiopia, Haile Selassie I, as the second coming.[41] Ras Tafari was Haile Selassie I's real name before his coronation; *Ras* means 'head' and *Tafari* meaning 'one who is respected'. Rastafari often attracts people from the poorest communities, but largely those with minimalist attitudes of all backgrounds. They have faced heavy discrimination from the police; I imagine because the Rastafari attitude of autonomy is a force to be reckoned with, but the relations between the Jamaican government and the Rastafari community continue to grow amicably. I recall while watching a documentary, a Rasta stated, "people don't love Rasta, because they don't know how to love themselves." Rastas undoubtedly carry a vibe of gratitude even when having little to nothing. Many Jamaicans have adapted the Rasta attitude without being strict adherents to the religion or lifestyle. *Don't Haffi Dread* by Morgan Heritage is a legendary song that explains this. The attitude of the Rasta is indicative of their influence on music. Rastas are known to use music to self-identity and rebel instead of using violence. It is noteworthy to mention the term Rastafarianism is considered offensive to some Rastas who are widely known to oppose '-isms'.

Religion is somewhat of a paradox. I do not label any religion as good or bad. Religion can bring division, but it can also establish a human connection and connection to God. This paradox explains why so many religions are practiced in Jamaica today. "The defiance by the slaves resulting from such an attempt at indoctrination explain the turbulent interface and clashes between the opposite sides of the argument and illuminates the reason for so many diverse religious groupings in Jamaica. Clashes between conformist and nonconformist churches resulting in a breakaway of the membership to form their own religious sect preceded the mass coming together in the vicious slave rebellions, which has become a common part of Jamaican secular and religious history."[61]

There is something more potent than a religious system that can link so many people who practice so many different religions. My thought is that the ultimate religion that exists in Jamaica is Love. Nowhere in the world do I see over 100 various denominations coexisting with such ease. These different practices exist in a way that is not immediately identifiable. Religious tension is non-existent except for Obeah, a practice frowned upon, with its most serious repercussions being raised eyebrows and major social distancing. With a further look into Obeah, it has a negative connotation. Perhaps, looking at Obeah as the Ultimate Power instead of just a tool is where the disassociation begins with Jamaicans and those who practice the controversial way of life. Not to take away the power of Obeah and what it speculatively did for their ancestors during slavery, but I think the Jamaican people also have found a more profound influence in something else, especially after The Great Revival in 1860-1862. "For slaves, it wasn't always simply *God* as their limit but often African religion as a whole, with its pantheon, ancestor worship, ceremonies, dancing, and magic. God as the limit is more evident in movements after the Revival when elements of Christianity openly fused with African religion on a large scale."[41] There was a shift in consciousness caused by the Revival, which distanced Africans from the magical and superstitious elements. However, shouts, spirit possession, music, and dance were still used for expression. The numerical results of conversions, confessions, baptisms, and overall church attendance, were so high that it seemed to have wiped out old superstition beliefs connected to Obeah.[60]

I have initiated conversations with my mother regarding Obeah, only to be quickly dismissed. This is common amongst a lot of my Jamaican family and many Jamaicans today. According to my mother, Obeah does not exist. She has shared stories of getting whooped by my Granma for simply fearing a local Obeah-woman in her childhood. My grandmother then proceeded to the Obeah woman's house and challenged her to come outside and kill her if she's bad (my grandmother is strong advocate for God). The woman never came out, and it wasn't long after that she moved ouy of the community, a community near Black River, St. Elizabeth that I find very high in consciousness. I believe my grandmother's spirit was too strong for the Obeah woman. My grandmother is still alive today. This is how seriously elders took the influence of Obeah on their descendants, and continue to. Why? It is unclear to me as of right now. I will admit it is quite mysterious, and that mysticism perhaps evolved into a more powerful tool for defense than fear.

After doing more thorough research on The Great Revival and its influence on Jamaica in its time, I believe this movement, too, had a profound impact on Jamaicans' future affairs, including their attitude, desire for unity, and overall pride. Their value on redemption, which I noticed not to be as favorable among other societies in the world as it is in Jamaica, is unique and should draw more human studies from anthropologists and sociologists. It may have connections stemmed from Pocomania, as I read in Elizabeth Nelson's insightful work, "the Zionists saw great similarities between the suffering of Blacks in Jamaica and the plight of the children of Israel in bondage." They also believed that oppressed Africans would regain their humanity through spiritual redemption.[41][42]

Education in Jamaica is modeled after Britain's system. It was initially designed to integrate formerly enslaved people into the empire and maintain peace with the lower class, though enslaved Africans and indigenous peoples to the island were not educated in significant numbers until Jamaica emancipated slavery in 1834.[59][66] The Ministry of Education was eventually put into place in 1953, then called the Ministry of Education and Social Welfare. The Jamaican government has been working towards a better education system in the country ever since. There are four levels of education: early childhood education (preschool), primary education (elementary), secondary education (high school), and tertiary education (college/university).

There are both public and private schools throughout the island. Generally, private school curriculums must adhere to the same standards as the public curriculum. There is a stark difference in primary education in that it is possible to see public students leave without knowing how to read or write.[68] The national debt continues to consume a larger portion of the government's budget each year, continuing to bring obstacles to those working towards enhancing the educational system. Many children tend to drop out of secondary (high school) and higher education institutions so they can work to survive in Jamaica's reality.[66] Despite these obstacles, the government has been making significant progress and is committed to Jamaicans receiving a quality education. Since 2009, the Minority of Education has been demonstrating its commitment to implementing the Education System Transformation Program, giving more power and accountability to localities throughout the island under the Ministry of Education.

Jamaica has been highly successful in ensuring access to pre-elementary early childhood education. The country was recently recognized by UNICEF as "a model for early childhood development, thanks to the results of a pioneering early childhood program and near to 100 percent enrollment in early childhood institutions."[66] By the end of the 6th grade, every primary Jamaican student must take the Grade Six Achievement Examination (GSAT) to move onto secondary (grades 7-11). The new millennium began a pivotal century for the Ministry of Education, in 2018 Primary students taking the GSATs throughout the island showed tremendous improvements and nearly perfect stats.[68] Stefanie Babb pointed out Senator Ruel Reid's review, "Education Minister, Senator Ruel Reid, says that an overall increase in four of the five subject areas tested has seen significant improvement. Furthermore, 100 percent of the students registered for the examinations will be placed in seven-year high schools."[68]

The secondary is broken up into three parts: lower-school, upper-school, and an advanced post-secondary program, also known as Sixth Form. The Sixth Form covers grades 12 and 13, and though it is optional, it is very competitive in suburban and rural areas that serve a large number of students but with few schools.[69] First, the government is working towards making secondary education for all children under 18 both mandatory and financially accessible for all in the future.[68] Upper school education (grades 10 and 11) is designed to prepare students for the external Caribbean Secondary Education Certificate (CSEC) examinations conducted by the Caribbean Examinations Council (CXC), marking the end of secondary education.

If they want to move onto tertiary education to potentially receive a bachelor's degree from one of Jamaica's 20 institutions,[66] students must take the Caribbean Advanced Proficiency Exam (CAPE). In addition to the 20 institutions on the island, there are also 14 community colleges, one dental auxiliary school, one vocational training development institute, 29 vocational training centers, and six human employment and resources training vocational training institutions (HEART). A significant number of Jamaican students also have the opportunity to study abroad, whether through merit, visa-advantages to travel or study abroad, or financial background.

It is common to see many Jamaican students study abroad, mostly from upper-class sections. As the years pass, Jamaican students are enrolling less in US Institutions and more at Canadian institutions.[66] It's also noteworthy to mention that most Jamaican students are women, per a 2015 UNESCO statistic Trines shared in his *Education in Jamaica* article. "According to the latest 2018 Global Gender Gap Report of the World Economic Forum, 34 percent of Jamaican women enroll in higher education programs compared with only 20 percent of men. That's one of the highest such disparities in the world."[68] As a result of the changes that have been happening in the education sector, and taking into consideration the turnaround time, other Caribbean countries have consulted Jamaica's Ministry of Education.

I also wanted to touch on the country's approach to special education. Until 1974, the special education sector was run by voluntary organizations that took financial responsibility for exceptional children's care.[65] Today, the government intends to continue to appoint special education teachers to primary and all-age schools until all students who need such services have access.[65] Vocational training for young adults with disabilities is provided by private voluntary organizations and NGOs.[65]

The Jamaica Tourist Bsm is a course level developed within the last few decades that is offered to early childhood, primary and secondary students, ranging from age 4-20. The program allows Jamaican students to study further, *Who is a Tourist, Why People Travel, the Importance of Tourism, Anti Harassment, and Culture.*[69] This is an excellent program that further advances the understanding of Jamaica's impact on the world and the lucrativity of tourism. This program gives students an advanced view into the world of international business and how to form connections in a respectful and accommodating manner. Accompanied by at least one teacher, the top students get to stay in hotels and tourism-related organizations for one month. They cover the following topics while there: Tourism is our Business; Attitudinal Development; In Tourist's Shoes; Tourism and the Environment; and Trends in the Industry.[69] Students generally go on field trips to local tourist attractions as it is also a part of the curriculum for this subject.

Jamaica has several security forces, most prominent are the Jamaica Constabulary Force (JCF) and the Jamaica Defense Force (JDF). The JCF is a police officer force responsible for internal security, while the JDF is a force of soldiers responsible for major disturbances and natural disasters that disrupt the natural order of the island. There is also a small military present, consisting of the army, air force and coast guard services. Indecom is also considered a security force designed to be in protection of the people against unlawful or unethical behavior performed by the JCF or JDF. As their site states, "INDECOM, is a civilian staffed state agency tasked to undertake investigations concerning actions by members of the Security Forces and other Agents of the State that result in death or injury to persons or the abuse of the rights of persons; and for connected matters."

Jamaicans' style of dressing can get quite unique and has become famous, and it is an important element of the Jamaican lifestyle along with good hygiene. Being of excellent hygiene was and is of the utmost importance. Jamaica's first known inhabitants, the Taínos, wore very little clothing; men and unmarried girls were most often naked, though the islanders sometimes wore palm leaves, flowers, and short cotton skirts. The little gold that the Jamaican Taínos had was collected from the rivers. While they enjoyed wearing ornaments and decorations, they saw no need for the gold and traded it away for beads and other trinkets. I suspect Africans also coming from hotter climates dressed in a similar, scantily way. If we go to Jamaica today, people pretty much dress as anyone else dresses in a free country. Some are fully clothed, some are often not, ranging from religious or professional purposes to climatical reasons. One of the earliest understandings I had of Jamaican people in addition to talent and skill was the importance of style.

Fearless

From my experience, most people I see working in Jamaica do not work in corporate offices. People work as taxi drivers, they work in factories making goods, and they work in service positions for the hotel and tourism industry, if not working self-sufficiently as farmers and similar roles. My family have their farms in the hills of Lumsden, St. Ann and the red-dirt grounds of St. Elizabeth. When nighttime falls and the work day ends, everybody, no matter what profession, wears their best-dressed, or clean apparel. I recall seeing this day to night transformation during my childhood in St. Elizabeth. All the local guys working on farms surrounding my Granma's house put extra care into their nighttime wardrobe when it was time to relax, chill, play dominoes or Ludi (a popular game in Jamaica influenced from Indians) and get rambunctious with one another; and listen to music spewing from loudspeakers. It's all a part of the vibe.

During holidays Jamaicans are in their best clothes. During slavery, they also appeared during their holidays, "decked out with a profusion of beads and corals, and gold ornaments of all descriptions. Where the gold came from is not indicated or suggested. Is it possible that it could have been smuggled over on slave ships and accumulated over the years on the island?"[20] I do believe there is a possibility that Africans brought gold over from their countries. For instance, Ghana is one of the world's leading exporters of gold, and as we now know, a large portion of Jamaicans originated from Ghana, also known as; The Gold Coast. The same was true for Indians who came decades later, where elements of traditional Indian dress can be found in Jonkonnu processions where Jamaicans dress up in elaborate masks parading public streets, that are known to invoke scary memories for Jamaica during their childhood.

Fearless

When it comes to parties today, it is prevalent to see women amongst all classes in revealing clothing because Jamaica has a hot climate. Not all Jamaican women dress risqué, but those who do can be found everywhere, every day. I view judgments on the way Caribbean women dress as being dramatic and ignorant of other cultures outside of what they know, typically by non-natives. There is no oddity about this way of dressing. "Slave children, as children in West Africa still do, wore party-colored beads tied around their loins; sandals, cut from ox-hide, which they bind on with things, were also worn on occasion by adults. In general, however, slaves went barefoot, and many of them, especially 'new' Africans and/or field slaves when working, were described as being naked or almost naked."[20] With the hot climate enslaved Africans were accustomed to in Africa and now Jamaica, this was the norm. Today, the "batty rider" is popularized by Jamaican women, a type of shorts that leaves a tiny bit of flesh from the bottom part of the bum out. *Batty rider* is a term popularly enhanced by Buju Banton's song *Batty Rider*.

During slavery, the colonial government demanded sufficient clothing be given to enslaved people, and penalties were given to slave owners who disobeyed. "In general, the Negroes in Jamaica are weakly clothed, and there are very few Sugar Estates where the Negroes do not from their own private earnings provide themselves with extra clothes for Sundays and Holidays."[20] Perhaps along with harsh treatment, apparel judgments imposed on society by man, in this case, the British, resulted in the way people still dress today, and were the result of temptations, jealousy, and/or simple misunderstandings.

Jamaicans set high standards for their physical appearance. One cannot come "outta road" without a fresh bath and dressed in some of their best clothing. I've come to appreciate this quality of Jamaican life because it adds more vibrancy to the island. It is evident in the way both men and women take hygiene and physical appearance seriously that Jamaicans appreciate the splendor of life, even in poor circumstances.

The country's official languages, being a bilingual nation, are Jamaican English and Jamaican Patois. During slavery, Africans learned to communicate both with one another and with the colonists. We must remember many different African groups that speak different languages were brought to the island and were split up to avoid revolts. Finding a form of communication was essential to foresee a future without slavery. The forming of Jamaican patois is a combination of their past rulers, the Spanish and the [British] English, and African terminology. The Jamaican language is exaggerated with added facial and hand movements and uses phonetic spelling.[24] Their use of words is very intentional. Due to the considerable Irish influence at early points in colonization, most Jamaicans speak with the lilt of an Irish accent. Dread talk, also known as 'soul' or 'ghetto' language, is also popular, with words being often used, such as *brethren* (brother) and *Jah* (God). Rastas are also very well known to change their words because of their questionable connotations. They use words like *overstand* instead of *understand*; *Truebrary* instead of 'library'.[62] Rastas take things as small as words quite seriously. The general Jamaican population has caught on to the same trend, especially amongst men, changing words like 'Montego Bay' to *Galtego Bay* or disc jockeys using the term *1s and 3s* instead of 1s and 2s, because, for some reason, the number 2 is associated with homosexuality, and Montego Bay has the word "man" in it when we pronounce it. Jamaicans still use the term *pagan* but as a tool to condemn another for having the behavior of the devil. Having etiquette and manners is standardized throughout the country, especially within government establishments and amongst elders in general. Overall Jamaican etiquette is rooted in West Africa with greetings such as, "good morning; how is family," followed by the asking after each member in turn; they're polite loads of address-' compliments of respect and friendship, went speaking of or to each other' (uncle, auntie, granny, Tata), have their roots in West African forms of etiquette.[20]

Jamaicans apply their energy to their words, giving each syllable a definitive tone. The tone is often so powerful that it often overshadows the misuse of words, which is common and evident sometimes in Jamaican music. This is evident in regular conversation and in songs. An artist will use an incorrect word in a sentence not related to the content, but somehow, we'll understand the point attempted to be made through the energy elicited. I find that today, the attitude of not necessarily caring about the accuracy of a word, and instead, the point one is trying to get across to be rampant and especially so amongst older Jamaicans. A person with a more expansive vocabulary was assumed to be educated or in a better financial position, giving way to power. This mentality is linked to slavery, though grammar and usage is not as much a concern to poorer Jamaicans. Artists are not criticized for improper usage either. Yes, words have dictionary definitions, but it is the energy behind them that holds more life in Jamaica, that seem to supersede the importance of pronunciation, word usage, and overall grammar.

Jamaicans are known to be storytellers, a respected art and skill that survived from West Africa and was a poignant tool in keeping the traditions amidst slavery. Ms. Lou was Jamaica's most beloved storyteller, actress, radio personality, and educator; and notably brought Jamaica to the forefront of the literary world. She believed artists should express themselves in their native Jamaican language to encourage people to value their heritage and identity. When she returned home [from studies around the world), she became more interested in her native culture and decided to write and perform only in the Jamaican language. [24] She set the standard for Caribbean literature and paved the way for countries to claim their own identities separate from European rules. She was a true heroine, audaciously sharing her art in the manner she knew best when British hegemony reigned on the island. Miss Lou's contributions to the respect of Jamaican literature were so powerful that "the fact that its literature is universally recognized and respected is a disparaging clap-back to the [British] empire," or rather those that plagued the world with colonizing mentalities.[59] Her work continues to be studied and performed amongst Jamaican children in schools today. Even after moving to the States for better healthcare, her Jamaican pride never ceased as she saw Jamaica as a more spiritual realm than a physical place: "Any which part mi live — Toronto -o! London -o! Florida-o! —Jamaica mi Deh!"[59]

Enslaved Africans brought with them the tradition of orally sharing literature from West Africa. One legendary character is the West African spider Anansi, a trickster understood as a hero. It is probably the most essential and famous character in Jamaican folklore. Anansi's stories changed and developed into different plots throughout time, but Anansi represented empowerment for enslaved Africans and still holds significant relevance in Jamaica today. Anansi's characteristics include, but are not limited to, being clever and fearless in order to survive. Sound familiar?

One could also say the entity *duppy* is another important part of folklore culture. One will often hear Jamaicans talk about duppies or ghosts. It is primarily associated with people who have passed on but come back in ghost form to haunt people, although it is said good duppies come to send important messages and give advice. Maroons adapted the word *duppy* from the Taínos, but the elements mix from both African and Taíno cultures. It is a widely used word today, and it feels like many believe they are not real, as much as those who do!

Ganja has become synonymous with Jamaica and is probably Jamaica's leading stereotypical representation, if not dreadlocks. But ganja was not birthed in Jamaica. Indians came to Jamaica as indentured servants and introduced both ganja and the chillum pipe. The word ganja dates back farther than 1689 and is derived from the Hindi word *ganja*. Myal dances were often aimed at recovering spirits trapped by duppies, and marijuana/cannabis (better known as ganja/weed in Jamaica) and other hallucinatory drugs were used to enhance and enable the trance state.

For Rastas, the herb is smoked as a form of thanks to Jah, and the smoke rising from the burning herb is said to carry hopes and prayers of the Rastaman up to Jah.[41] Ganja was banned in Jamaica under the 1913 Ganja Law by the white elites and the Council of Evangelical Churches in Jamaica.[96] In 2015, just after a century later, laws started to change and the government began to allow limited cultivation and possession without it being a criminal offense.

Jamaicans aim to live a fulfilling life where when it ends, people can say "he/she was a good man/woman" or "he/she accomplished ___ in life." There is an insatiable need to acknowledge God and live by God's guidance. When one passes, celebrations commence the death of the physical body and the journey of the spirit. *Nine Night* is the custom to celebrate the ascension of a Soul from physical to spiritual for nine nights leading up to the burial. White observers described it as "'every kind of tumult and festivity'— dirges, drumming, horn-blowing, in the West-African Style."[20] The following closing paragraph from *Folk Culture of the Slaves in Jamaica* about the island's rich lifestyle is compelling.

"It should be clear by now that the life of the slaves in Jamaica was not devoid of ceremony and custom, as is popularly imagined, but, on the contrary, was especially rich in these respects. The survival of the Negro in the New Worlds, in fact, as well as his contribution to its emerging contemporary culture, is closely linked with this fact. This paper has tried to illustrate, sometimes by direct quotations, sometimes by implication, that this folk culture of the slaves is indeed part of a wider living tissue extending back to a great tradition of Africa and moving forward into the quick of our contemporary life and value systems. The presence of this rich tradition has been obscured by the ignorance of our literate education which, since emancipation, has been concerned with establishing the concept of darkest Africa and void's slavery, and providing us with the notion of that in view of the vacuum of our history, the only solution is salvation for us out of the impasse, lay in the acceptance of European cultural norms, even though these norms would, in the circumstances, lead only to the appearance of mimic-men, a bastard imitative culture, or as many would have it, no cultural integrity at all. With this in post orientation, it was perhaps only natural that we should have dangerously self-fulfilled this prophecy income to believe that we have, in fact, no way of doing things; or that we do, is relevant to the modern industrialized world of the business executives in that the manifestations of our culture in the life of the folk was something to be despised ignored and eradicated."[20]

CHAPTER ELEVEN

Love

Jamaicans Find And Show Joy In Reality, Despite Their Circumstances

♪ *Johnny Nash – I Can See Clearly Now*

♪ *Etana – Blessings*

Jamaicans find and show joy in reality, despite their circumstances. Love is arguably the world's most substantial value when it comes to coexisting. Jamaicans believed that love is the foundation for acceptance of Self, others, and the environment from the beginning of their culture development. Visitors notice quickly that poverty is prevalent in certain areas. In the same instance, visitors see that Jamaicans do not carry poverty on their shoulders. They remain grateful in their attitude toward life. It would be understandable if a visitor could not grasp how a person could show any contentment in such dire conditions because of the standards that Westernized environments set for their societies. While one may grapple with this, one would also challenge themself on what happiness is, and whether their posessions is really needed for happiness. Jamaicans are unforgettable in their attitude towards life's difficulties. It is hard to decipher who is poor on the island if one is not looking at their living conditions, because the focus seems to be on love, peace, and gratitude. Beggars are hard to find in certain areas because their gratefulness often leads to pride and abundance in some form. Communities often look out for each other.

In the documentary *Man Free,* a woman named Donnette, who founded her own baking business, does an excellent job explaining the attitude many Jamaicans exude.[70] "Being happy comes from inside, and if you don't have this get rich quick attitude, then you'll always be happy. Because I think it is your family or having someone around you that really cares, that really makes you happy. If money is the only thing on your mind, then you'll never really be happy. You have to be happy before the money; then, when you have the money, then you will be happy. And if you don't have the money, then you'll still be happy. My advice to young people like myself is to work very hard. Even when times get really rough, because it will... Sometimes it's gonna be hard, sometimes it's gonna impossible, but just continue work and you know if you believe in God then he is gonna pull you through. Sometimes the hard work, and this thing that looks so impossible, is just like getting you prepared for the roads ahead. My advice is never to give a head up and just keep on moving. I don't believe in failure, so I won't say anything about that. Just continue to work. If it's a million, out of one chance you get, work the entire million, and you'll get your own chance, that's it."

Donnette's thoughts perfectly summarize the Jamaicans approach to living intentionally, aware of their power to choose their emotions.

Jamaicans demonstrate an innate power and desire to serve in their everyday lifestyle. When Perry Henzell passionately explained his views on Jamaica, in part, he shared, "if your car breaks down in Europe, nobody will even dream of stopping and helping you. In Jamaica, if your car breaks down, five people will stop in the course of a few minutes to help you. Where does that come from? I don't know." This spirit is evident in the relaxed Jamaican way of life. Manners are an easy example to refer to as it is practiced everywhere, especially in public places, and is expected of visitors. Once upon a time, my mom told me when she was young, she would get whooped if she didn't greet a neighbor on her way to or back home from school. One man, *Mas*____ (shortened for *massa/master*, a term still used predominantly in the countryside amongst the elderly although it's becoming extinct) came back to my grandma and told her my mom didn't say hi. She got a whooping right after. Jamaicans encourage a supportive environment, and neighbors often look out for one another. We can link this power back to Africa; before introducing Christianity, "while individual success was not discouraged, it lacked importance if it did not benefit the common good of Akan society."[73]

Redemption seems to be a favored value in Jamaica. Redemption has ties to the strong religious presence on the island, and it is an essential principle in Christianity, Judaism, Hinduism, and Islam. Constant punishment is not a favored process in Jamaica, though it is necessary to combat crimes. Children are generally taught right from wrong and punished when making a wrong choice when growing up in a structured and disciplined household. Children are expected to and welcomed to improve their behavior through the constant love they receive. Notable reggae artists who have served time somehow have maintained or restored a good reputation and have continued respect amongst the public with their will to express their truth; especially so amongst younger crowds, most notably demonstrated by Jah Cure's, Vybz Kartel's and Buju Banton's charges.

Energy is contagious in Jamaica, as it is elsewhere, and with her strong spiritual foundation this works in her favor. It is normal to notice someone expressive with vibrant energy in public. It is common to see one person with high energy interacting with another whose energy may be more reserved and subdued, but accepted and revered. Yet, the respect and adoration within the interaction remain. In public places where shoppers, taxis, workers, hustlers, etc., are in motion, it is enlightening to watch how people connect in the most mundane activities. People work together in public to keep things in flow, with little governmental influence. Everybody has somewhere to go and something to do, and it is an unsaid spoken rule to proceed everyday with respect and manners, because there is no tolerance or anything else. The main town or marketplaces throughout each parish is an excellent way to see the coordination, as well as taxi stands, tourist adventures, and wherever you encounter everyday traffic.

Africans and Indians, as explained before, were smoking marijuana before they arrived in the Americas. Marijuana, also known as ganja, is not socially considered a drug in Jamaica, but rather a herb. Drugs, specifically cocaine, are discouraged. "We don't classify it as any drugs you know, 'cause it's so natural. We just put it in paper and smoke it. Where cocaine is not that way. Cocaine is like, it's so dangerous to the people dem weh you see use it. They get so very lackadaisical that they would prefer to steal and kill in order to get it, more than to get themselves constructive and do something constructive."[70] A Rasta shared this perspective from the *Man Free* documentary, echoing similar sentiments many Jamaicans share on the drug. Although ganja "Cocaine seemed to be the perfect companion for a trip into the fast lane. It provided energy and helped people stay up."[71]

Spiritually speaking, marijuana is perceived as a way to be more connected to the present for some, and for others, their ancestors.

Humor and sarcasm are embraced as a tool for growth. It's a form of exaggeration used to heighten the moment. Laughing is a sign of being present and showing appreciation for the present. Coupled with the use of sarcasm, Jamaicans use laughter as a smooth way of sharing wisdom and being critical of one's actions. There is a healthy sign of release from observation when expressing the truth and coming to terms with it. Even if someone tells us something we don't want to hear, it's difficult to be upset when laughter takes over. Laughter and sarcasm provide the space for being fearless in any environment. I find sarcasm to be a common vibe in music as well, with artists like Red Cat and his hit tunes *Shelly-Ann* and *Dwayne*, Beenie Man's *Romie*, or even Left Side & Esco's *Tuck in Yuh Belly*. Oliver Samuels, Miss Lou, Itty & Fancy Cat, Shebada, Majah Hype, are just some of the well-known comedians commonly known throughout Jamaican households. Majah Hype, a current hit comedian who is rumored to be Jamaican, doesn't disclose his nationality as his goal is to unite the entire Caribbean community without the interference of divisive ideas. He is known for doing skits in nearly all of the Caribbean dialects. Along with him are a rising group of incoming, talented, young faces taken over the social media world, slowly and strategically bringing their talents to other platforms while building larger audiences.

As I researched the Maroon's evolution and their forced move to Nova Scotia after the Second Maroon War, I retrieved a portion of their petition to be removed from Nova Scotia due to the cold weather, among other factors. "In the April 1798 petition to the government, the Maroons wrote, 'the Maroon cannot exist where the pineapple is not.'"[72]

I find the petition's text an example that Jamaicans have always found sarcasm and humor as a valuable survival mechanism no matter what the situation is. The art of sarcasm and exaggeration is completely normalized in Jamaica. It's a palpable and joyous phenomenon that contributes to their evolution, despite their environmental circumstances and lack of opportunities, in unique ways. Sarcasm separates the truth from the situations. It's a very abstract tool that can be used to draw out the truth if used properly (and of course, can be dependent on how hard one would want to hide the truth). We hear it everywhere, in music, in bars, in the airport, we can't escape it. I read a popular book called *Conversations with God* some years ago, and I recall Neale Donald Walsch, or God - one of the main characters, telling us readers that sarcasm was one of God's favorite things. I never forgot that, and it was only until recently that I've been able to make that connection. Exaggeration is a creative theme in Jamaican society that is commonly translated into sarcasm, and strategically so, the truth.

The respect for the hierarchy system is traced back to both the Tainos, mentioned earlier on in the book, and the Akan culture and its many tribes, including the Ashanti, Akuapem, Akwamu, Kwahu, Akyem, Agona, Wassa, Fante, and Bono tribes, who believed in having a large centralized governing hierarchy. They favored an order because they thought it put the community's welfare as a priority before the individual. "This may lay credence to the theory that many of the large plantation owners in Georgia and South Carolina preferred Akan captives to work their fields because of their reputation to adhere to a hierarchical system."[73]

CHAPTER TWELVE

Sound

Jamaicans Use Sound As A Tool For Peace

♪ *Beres Hammond – Rock Away*
♪ *Elephant Man – Higher Level*

Jamaicans use sound as a tool for peace. Music has always been known as one of the seven liberal arts and sciences of the universe, along with Grammar, Rhetoric, Logic, Arithmetic, Geometry, and Astronomy since medieval times in ancient Roman and Greek cultures. People are learning more about the healing benefits behind sonic frequencies, and it's not surprising to find songs like Louie Armstrong's *What a Wonderful World* or Coldplay's *Paradise* and *Viva La Vida* in the 432 HZ range, a frequency said to be the natural frequency of the universe. In science, we have learned that the universe was created from a "Big Bang" or an explosion that further expanded space. We will not derail far off from the topic of Jamaica, but this book emphasizes the importance of sound in our lives throughout history. Sound has played an instrumental role in developing and maintaining cultures, but practices get lost over time due to outside influences and pressures. However, things change once knowledge is in hand and ancestral awareness begins to increase.

Fearless

There was a connection between music and spirituality during slavery. Sound was used as a tool used amongst enslaved Africans to communicate with one another for revolutionary movements. Enslaved Africans used the drum to communicate, incite unrest, and cause revolts throughout the island.[20] In Maroon communities, they used the abeng to communicate with enslaved people over great distances, in addition to drumming instruments such as the gumbeh, bass, and repeater drums. Colonists were said to have been bothered by the "heathen" sound the drum brought and feared its influence over unifying enslaved people. The sound was such a powerful tool that complaints were rampant enough to have drumming banned, especially once the energetic effects on the enslaved was exposed.

Bass, or the drums, was the most popular and essential instrument in what would become one of the world's most influential genres, reggae music. Its roots were cultivated during slavery, beginning with the Kumina and Burru drumming styles. Kumina music stemmed from the Congo region, and drumming styles incorporated the Kbandu, and the Playignkyas used to evoke spirits. Burru music originated from the Akan-Ashanti tribe and used three drums for traditional dance: the thunder (bass), the fund, and the keteh (repeater). The funde, for instance, focused on carrying the heartbeat rhythm, so less improvisation on drumming was used (although improvisation turned out to be a feature of the enslaved Africans' songs and later birthed the art of freestyling and toasting). The Tambu also originated from the Congo, and it was used to communicate with the ancestors.

No efforts from the government nor pleas from colonists could overpower the drum's influence, nor the gatherings where drumming took place. Instruments played a vital role in the development of culture. The possible connection between instruments and frequency of behavior is a speculation to pursue seriously. Africans found ways to stay alive in the Americas by practicing their drumming customs. No matter how oppressive the environment was, the African rhythm thrived, although the extent varied across the Americas. We will focus on Jamaica and later touch on America's regions that had a heavy enslaved African population and what their musical environment was like in those areas.

The term reggae is broadly and loosely used to cover all sounds from Jamaica. Perhaps this is because it is the most influential genre to have been exported out of the island. Some clarifications need to be dissected and understood so people can know the various types of Jamaican music. Reggae is not the first official genre to be fostered out of Jamaica, and the styles that preceded it are often referred to as 'pre-reggae' styles due to the general misuse of the word 'reggae'. Reggae subgenres such as roots & hip-hop assumed similar responsibility of educating and awaking the people like reggae itself did. The genres gradually became more daring and expressive. They currently carry an accepted roughness that incites movement of the body. These different music styles should be studied extensively on their own as they each have a unique story about their development and influence on the world.

Folk music is the most indigenous music to Jamaica. Folk is a genre filled with tales often associated with life lessons to learn. Pre-reggae genres also first included **Mento**, a Jamaican folk music style brought over by enslaved West Africans that emerged in the 19th century but didn't gain popularity until the 1940s and 1950s. It also has European influences, as enslaved Africans were forced to entertain masters at the request of their favorite songs. The genre covers the people's social lives with a humorous touch, and the rumba box is used for bass. Mento is similar to Trinidad's Calypso music, where tropical rhythms are used. It was a celebratory and family-friendly type of music. Byron Lee and Harry Belafonte are two famous Jamaican musicians who often get grouped into both genres. One may be familiar with Harry Belafonte's *Banana Boat*, which became a worldwide sensation. Mento music played a pivotal role in the development of reggae music. Several influences marked the beginning of a newly evolved music culture in Jamaica. Long before reggae was cemented in history, Jamaican musicians were shaping their formative years through the likes of blues, jazz and R&B from artists like Fats Domino and Nat King Cole amongst other legends. Hearing R&B sounds through Jamaican sound systems in the 50s was the norm, and still is. This lifestyle paved the way for Jamaicans to further add to their musical culture in magnifying ways as musicians would often be influenced by American R&B in the 40s and 50s, before soul and funk took over in the late 50s and early 60s. This left Jamaican musicians to get more creative, and ska musicians emerged.

Ska music was developed in the 1950s specifically for dancing. It is characterized by syncopated drums and bass with offbeat rhythms often with no words, also known as instrumentals. It gained popularity in England in the 1960s and then in the US in the 1980s. Pioneers include The Skatalites, Desmond Decker, Toots & The Maytals, Prince Buster, Derrick Morgan, and they are just a few of the artists who have contributed to the development of ska. Ska moved into rocksteady as words reflecting what society was thinking began to have a greater impact on the people.

Albums to listen to: *The Skatalites – Hip-Bop-Ska, Ska Authentic; Toots & The Maytals – Funky Kingston; Desmond Dekker: The Israelites; The Wailers - The Wailing Wailers*

The sound system and selectors play a significant role in Jamaican entertainment. The sound system unit is a critical staple in Jamaican culture and developed on the island in the 1950s. It is a group of different selectors, MCs, and sound engineers along with their sound equipment, playing all different music styles. A selector is a Jamaican term for a disc jockey (DJ), and it is used more often than the term 'DJ' within the culture. Both the selector and the MC roles play a major role in the development of the entire Jamaican culture, and these roles garner much respect and attention amongst artists and fans alike. Sound systems once took the place of radio as radios were inaccessible to many Jamaicans. The sound system culture paved the way for more economic opportunities and is very much still alive today, making its way through the Americas, Europe, Africa, Asia; as far as Japan and Scandinavia. It is prevalent in rural areas throughout Jamaica and amongst the lower classes, including Kingston, where it all started in the famous Tivoli Gardens. The sound system's most notable characteristic is the loud bass sounds coming from the speakers that can stretch its sound over multiple communities.

Toasting began in the late 1960s by deejays and singjays. This music style is characterized by artists creatively and lyrically chanting over a *riddim*. Riddim is the Jamaican term for 'rhythm', and it gained its popularity in the 90s and early 2000s through the likes of labels like VP Records, currently one of the biggest independent labels for reggae and dancehall. In toasting, multiple artists share the same beat during one song. The toasting style greatly influenced Jamaican DJ Kool Herc, who used toasting in New York City in the late 1970s to pioneer hip-hop & rap. Pioneers also include U-Roy and Dennis Al Capone who would rap over King Tubby's mixes.

Albums to listen to: *U-Roy – Version Galore*

Rocksteady emerged as a dance style in the mid-1960s after Alton Ellis released his song *Rocksteady* with pioneering labels like Treasure Isle and Studio One steering the way, similar to Ska. As a predecessor of ska and a precursor of reggae, the style only lasted a few years, but it remains a beloved genre in Jamaica. During its popularity, new sounds and styles from new technology were introduced to producers and engineers. Sound effects like the horn were introduced, and the bass patterns became increasingly complex, giving rocksteady its famous bass lines. Alton Ellis, John Holt, The Heptones, Slim Smith, Bob Andy, Delroy Wilson are just a few names to be familiarized with. The term *rude boy* was coined during this musical period as Jamaican people's energy began to shift when the UK granted independence to Jamaica. The subgenre eventually morphed into reggae as the Rastafari movement became more popular. Its influence continues to be heard in reggae, dub, and dancehall riddims today, like Barrington Levy's remake of Bob Andy's 1970 classic, *Too Experienced*. Rocksteady artists begin transitioning into making reggae music leading to the end of an era.

Albums to listen to: *The Heptones – On Top, Alton Ellis – Sings Rock and Soul, Bob Andy – Song Book, Paragons – On The Beach*

Reggae in the late 1960s emerged as Black consciousness became more of a focus for the people, reaching its heights in the 70s when music started to take a political direction. This is where we begin to see the musician's role evolve into that of a messenger. The *rude boy* attitude was now met with a more relatable one. When we sing about reality everyone can relate, and this theme is often the trend that is most popular in Jamaica.

Reggae was developed with a rhythmic style led by the bass and drum. It is characterized by beats known as the skank. Leaving Jamaica in the late 60s, Bob Marley returned to Jamaica in the 70s after working in the US to embark on his evolved position from a ska to reggae artist, now as a devout Rastafarian. His experiences growing up in Trench Town and the US system is a great example of how one's environmental circumstances shape one's perspective; and in Marley's case like so many others before him and after him, his music.

The sounds of Jamaica and reggae deservingly need its own book to highlight all the pioneers and contributors that continue to keep the trailblazing genre alive, but I want to share a few for a start before our preferred digital music platform, and hopefully additional research, leads us further on a storytelling journey. From the 1970s emerged Jacob Miller, Burning Spear, Sugar Minott, Inner Circle, Jimmy Cliff, Peter Tosh, Bunny Wailer, Bob Marley, Dennis Brown, Gregory Isaacs, Mighty Diamonds, Third World, Culture, and Barrington Levy. The 1980s: Black Uhuru, Ini Kamoze, Frankie Paul, Cocoa Tea, Beres, Sanchez, and Freddie McGregor. 1990s: Garnett Silk, Buju Banton, Tony Rebel, Morgan Heritage, and Luciano. Reggae also had a strong impact in England, producing world class acts such as UB40, Steel Pulse, and Aswad. The arrival of a new millennium additionally added to the current with Munga, Bugle, Dre Island, Protoje, Jesse Royal, Kabaka Pyramid, and Chronixx, and just too many to list. This a genre where musicians actually live what they sing about.

Albums to listen to: *Peter Tosh – Legalize It, Ken Boothe – Everything I Own, Bunny Wailer – Blackheart Man, Jimmy Cliff - The Harder They Come, Garnett Silk – Give I Strength, Buju Banton – 'Til Shiloh, Sizzla - Black Woman and*

Child, Luciano – Where There Is Life, Dennis Brown – Love Has Found Its Way, Freddie McGregor – Big Ship, Bob Marley – Survival, Anthony B – Real Revolutionary (aka So Many Things), Burning Spear – Calling Rastafari, Richie Spice – Universal, Everton Blender – Rootsman Credential, Richie Spice - Damian Marley – Stony Hill, Chronixx – Chronology, Protoje - In Search of Lost Time

Roots Reggae is the name given to a spiritual type of music whose lyrics predominantly praise Jah (God) and narrates the story of past and present-day slavery and the economic exploitation of the poor. Recurrent themes include all forms of social injustice, including poverty, capitalism, racism, political intimidation, and police brutality. The Rastafarian culture tends to dominate this movement, focusing on liberating the minds of Black Jamaicans. "Roots reggae gave Rastafarians a prominence that they had never enjoyed in the past."[41] Rockers were the theme of a sound under roots reggae that gained popularity in the 1970s by Sly & Robbie. Nearly all the artists mentioned under 'reggae' can be labeled as 'roots reggae' artists. Reggae ignites revolutions beyond the shores of Jamaica. Today it has continued to have a powerful influence on people of all backgrounds and other music genres, with other notable Roots Reggae artists born outside of Jamaica, like Akae Beka of St. Croix.

Dub, another unique style of music rooted in reggae, emerged in the 1960s with pioneers such as King Tubby, who had a pivotal impact on the development of dub music, and producers Dave Kelly, Gussy Clarke, and Donovan Germaine. Dub emphasizes heavy bass on preexisting songs with most of the vocals removed, sometimes popularly done with an echo effect. Mixing employed in dub music techniques by legendary engineers like the Scientist have also influenced genres such as hip-hop, punk, disco, house techno, and dub poetry. Dub poetry evolved in the 70s out of both Jamaica and England. It is characterized by rehearsed poetry or 'spoken word', with dub poets often chanting rhythmically without a background beat. Like reggae, subjects varied from police brutality, ganja, to Rastafarian themes. Pioneers include Linton Kwesi Johnson, who coined the *dub poetry* term, and Oku Onoura; leading the way for today's Benjamin Zephaniah, and Mutabaruka, a famous dub poet now turned radio talk-show host.

Albums to listen to: *King Tubby Meets Rockers Uptown, Lee "Scratch" Perry and The Upsetters – Super 8*

Dub plates emerged in the 1970s on the helms of the sound system and clash culture. A dub plate is a track remixed with heavy prominence on the bass. Jamaicans regularly pay for artists to remix a song for them. Of course, the more exclusive the music or the artist, the higher the price. Authentic dub plates could hold only a certain amount of songs, which presented exclusivity purchasers depended on. The exclusivity produced the sound clash culture, which is now a craze to look forward to at events. A sound clash is identified as two opponents (often as teams) playing their remixes, called *dub fi dub* until a winner is chosen.

Lovers Rock is a reggae music genre that emerged out of England in the 1970s following the mass immigration of Jamaicans, which prompted Britain to focus on repairing relations with Jamaica. When Black people could not go to the local pubs due to the "No Blacks, no dogs, no Irish" rule, they started their sound system parties in the 1950s, which became an immediate trend. When Jamaicans came to Britain, they realized they were more potent than many white men.[27] White people started leaving neighborhoods shortly after, and British Blacks established their identities from Jamaica. The Bamboo Club was the first Black club in Britain, where

Black legends such as Bob Marley and BB King appeared. Racism was present in Britain, but reggae music unified Jamaicans with other cultures.

Love has always been a prominent Jamaican music theme, but lovers rock became an official style for love songs. The focus of the bass became the heartbeat. Lovers rock proved to be a lasting style, and it became a popular genre for female musicians. Young and confident female artists emerged within the genre. Lovers rock challenged racism and female oppression. In response to the Black masculinity associated with roots music's Black power, women utilized lovers rock to challenge this rough masculinity with emotion, heard in songs like *Men Cry Too* by Beshara. Lovers rock gave women a stronger voice in music and paved the way for women to take control in the industry in a non-aggressive manner, as it did for Carroll Thompson, popularly known as the Queen of Lovers Rock; and also influenced artists outside of Jamaica, like it did for Janice Kay's *Silly Games* by famed producer Dennis Bovell. The genre has remained rooted in righteousness, never straying from being heart centered. Powerhouses such as Sade and Estelle were inspired by this genre that gave name to both of their *Lovers Rock* albums. It's important to keep in mind that before lovers rock, reggae singers were making romantic songs long before, such as Ken Boothe, John Holt and Alton Ellis. Today, reggae love songs are now generally grouped under the UK-coined term, 'lovers rock'.

Albums to listen to: *Johnny Nash - I Can See Clearly Now, Gregory Isaacs – Night Nurse, Beres Hammond - Can't Stop a Man, Sanchez - One in a Million, Maxi Priest - Maxi*

Dancehall emerged in the 1970s and is characterized by faster rhythms than the other types of Jamaican music that came before it, following the development of music technology. However, the drum is still the most prominent instrument in this genre. Roots reggae was taken over by the force of dancehall in terms of popularity when it emerged. Both continue to hold their weight amongst different crowds and have more similarities than differences. One notable difference is the explicitly sexual and violent language often found in dancehall that is not in roots reggae. Dancehall with explicitly sexual and violent content was banned from the airwaves by the Broadcasting Commission of Jamaica. Today artists still create dancehall music but with highly conscious themes.

Dancehall is the most influential genre out of Jamaica amongst Jamaican diaspora communities and most popular among the younger generations. "Through dancehall, ghetto youths attempt to deal with the endemic problems of poverty, racism, and violence, and in this sense, the dancehall acts as a communication center, a relay station, a site where Black lower-class culture attains its deepest expression" and connection.[78]

The DJ and MC hold crucial roles in the dancehall culture. A disc jockey is known as a selector in reggae that plays the music, and a DJ is the actual MC (or the rapper) that deejays over the music. Though the musician is the messenger, the DJ and the MC also assume the responsibility for explosively delivering the song's message coercively by way of blending rhythms and content. During live performances, in a collective effort, all three artists hold the attention of the audience. This combination of both crafts adds to the effect of the lyrics. I believe what undoubtedly makes it easier for all the roles to be executed masterfully is the truth behind reggae music's messages and how the average Jamaican finds connection to it. Dancehall often, if not entirely, reflects reality in Jamaica, from the vibrant sides to the darker sides, especially with poverty-related themes. Like it's parent-genre reggae, it reflects real life, but at times add flares of hope. Pioneering dancehall producers include, and are certainly not limited to: Henry Junjo Lawes, Winston Riley, Joe Gibbs, Lee Perry, Bunny Lee, Papa San, George Phang, and Richard Hoo Kim. The same goes for pioneering and contributing artists: Yellowman, Sister Nancy, Shabba, Ninjaman, Lady G, Beenie Man, Bounty Killer, Shaggy, Capleton, Super Cat, Patra, Nadine Sutherland, Tanto Metro & Devonte, TOK, Elephant Man, Mr. Vegas, Lady Saw, Wayne Wonder, Assassin/Agent Sasco, Baby Cham, Vybz Kartel, Mavado, Gyptian, Konshens, Popcaan and, as I've said before, it is impossible to include everybody without writing a separate book. Additionally, the list will always grow.

Albums to listen to: *Shabba Ranks - X-tra Naked, Beenie Man - Many Moods of Moses, Mad Cobra – Hard to Wet, Easy to Dry, Patra - Queen of the Pack, Baby Cham – Ghetto Story, Vybz Kartel - Pon Di Gaza 2.0*

Ragga or **Raggamuffin** music emerged in the 1980s as a subgenre of dancehall music with pioneers like King Jammy behind Wayne Smith's hit *Under Mi Sleng Teng*. It is derived from the colonial British word *ragamuffin* used to describe ghetto dwellers. The style is characterized by electronic music, and sampling is a prominent tool used by deejays. Reggae, its precursors, and subgenres have given birth to other genres not categorized as Jamaican music, but whose influence is often detailed when being defined.

Hip-Hop/Rap music arose in the 1970s from the connection and exchange between the Caribbean and African American youth in Bronx, New York City. There are several contributing influences to the emergence of hip-hop. With the influx of Jamaicans arriving in NYC in the 1990s, DJ Kool is said to have created the blueprint for hip-hop music and culture by building upon the Jamaican tradition of impromptu toasting, a spoken type of boastful poetry and speech over music.[78] He also introduced the style of scratching and break-beat deejaying, repeating the dance part of songs. What became known as scratching in New York was already known as dubbing in Jamaica.

Albums to listen to: *KRS One – Criminal Minded, Busta Rhymes – The Coming, NWA- Straight Outta Compton, Dr. Dre – The Chronic, Biggie Smalls – Ready To Die, Common - Be, Red Man – Muddy Waters, Mos Def & Talib Kweli – Black Star*

Reggaeton emerged in the 1990s and originated from the reggae scene in Panama before further developing into its official name in Puerto Rico. It blends its primary influences from hip-hop, reggae, dancehall, and soca, with sounds more native to Spanish countries like bomba, salsa, merengue, Latin pop, and bachata.

Albums to listen to: *Barrio Fino - Daddy Yankee, The Last Don - Don Omar*

Reggae Fusion developed in the 1970s and 1980s, but the term was coined in the 1990s. The term is used to describe reggae artists who have crossed over to other genres and other genres being fused with reggae, with artists who deejay over non-Jamaican music. This has been seen in reggae's earlier stages already with artists like Mad Cobra, Shabba, Bounty, and Super Cat. Some exemplary reggae Fusion genres are reggae rock, reggae funk, reggae disco, and Hawaiian reggae, but is also fused with hip-hop,

R&B, jazz, rock, drum and bass, punk, and polka. Shaggy, Sean Paul, Sean Kingston and Rihanna have all been known for their work in this genre.

Albums to listen to: *Shaggy - Hot Shot, No Doubt - Rock Steady, Diana King - Tougher Than Love, Wayne Wonder - No Holding Back, Sean Paul - Dutty Rock, Damian Marley & Nas – Distant Relatives*

Although we've already mentioned a few through different genres, the impact women have made in reggae, its precursors and its subgenres weigh heavily. "When women come through that door, they end up making some of the biggest records ever," legendary Boston reggae DJ Junior Rodigan shared with me as I hurriedly tried to jot down some of the gems he had to share about reggae music's impact. Women and their arrival on the scene often bring balance to reggae. In her book, *Black Popular Music in Britain Since 1945*, a sociologist by the name of Jon Stratton details the patriarchal structures women had to navigate around. He shared how Caroll Thompson, known as the queen of lovers rock, started her own company for creative control to avoid and deflect the aggressive patriarchal attitudes and pushback she experienced on her rise in the industry. Jamaican female pioneers in Jamaican music include one of Bob Marley's I-Threes, Marcia Griffiths (who I've met in my home while my father managed artists), and learned was a hitmaker before becoming an I-Three. Her hit 'Electric Slide' is still a worldwide sensation. Rita Marley, Sister Nancy, Lorna Bennett, Lady G, Lady Saw, Patra, Tanya Stephens, Queen Ifrica, Nadine Sutherland, Cecile, Macka Diamond, Etana, Spice, Tami Chin and Tessane Chin, Ishawna, and as of recently, Koffee, Shenseea, Lila Ike, Jada Kingdom, Sevana, amongst so many others; like their male counterparts, they don't play once they step on the scene, always leaving an impact no matter how silently we forget about them. Who would've thought Diana King wrote for Biggie Smalls?

The art of sampling music has been popular frequented since the 80s, similar to ragga.

Acts from all different coasts in the USA have sampled reggae songs repeatedly in their musical career but nowhere is as influential as New York City and the artists from there. Nas has sampled Super Cat's *Dance Inna New York* in his song *The Don*. Dipset has sampled Sanchez's *One in a Million* on their *Dipset Anthem* hit, along with Ini Kamoze's *World-A-Music* on *Murda Murda* during the heights of their career. Sizzla's *Solid as a Rock* is on Jay-Z's *Crown*, along with John Holt's *I Will* on *Encore* and Max Romeo's *Chase the Devil* on Lucifer. LL Cool J's sexy hit *Doin It* samples Grace Jones' *My Jamaican Guy* and the head-bopping classic *Oh Yeah* by Foxy Brown & Spragga samples *54-46 Was My Number* by Toots and the Maytals. We can't get forget Nicki Minaj sampling Mr. Vegas' *Heads High* on *Megatron;* or her collab with French Montana on *Freaks,* sampling Lil Vicious' *Freaks* and Chaka Demus & Pliers' *Murder She Wrote.* If there's any place in the world other than the UK that had Jamaicans and reggae as a major contributor to the development of their culture, it's quite noticeably NYC. The energy had such an impact in New York City that when gangster turned music executive Haitian Jack, arrived to NYC as an immigrant and faced discrimination for his ethnic background while trying to survive in the streets, he shared that he begun to run with the Jamaicans because there was no long talking, they just fired, and he wanted "that respect." I caught that on a recent series called Hip Hop Uncovered and had to jot it down (for this very purpose of sharing it) before forgetting. I instantly thought about how Jamaicans have such a large impact on the NYC lifestyle and culture.

Although I don't think Yellowman's Zungguzungguguzungguzeng (with at least 30 different artists, including 2Pac and Junior Mafia) can be out-sampled; one of the most sampled reggae songs, if not the most, is Sister Nancy's *Bam* which we can hear on Lauryn Hill's *Lost Ones,* Guerilla Black's *Compton,* Jay-Z's *Bam,* and Kanye West's *Famous.* There is something about that song! Both Kanye West and Jay-Z have sampled a number of reggae tracks. Kanye West has Beenie Man's *Memories* on *Send it Up,* Super Beagle's *Dust a Sound Boy* and Barrington Levy's *Under Mi Sensi* on *I Don't Like Remix.* And who in my generation can forget ASAP Ferg's *Shabba,* not only a song title, but a sample and a video appearance! If we head to the West Coast, we see early examples of Jamaican influences in rap with Dr. Dre's *The Day The Niggaz Took Over* and *Let Me Ride,* as well as Easy E sampling Yellowman in *Nobody Move.* Some popular collabs between reggae and hip-hop span back to hip hop's beginning.

The genres and sub-genres originating out of Jamaican music, such as dancehall and hip-hop, show respect to its parent genre, evidently so with continuing collaborations. So one can understand how strong the influence is on genres and people outside of Jamaica, I think it's important to show how far all the different ways Jamaicans and/or its products have influenced its surroundings. We see a lot of the same names come up repeatedly in collabs: Bounty Killer & Gwen Stefani, Lady Saw & Gwen Stefani, Swiss Beats & Bounty Killer, Beenie Man & Mya, Beenie Man & Janet Jackson, Beyonce & Sean Paul, Shaggy & Sting, Nas & Damian Marley, Jay-Z & Damian Marley, DJ Khaled & Buju Banton, DJ Khaled & Mavado, and Drake & Popcaan, just to name a few of a fast-growing list.

Fearless

In the recent years, we have seen international superstars like Drake and DJ Khaled show credit to Jamaican musicians and the genres for their own success, loudly and proudly so, continuously collaborating with legendary and top Jamaican musicians. And they weren't the first, although their stardom might outshine others who have strongly represented their association with Jamaica, like Swizz Beats, Snoop Dogg, and Busta Rhymes (just to name a few). The secret behind Jamaican music's strong influence is primarily from the energy of the Jamaicans making it. So, it is interesting to see how far power can reach around the world through music, and most notably, it can bring out a different type of creative energy and invoke power within oppressed people all over the world. Reggae music has become so powerful that it has influenced non-Jamaican cultures everywhere, without interfering with their unique roots.

Drake himself is an interesting topic to study when it comes to his connection with Jamaican musicians, often being called a culture vulture. There are many reasons to believe that Drake uses Jamaica and its most influential product, reggae, as a blueprint for his ultimate Toronto and world takeover. I notice the duality he gets slammed for by those who thinks he's too feminine with his music at times, is a quite normal characteristic for dancehall musicians to exhibit in their music too, and thus accepted in Jamaican culture. 'Rude boys' have been making romantic songs in Jamaica for quite a long time; and it's almost expected to be made along with the typical 'badman' tunes. I think this is one of his key formulas that led to his fast domination in music, and this formula has more of a positive effect than it does a negative on the public. Being soft is a residual of toxic masculinity that this formula can reverse if one is brave enough to in such patriarchal-dominated societies where Drake endured much of that backlash in the beginning of his career. People, especially men, have evolved with him now, and we hear less of the "soft" chat. He has often connected musicians from his side of music to Jamaican musicians and has countless songs with either a Jamaica-reference or they are Jamaican-influenced. Some of these songs feature collaborations with Jamaican musicians such as Popcaan with *Controlla* and *Twist & Turn* and Mavado with *Find Your Love;* both of whom have been expressing the same duality I speak of Drake in their own music. Drake signed Popcaan to his OVO label in 2018. DJ Khaled did the same with Mavado in 2011, and Roc Nation did the same with Buju Banton in 2019. This is a growing trend and good for Jamaican musicians, as their pay often doesn't align with the influence they have on the public as other genres based out of more lucrative communities do.

Visits to the island from artists are frequent. Several hip-hop and rap artists have visited Jamaica on what I would call musical pilgrimages. DJ Khaled, Beyonce & Jay-Z, Drake, Solange, Nas, Kendrick Lamar, J.Cole, Kanye West, Snoop Dogg, Alicia Keys, Lil Wayne, Diplo, Future, Young Jeezy, Gucci Mane, Migos, Rich The Kid, H.E.R., Skip Marley, are just a few artists who have spent a considerable amount of time there, whether studying the greats, taking in the energy (like Gucci Mane who frequents the island due to his wife being Jamaican), or working with other Jamaican musicians. Solange spent a significant amount of time in Jamaica creating more content for her fourth studio album, *When I Get Home,* where she expressed her love for Runaway Bay and several other areas throughout Jamaica. She has stated she finds "good vibrations" and can feel "strong" on the island. She closes her album by thanking the island for "giving so much, sharing so much, and being a constant place of refuge and retreat when I've needed it the most." All artists mentioned above either have collaborated with a Jamaican musician or have written, sang, rapped, or sampled a reggae-influenced song.

Other forms of reggae have emerged in different regions and other countries, producing exciting versions of the genre. I was introduced to Hawaiian reggae while on my visits there. In Japan, the Japanese reggae has been around since the 1970s. I have learned from my brother's visits that it is the primary genre played in coffee shops, especially in certain towns like Yoyogi and various parts of Shibuya. Chinese reggae and Italian reggae popularly exist in underground scenes in lower class areas that you normally wouldn't see advertised. I've experienced the Italians love for reggae at a massive Sizzla concert in Rome in addition to several underground clubs and I was in awe of the interest in roots reggae, and the dancing to dancehall music by Italians. Upon my research, I've discovered Nigerian reggae, Ethiopian reggae, Irish reggae, amongst a unique list of different types of reggae around the world.

I think one reggae artist uniquely invited other cultures and other countries to experience music the way Jamaicans do; that is Bob Marley. He was a welcome sign for the non-African diaspora into African culture with his drive to push reggae music and all that it represented. He was representative of how one person could become a peace symbol for the world. If we were to ask the question, "When you think of Jamaica, who is the first person that comes to mind?" Most people would probably respond with "Bob Marley" if not Usain Bolt by the newer generations. He aided his ancestors in paving the way for both Jamaicans and Jamaican music to be accepted with respect worldwide. It is no surprise that different versions of reggae exist around the world. Bob Marley was a messenger for oppressed people, had a far international reach and perhaps improved the island's image while doing so. His famous 'One Love Peace Concert' in 1978 was a revolutionary one when he joined the head leaders' hands of Jamaica's two opposing parties, People's National Party (PNP) & Jamaica's Labor Party (JLP), whose campaigns were causing a violent divide in Jamaica at the time. As I was randomly watching a Netflix show called The Outer Banks, I watched how they showed their respect and adoration for Peter Tosh, one of the Wailers, when the character Kiara says, "The spirit of Peter Tosh will never die." Talk about random! As well as highlighting the artists who garnered international attention, the show addresses the social justice issues of rich islands owned by white people. These issues remain vital themes in reggae material.

Music triumphs in everything, including the government. Since it is said that music is one of the seven sciences of the universe, if this holds true, then Jamaica may have put itself in a position where they are going in the right direction in terms of universal advancement towards peace. The government respects and supports the export of reggae music. Its influence on both the community of Jamaica and the world has earned its declaration of being a global treasure on **UNESCO'S** *Intangible Cultural Heritage List* back in 2018. Many artists are known to give back to their community, like the popularly known musician Shaggy, who throws his Shaggy & Friends concert to benefit Jamaican hospitals and lowly-maintained areas on the island. Legendary artist Bounty Killer has always expressed his passion for ghetto youths to rise, "youths don't take up violence because mommy and daddy have to go spend money dee Nah have on lawyer fee" and backs it up with action in the community. He also is a role model with his community work with hospitals and care packages to poor families. He has earned his name as the general of dancehall by regularly keeping his fellow musicians accountable if they derail off reggae's initial purpose of being a message portal to uplift people, a popular thing to do amongst the vets of reggae music. Sizzla has invested large amounts of money into his community, Judgement Yard and is a known advocate for child literacy amongst other things. Musicians regularly organize or are participants in entertainment, school, and cultural events within their communities as well.

Musicians often have a more powerful voice, especially if the musical content speaks on oppressions people face regularly. Music has so much power over the people that the government may have to step in if a disagreement becomes too personal and grabs fans' attention or support extensively, as the Mavado and Kartel feud in 2008 so lucidly highlighted following the violence their music and personal feud was causing between their 'Gully' and 'Gaza' fans, respectively, throughout Jamaican communities. Throughout the year, there are annual, quarterly, weekly, and daily events that celebrate reggae music, like the famous Reggae Sumfest that happens every summer and highlights Jamaica's most prominent and rising stars along with international acts. The Prime Minister regularly participates in events commemorating the treasure that has afforded Jamaica so much global traction, especially so during Reggae Month in February.

Simply, Jamaicans love good sounds. Jamaicans have a long history of remaking songs from other genres since the development of mento music. To this day, artists like Terry Linen remake classic American and Canadian-based songs like Whitney Houston's *Your Love is My Love*, just as we will have superstars from other genres remake classic reggae songs.

Sound systems often played R&B and soul hits when they first erupted on the scene, and the same continues to this day. Celine Dion, Cyndi Lauper, are just a couple of artists most Jamaicans are very acquainted with because of the popularity of their songs on the island. Celine Dion's concert on the island was legendary. Their love for a good sound is traced back to slavery with this observer's perspective on the effects sound had on enslaved Africans, even through just regular conversation. "So susceptible are the Africans of the influence of that art which variously affects the mind by the mysterious power of sound…they will scarcely give any attention to any religious instructor who possesses a harsh or discordant voice. Every good speaker, independently of the softness of his tones, raises and lowers them in strict musical intervals; so that his disclosure is as capable of being noted in musical characters as any melody whatever, becoming disagreeable only when those intervals are uniformly the same, or when the same intonations are used to express sentiments, of the most opposite import."[20]

Music is by far Jamaica's biggest export, but an export whose return value still does not measure up to its influence on the masses. Despite Jamaica's groundbreaking years in music and the world's reverence of the music, the island made a copyright act in 1993. The stagnant move to creating a copyright act stifled the profits of Jamaican musicians. Perhaps the reason for the stagnation is rooted in oppression. Jamaican musicians, for instance, aren't able to obtain visas despite the influence the music and its content might have in other countries.

Kingston is the best place to get a taste of all the sounds Jamaica has produced. The Kingston area is where we will find many of the studios that sculpted the Jamaican musicians we have come to love today. But establishments where musical developments occur can be found throughout the island, even in the poorest of communities. Before reaching immigration, as we exit the plane, we are sometimes greeted with live reggae singers. Upon leaving the airport, we instantly hear sound systems in cars exploding with heavy bass. The same music volume can be heard in the countryside and mountainous areas. These examples relate to Jamaica's early history of using sound as a tool for power. The following is a quote from a white slave owner who expressed his disapproval of enslaved Africans using the drums when he was trying to sleep, "these damn Negroes, they make so much bloody noise with their nocturnal activities!" Possibly what we call *partying* and *clubbing* today, might have been the enslaved Africans' form of "nocturnal activities." Colonies banned those "nocturnal activities" because they realized it was a power source for slaves to stay connected to the Motherland, devise freedom plans, and unite as one people. This reveals that Jamaicans have been partying, and have never stopped, since time.

CHAPTER THIRTEEN

Dance

Jamaicans Have Never Stopped Partying

♪ *Chronixx – Cool as the Breeze/Friday*

♪ *Bob Marley - Jamming*

Jamaica has been dancing since the beginning of her time with the same energy. Dancing is a vital component of Jamaican culture. Different African tribes also brought their dance traditions with them to the Americas such as the Akan with the *kumina* and the Congolese with the *Dinki Mini*, energetic dances used as tools for things like cheering up mourners after a death. The link between dancing and spirituality was especially demonstrated during the 18th and 19th centuries during Pocomania and Kumina's rise. The British were vigilant in spreading Christianity while Africans continued to hold on to their spiritual beliefs and practices, birthing Pocomania. If we recall from earlier chapters, Pocomania was the most prominent religion indigenous to Jamaica before Rastafarianism. Pocomania was characterized by exaggerated body movement. Pocomania ignited fearful curiosity among the colonists and prompted the government to take legal action out of fear. "The thing itself is worse than any picture of it could be, and it is no wonder that he wants to know whether these practices are not a form of Obeah, even if carried on under the guise of

Fearless

Christianity. He suggested that legislation be brought to bear Pocomanism and that the island's ministers needed to unite to crush the Pocomaniacs, "an ignorant set of dancing, prancing, steppers, a set of howling...."[52] Another source describes the dancing demonstrations observed from Africans while in church, "during the sermon, a heathen woman began to twist her body about, and make all manner of Grimaces. I bore it all for some time till she distributed the congregation, when I desired one of the assistants to lead her out, thinking she was in pain. When the service was over, I inquired about what ailed her, and was told that it was a usual thing...and called by them Conviction."

While negative connotations were attached to how Africans used drums and dance to connect to God, some Europeans yearned to understand their methods. "...Each man was also, in a way not understood by Europeans...a priest in through possession (induced by communal dancing to drums) could not only communicate with the gods but assume a god's position. In Jamaica, Black baptist worshipers were often possessed, as were pagan cultists always under the prompting of the drums."[20] Kumina that emerged in 19th century Jamaica is also characterized by dancing. "When under full possession, a revelation is given by the ancestors concerning the occasion for which the cumin is called."[41] Maroons still practice Kumina today to drive out evil spirits.

Music and dance served both as a recreational and functional purpose, as done in Africa. Enslaved Africans danced and sang at work and at play.[20] Despite the controversies that once existed during early England's rule, dancing has been a unification tool. "According to Michael Mullin, Whites witnessed Maroon dances and other ceremonies, enjoyed their hospitality, and slept with and married some of their women." It seems like commonalities were revolving around this peace. Mullin further claims, "white visitors were aware that they would be welcome in Trelawny Town whilst Cudjoe was alive because a rule with Cudjoe was always never to provoke whites." Whites found a comfort then amongst the Maroons as they do now on the island. It was likely that Cudjoe could see the benefits of a non-violent co-existence with them.[23]

The Maroons once performed the Kromanti dance as a ritual for spiritual protection, a dance from a religious aspect that embodies music, possession, and ancestral spirits. The style had elements derived from past African religious traditions and was viewed as a form of metaphysical warfare against their oppressors. Although the Kromanti dance is no longer practiced amongst the Maroons, aspects of the dance have influenced later forms of Jamaican dance. The Kromanti dance began after nightfall and finished at daybreak, quite similar to the Jamaican partying style today.

Skanking was developed in the 1950s for the ska music scene. Variations have changed since its original combined format of the running man motion, taking up a particular foot of radius to rock with elbows swaying on the beat comfortably. Reggae and roots music usually requires skanking, weaving, and a swaying vibe. These forms of dancing are much easier as there is no particular way of performing the dances, one can incorporate their own style. Lovers rock usually requires more intimacy between opposite sexes, with various winding movements. The only demand with these types of movements is making sure the execution of moves falls on the bass. Even in films that mirror real-life back in time, we see the same patterns among the enslaved and how they preserved their intense energy and customs through their roots. In the movie *Palm Trees in the Snow*, when an enslaved Black man teaches an enslaved Black girl how to dance, he goes, "don't look, listen to music." The power of the drum is a recurring theme and a massive connection between many African diaspora cultures.

Dinki Mini is a West African dance historically performed during Nine Night. As mentioned earlier, Nine Night is the 9-day celebration of the deceased through dancing and having other forms of entertainment.

With the help of dancehall, Jamaican dancing today has had significant international influence. Dancehall has become a craze that has created new income avenues for Jamaicans. They are often in demand at staged shows and events of various magnitudes. The ability to move to dancehall music has taken many from impoverished communities into improved financial conditions. As a result, street parties have been created to attract all types of dancers and audiences. Jamaican dancing's current style is similar to how their ancestors on the island once came together centuries ago. "Dancing usually took place, as in Africa, in the center of a ring of spectator-participants, performers entering the ring singly or in twos and threes. Sometimes male dancers express themselves acrobatically; but more often, especially at private entertainments, the shuffle staff were employed, the dances stylistically confining themselves to a very restricted area indeed." [20] Jamaicans can surely get acrobatic on the dance floor. Dancing is not new to the inhabitants, but its evolution continues to add to Jamaica's reputation.

While dances became more creative and popular, so did the names to identify each dance style. For example, daggering is characterized by exotic, aggressive moves. Wild moves can range from males mounting onto females spreading eagle to dry humping. It is also common to see women jumping on the men to perform sexually explicit moves. It seems as if Jamaicans subconsciously take their passion for heterosexuality to a very visual extreme. Regarding Kumina, spirit possession was achieved through tireless dancing and was accompanied by rhythmic drumming. "The drum is the heartbeat of Africa, the heartbeat of the ancestor, and the dancing is the African body partaking in an ancient expression of identity. The dancing becomes so rigorous that the spirit of the ancestor takes control of the dancer's body until the dancer loses control of their agency and becomes the ancestor."[42] This type of behavior is reminiscent of today's intimate man-to-woman dancing, including the intense daggering, though Kumina was more associated with religious purposes. Daggering songs highlight Jamaicans' ability to say exactly what is on their colorful and lively mind. Songs related to daggering are heavily censored on the radio. Daggering is most popular in the ghetto or downtown areas.

Jamaica has been known for the production of its Dancehall Queen contest every year for decades now, starting in Jamaica in 1992 with Carlene Smith as the winner and spreading the competition to almost every continent. Carlene was a game-changer as the title 'Dancehall Queen' became one of the most important entertainment fields. The film and hit single *Dancehall Queen* by Beenie Man and Chevelle Franklin had a strong influence on the growing impact this aspect of dancing had on the culture. Women utilized dance halls to express their attitude towards their sexist experiences within the culture. Of course, along with the popularity of women taking over the dance floor, we have dancehall songs encouraging, uplifting and empowering them by their male counterparts in songs like Mr. Lexx's and Mr. Vegas' *Video Light* and *Pickney Nah Hold Yuh Down* (having kids doesn't stop your power) by Beenie Man. For women in the dancehall, dancing is undoubtedly a way to express oneself freely through physical movement. It is a form of women's empowerment. Danger, a dancehall queen and the winner of the International Dancehall Queen Competition in 2014, expresses her power through dancehall as she explains: "We are queens, we are not afraid to go out there to do what we want to, demand what we want, and to live how we want, and represent women all over the world and to let them know it is okay to be yourself and that it is ok to not hold back." The influence of Jamaican dancing and dancehall queen competitions can be found throughout other Caribbean countries and throughout America, Europe, Asia, and of course its roots, Africa.

Jamaicans still dance and celebrate life in various ways, with more creativity as the way of life evolves. Most popular in Kingston but found throughout various parishes on the island are all-inclusive parties throughout the day or the night into the morning. Daybreak parties can start as early as 4 AM and last until 3 or 4 PM. Day parties can begin anywhere around 11 AM or 3 PM and last throughout midnight. This lifestyle has translated over to the Miami/Fort Lauderdale area with ease because of its large Jamaican population and close proximity to the island, and it is now a growing culture in Atlanta, NYC, Los Angeles, Connecticut, Jersey, amongst other worldy cities. The all-inclusive vibe is prevalent throughout the Caribbean. This lifestyle compliments the energy of its inhabitants. These all-inclusive gatherings have become a lucrative income stream for islanders and a popular gathering for inhabitants to look forward to.

Easter, the original ATI Weekend, and the innovative Dream Weekend have popularized Jamaica's holiday weekends. The latter two are just two of many famous party weekends where partygoers often pay an all-inclusive price, including unlimited food and drinks, to party between 3-5 days. This is most popular in the three main tourist towns of Jamaica, Negril, Ocho Rios, and Montego Bay. During Christmas time, *junkanoo*, pronounced as 'john-canoe', is celebrated. Junkanoo is a street parade filled with music, dance and costumes influenced by masks and gear Akans once wore in battle in Africa; one famously led by an Akan named John Canoe who turned his back on the allied-Germans for his people. Parties are held on the beach, throughout the streets, or in large empty spaces. Dancing is the most important component of these events after sound, in addition to parties that take place throughout the island in uptown, downtown, and country communities. The aura of the parties is dictated by the price of entry or by the promoter, but we can always count on loud music, access to liquor, and partygoers dancing. Although Jamaica's classism is reflected in the different types of partying cultures that exist, no party scene restricts one socio-economic class from access. Generally, uptown parties have attendees from the upper and middle class, but those from lower classes who want to attend an uptown party will do so. Downtown parties are most popular amongst the lower classes and are the most energetic, as the ghetto is where we most often feel this raw energy Jamaica is known for. Street and block parties are most popular in the downtown and country areas, and upper classes aren't stopped from going to these either. What connects communities throughout Jamaica, no matter the background, is the love for music and dancing.

Hot Mondays, Weddy Wednesday, Passa Passa were once prevalent street parties that often produced and sold music anywhere there was a beloved dancehall scene, now we have Wet Sundaze, and Bounty Sundays operated by Bounty Killer. The most famous street flex we see in uptown areas is a carnival, which is more of an uptown favorite, as soca music from Trinidad is most popular with the upper class.

The introduction of carnival to Jamaica can be traced back to Ghana, heavily influenced by way of Trinidad. Carnival was and still is characterized by bold, courageous, and scantily dancing. "Once upon a time in Takyiman in the Bring Ahafo Region of present-day Ghana, young women celebrated the Bo me Too festival. Scantily dressed and dancing the day away along the main streets in a carnival fanfare mood, a young woman would raise one leg high towards an unsuspecting man and shout 'bo me too' (fire or shoot me). The idea was to receive potent rays of the Merciful God from the man that would render her fertile for childbirth. It's very likely that aspects of the Bo me Tup festival found their way to the Caribbean during the slavery period and merged with other cultures for the birth of Caribbean carnival. Scantily dressed women in contemporary Carnival festivities was not created in or from vacuum."[101]

We'll find more large family and community-oriented parties in the country as there is more land but fewer establishments to party at. Clubs are found throughout the island, but the most well-known clubs are in Ocho Rios, Montego Bay, and Negril. Montego Bay hosts the famous Pier One while Negril has long boasted Jungle Nightclub further down west of the coast, and Ocho Rios famously does the same with Ocean's Eleven and Jamaica's most legendary stripclub, Shades Nightclub. Margaritaville, also known as Ville, is found on several islands where both locals and tourists often interact and party together, with one in each of the three tourist towns in Jamaica. Ville is usually in tourist-heavy, public entertainment spaces that are often guaranteed safer with more enforced security. There are a long string of nightclubs throughout the island to accommodate the demand. But one can't visit Jamaica with the raw experience of partying where Jamaicans regularly party with the scene, and clubs catered to a more upper class, attracts Jamaicans from all over the island and toursists that dare to venture off tourist areas. Despite the different distinctions, again, the partying lifestyle in Jamaica does not discriminate against anyone.

The celebration of lifestyle aids Jamaicans in staying young and living longer. This is most obvious by watching people of all ages dance and party while still noticing their structured and respectful lifestyles they're still able to maintain. Bogle, the inventor of the *Bogle* dance popularly sung by Buju Banton was 40 when he died, and he was still dancing up until his last days. Elephant Man is still making hit dance tunes and he has reached his heights doing so with using his artist platform to promote dances like: *Log On, Gully Creeper, Blazay-Blazay, Pon de River, Pon de Bank, Spongebob, Willy Bounce, Sesame Street, Summer Bounce, Shankle Dip, Crazy Hype, Ova Di Wall, Signal Di Plane, Gi Dem A Run* amongst more, ushering in a new generation of artists with most of their musical content characterized by dancing. The current dancing king turned artist, Ding Dong, hasn't slowed down his energy in either the music or dancing arena since emerging in the new millennium, following the steps of Elephant Man and Beenie Man (with hits like *World Dance, Row Like A Boat, Swing It Weh*) creating hit dances and songs to compliment them like *Bad Man Forward-Bad Man Pull Up, Della Move, Genna Bounce,* and *Flairy*. These artists, songs, and dances' popularity spans over a long period of time, if they ever do die, often from decades before with dances like *Bogle, Tatty* and the *Butterfly*. And who can forget the current from Tony Matterhorn's *Dutty Wine* or Mr. Vegas' *Tek Weh Yuhself* and *Hot Wuk*. We can't mention dancing without the pivotal dancers who ignited the growing trend of Jamaican dancers being outsourced to teach, do shows, and influence non-Jamaican peoples all over the world. That list includes Marvin, Keiva Di Diva, Mad Michelle, Shelly Belly, Sample 6, Black Blingas, and Ravas Clavas (which includes Ding Dong and Desha Ravers) just to name a few. There are probably hundreds of popular dances out there and the list only seems to be growing. Jamaica has shown that dancing is for the old and young no matter the socio-economic backgrounds. It is a tool that unifies the island. To counteract struggles and as a sign of gratitude, Jamaicans prioritize dance to celebrate life. Jamaicans view rhythm as a way to align with the universe's flow.

Dancing has become a sport in Jamaica where dancers can get quite acrobatic. Athletes incorporate dancing into their celebratory expressions as a form of happiness, and even as motivation. If one doesn't know how to skank, bubble, wine, rock steady, one will want to learn quickly when feels the vibe at a party. Many of these types of dances aren't hard to get into especially in Jamaican-influenced environments. There are more lessons to delve into as far as how life was like for the Africans in detail before they came to Jamaica, going deeper into the origins of the Akan and Congo people, to trace their powerful understandings of dancing. What other information did they have that was useful for evolution (that possibly got lost over oceans and time) for them to understand that sound and dancing are a part of day-to-day life? Perhaps, the knowledge of how powerful and beneficial it is to never give up. Getting deeper into the myriads of high energy and its wondrous abilities.

CHAPTER FOURTEEN

Only the Best

Jamaicans See No Limits

♪ *Sister Nancy – Bam*
♪ *Jada Kingdom - Win*

Jamaicans see no limits. The aim is to be the best independently and collectively. We have learned the Akan people were thought to be the best workers and the most favored enslaved Africans to import despite their so-called unruly behavior. Jamaica has ancestral memories of their hardworking ethic that they have carried over from Africa and Asia. Their aim to be the best translates into many areas of life. Jamaicans take the art of competition to high yet adaptable levels from education, politics, sports, entertainment, food & culture, and even how they communicate. Legendary reggae musician Luciano said perfectly, "Jamaicans on whole, they love the competition. They love to prove to themselves that they can really outrun someone. It's just the nature of 'I and I' people. That's why you have so much creativity and so many great singers because the competition level is so high here."

Jamaica is the fastest nation in the world. Our sports abilities have earned us a worldwide reputation, especially with our track and field athletes, cricketers, and soccer players. We continue to compete against other First World nations in the Olympic Games vigorously. We have even shown tenacity by being the first Caribbean country to compete in the Winter Games with bob-sleighing and ice hockey. The movie *Cool Runnings* depicts the famous Jamaican bobsled team and their determination. The Jamaican bobsled team's performance over the years has been a phenomenon because Jamaica is a tropical island. Jamaica has also produced the world's greatest boxers from Jamaican birth or Jamaican parentages, like Lennox Lewis, Mike Tyson, Floyd Mayweather, and Errol Spence. Guinness World Record holder Natasha Chang and the young and vibrant Fraser McConell who just won his first supercar victory in 2021, continue to put us on the map for race car driving. In cricket, Jamaica has produced many of the West Indies' Team and the world's best players, including Jimmy Adams, Jeffrey Dijon, and Chris Gayle. The Reggae Boyz is the national soccer team of Jamaica and is controlled by the Jamaica Football Federation. From Lindy Delapenha, Theodore Whitman, to the late Luton Shleton and the promising-young Raheem Sterling and Leon Bailey; Jamaican players, both in and outside of Jamaica, have made a name for themselves in the most popular world sport. Though they have never won a World Cup, they continue to compete with optimism.

Some people speculate on how such a tiny country can produce the fastest runners in the world. My father once joked that Jamaicans are so fast because they learn in their youth how to run fast when running from cops or if they did something bad in general that an elder was against. One could even connect it to the escape mechanisms during slavery days. There's also a rumor that yam, a root vegetable with starchy flesh, may be a secret tool. Yam has been a constant staple in the Jamaican diet since the beginning of slavery. From Herb McKenley to Asafa Powell, Yohan Blake, and Usain Bolt; and from Merlene Ottey and Veronica Campbell-Brown to Shelly-Ann Fraser and Elaine Thompson-Herah, Sherika Jackson, and many medal-holding Jamaican track stars, they continue to set records on the world stage, making Jamaica the fastest nation in the world. Usain Bolt's wins since the Olympics in 2008 have cemented Jamaican domination in Track & Field. When athletes win, or any Jamaican on popular platforms, the pride throughout Jamaica is highly contagious, resulting in an abundance of celebrations and parties throughout the island. Jamaicans have continued to display their skill and will to win in different worldly arenas with years of dedication and preparation for competitions, while growing up on the island. Other Jamaican sports athletes worthy of mentioning are NBA stars Patrick Ewing, Roy Hibbert, Ben Gordon, Andre Drummond, and Tristan Thompson; MLB players Chili Davis, Devon White, and Justin Masterson; NFL's Patrick Chung; mixed martial arts fighter Aljamain Sterling; professional WWE wrestler Big E Langston; the late Olympic fencer Kamara James, and professional bodybuilder Heather Foster. Jamaicans continue to dominate in a variety of sports despite the size of their tiny island. To acknowledge and pay respects to all the Jamaican athletes worldwide who have made an impact on their country through their sport would require a book, just like music.

    Jamaicans have a reputation abroad as hard workers. In addition to having a reputable work ethic, Jamaicans are stereotyped to have multiple jobs, like our brothers and sisters over in Mexico. There is quite a noticeable number of Jamaican farmers throughout the states who are contracted from the island and granted work visas for farm work. Ironically, it seems as if they, too, still seem to be the preferred workers by systems because of their work ethic and willingness to do the work. Even in the U.S. for the summer, these jobs pay in several months enough to serve families back home for an entire year, so the opportunity turns out to be favorable amongst some Jamaicans. I look at trendy places for vacation in America, like Cape Cod, where there is an abundance of Jamaican farmworkers and restaurant workers. In certain parts of the Vineyard, many Jamaicans live and work for the wealthy. My brother and I visit the Vineyard frequently, and there is no doubt that this summer home sanctuary for many Americans, especially New Englanders and those in the Northeast, has an added vibe from the Jamaicans that coexist there.

One might question if Jamaicans' work on the Vineyard is a form of present-day slavery. Work ethic can be traced back to Akan's arrival. I discovered by my observations of interacting with Jamaican uber drivers, bartenders, and cooks on the island that the Akan in one way or another, are still heavily sought after in today's century, and now in different places than where they were originally brought to. On one of our visits to Martha's Vineyard, my brother and I had a conversation with an owner of a restaurant named Coop De Ville. We noticed the amount of Jamaican workers on the island and brough it up in what turned into a lengthy and friendly conversation. He boasted about how talented and hardworking his Jamaicans cooks are, including the head chef before bringing us to her to be introduced. At another nearby bar called Sand Bar, we interacted with a bartender from a white European background, and after sharing the same observations as we did with the restaurant owner, he jumped on the bandwagon and shared how different the New England island is because of the large amount of Jamaicans they share it with, and the impact they have locally. After slavery was abolished, the British created non-forceful work situations in Jamaica where Africans from different areas could volunteer to come work in the Americas. At this point, they were called indentured servants instead of slaves. Now, they are called whatever vocation they choose to take up.

I recall one of my employers telling me his favorite group to work with was Jamaicans because they did the "work well with little excuses but made the environment fun, as long as they got their pay." At the time, I did not realize the extent of his comment until I began my research for this book. My thoughts on the Jamaicans' work ethic and the stereotypes attached are shared with an author by the name of Aidan Neal. "There is a wayward kind of thinking applied to the Jamaican immigrant's sense of ambition. This is the notion, that if one is working hard then they are simply not working smart. While this may be the case for several persons, contrary to popular belief it is not the only, nor is it the frequent truth. Perhaps the best assets of the immigrant are their mild ignorance of a racially oppressive system and the true belief in the American dream. It seems those who buy least into the American dream are Americans themselves. For any immigrant, coming to America is like visiting a rich and somewhat ungrateful Aunt. She is not altogether impressed with the opportunities laid at her feet and obsessively comments on those who do so little and are rewarded so much more. When you grow with far less opportunities you simply don't get hung up on how little others are doing. You're more concerned with the fact that there are opportunities and concede to having to clutch at them until you are in the position you wish to be."[80]

Jamaicans are not bystanders and find themselves on all powerful platforms from politics to music, sports, and more. Their militant characteristics have had some influence in other societies outside of Jamaica around the world. Many freedom fighters and politicians are of Jamaican descent, including Louis Farrakhan - Leader of the Nation of Islam, Colin Powell — the 65th U.S. Secretary of State, and Kamala

Harris, the first female vice-president of the United States, all who have used their platforms to advance on humane issues, such as racism and equality, in the United States of America. In the arts and entertainment field worldwide, we have multitalented supermodel Grace Jones who has contributed to the American Foundation for AIDS Research, Children's Health Fund, and Elton John AIDS Foundation. We also have supermodel Naomi Campbell who founded two charitable organizations on top of raising millions of dollars for the sub-Saharan children of Africa, Hurricane Katrina victims, and poverty in Brazil by supporting local artisans. Usain Bolt has made substantial contributions to Jamaican communities following his fast rise to stardom, in addition to list of other notable Jamaican stars.

Perhaps for Jamaicans, competition and striving to be the best is where their mastery of exaggerations best displays itself. Often, Jamaicans will make up their own lingo, and sooner or later depending on how catchy it is, it will spread throughout the island and eventually become a part of the everyday lingo. "Go hard and done" is one of many Jamaican idioms characterized by high energy, and it translates into a "do your absolute best and just finish" type of vibe, somewhat similar to "go hard or go home." Another more widely-known Jamaican saying, "We likkle but we tallawah" also embodies high energy. I read one definition online that translated the famous expression into, "we're a small nation but we're strong-willed, we're determined, and we refuse to be restrained by the boundaries of our small island." I used to think my family members were exaggerating all the time with the way they express themselves, but as the term 'exaggeration' is often used to describe a lie, that is not the case here. I use the term here to explain Jamaicans pursuit to be the best and get the brightest of smiles, loudest of laughter, out of every moment possible. They understand there is a process in achieving a goal and they welcome and endure the process with ever-increasing excitement. This excitement is very often seen in communication for the listener and the talker. Listening might warrant exaggerated behaviors in laughing, telling jokes, and aggressive responses. The flow in behavioral vibrancy connects to their higher energy levels somehow.

It is safe to say Jamaicans use their heart and Soul in their work, communication, and even most mundane tasks. From the once Akan-dominated society to Jamaicans today, Jamaicans have a pattern of wanting to create a new future for themselves, eternal peace and freedom, and taking action in every way possible to execute those goals. To win, thrive, and achieve is encouraged and expected in Jamaican society.

CHAPTER FIFTEEN

War

Jamaicans Will Fight For Their Freedom Until They Win

♪ *Queen Ifrica – Lioness on the Rise*
♪ *Dennis Brown – Revolution*

The Maroons set a new position of power and respect for Africans in Jamaica. They standardized a new mindset of all the enslaved people surrounding their borders and beyond. They created a successful movement that started from the first invasion of Spanish intruders lasting until present-day 2020. The inner rebel was released in mass amongst all Jamaicans and shaped the dynamics of the way the island is structured today. Throughout history, specifically during the 16th, 17th, 18th, and 19th centuries, we had different groups of people forcefully brought to Jamaica to create and adapt to a new way of life. The Maroons were the first to reverse the initial oppression imposed on them by fighting for their freedom and eradicating oppression by signing the British's peace treaty. The Maroons' standard is a threat to any systematic society that dares not to serve the people justly. The standard in place is an example of the strides oppressed people can make in reclaiming their freedom. This example continues to hold its power until all nations that the African diaspora serves implement systems that meet basic moral needs and acknowledges us as worthy human beings.

Additionally, this historic and rebellious movement is the only one I know of that survived from the very beginning of slavery until now. Accompong, the Maroons' site settled on after the peace treaty was enacted in 1739, still operates today. They even operate independently from the Jamaican government and they self-rule their society with little to no crime. Also, they have their own bank and currency. Both the Jamaican people and the government can learn something from this group of predominantly dignified, self-ruling Africans, to perhaps come to better solutions for crime, for one; and at the very least respecting them as one-less troublesome group they have to worry about in the country.

As part of the peace treaty, the Maroons agreed to capture runaway enslaved people. This is a controversial part of the treaty because it did not serve all enslaved people on the island, only the Maroons. At this point in history, we must consider the Maroons' choices in the 1700s to retain equal power with those that once ruled them. Among all colonies that enslaved Africans were brought to, we must examine the numbers of Africans to British in each of the territories. The environmental restraints and sacrifices an oppressed individual faced, the personal will from each oppressed individual to retain their freedom and the level of freedom that satisfied their peace of mind must also be examined. Jamaica benefitted in a way where they had strength in the numbers, but a large density of the oppressed possessed a militant resiliency cultivated in West Africa. Resiliency contributed to the level of freedom they fought for in Jamaica and their strategy to ensure a type of eternal peace for themselves. "It is not hard to understand why Maroons may have been more eager to form alliances or relationships with these planters rather than overseers, or indeed with enslaved peoples themselves. Amicable interactions with white society, and with wealthy planters, in particular, would have helped to achieve the goal of creating a unified Maroon identity. By allying with local white growers, Maroons distanced themselves from their former identities as the colony's enemies and re-characterized themselves as associates of the elite Jamaican society."[23]

In terms of numbers, money, influence, and power, the British outweighed Africans. However, Africans were able to hold on to their spirituality in the new oppressed world and ultimately outweighed their oppressors' evil spirits. We could speculate that the Maroons could have refused to sign the peace treaty and chose to pursue with vigor onto the British. With an exhaustive list of possible options, we will never know. What is known is the Maroons showed how powerful African spirituality was beyond the continent's borders and the benefits of retaining those spiritual systems. As discussed in earlier chapters, ancient spiritual customs are still heavily practiced by the Maroons and Rastas. Overall, the Jamaican people apply spiritual factors of music and dance to their evolution.

The Africans showcased their strategic and militant skills against the British and Spanish by choosing sides that secured the most freedom during the war over Jamaica in the 1600s. Jamaica experienced as many slave rebellions as all the other British colonies put together, with the 33:1 an enslaved person to slave owner ratio on the island.[81] The exact numbers of enslaved Africans that arrived in Jamaica are hard to pinpoint within all of the research I gathered; however, the range of six hundred thousand to one million is constant throughout various sources.

Fearless

The journey of the Maroons was a great demonstration of Akan's power out of the Motherland. Most rebellions were Akan-led. The colonial government did not perceive certain situations as acts of violence towards the colony and quickly pardoned the Maroons after signing the treaty. One occurrence backing this claim is a dispute that happened between a Maroon, Quao, and the leadership he attempted to overthrow led by Ned Crawford, killing Crawford in the process. Because the attack was not an attack on white society, the government pardoned Quao and his followers. These pardons perhaps highlighted the fear, or respect, many colonists and the colonial government still had of the Maroons.[23]

From the beginning of Maroon history in Jamaica to present-day Jamaica, we have a pattern of producing militant people. "The boldness of the Maroons, their prowess in guerrilla warfare, and their knowledge of the terrain made them a serious threat to English colonization, the plantation economy, and slavery itself. They plundered and burned plantations, captured enslaved people, took arms and ammunition, and killed English soldiers who ventured into the interior. Their continued successes against English forces inspired enslaved people, many of whom escaped the plantations to join maroon communities or establish new ones. The Maroons were such a formidable force that the English were unable to subjugate them after 85 years of intense, bitter struggle. The English conceded defeat in 1739, ending the First Maroon War. In the peace treaties, the Maroons won their independence and freedom." They were instrumental in taking down the famous Tacky's Rebellion in 1760, amongst other slave revolts, which earned both fear and respect in the colony. Maroons were employed to hunt runaways so extensively by white Jamaicans that the Maroons could be looked at as a police force.[23]

Jamaicans continue to hold key positions in defense agencies worldwide, taking their militant skills past the Jamaican border. In the US, that includes the CIA, FBI, and state and city law enforcement forms that defend the people.

The attempt to halt the importation of Akan enslaved Africans is a significant and often overlooked event in slavery that highlights the fear colonizers had of African people. This is an essential part of Black history that is not examined enough. The British nearly banned the Akan importation because they were the main forces behind all the rebellions in the 18th century that psychologically terrorized both Europe and America. They were dispersed across the island and were the majority, having been imported to seven of fourteen of the island's ports. Research shows a noticeable decline in imports from the Akan people in the 19th century compared to the 18th century. The British were afraid of Black domination and took notice of the power Akan had in the Americas. As a result, they moved down the coast to largely import Igbo people in the early 19th century. Reasons for the Akan's steep militance and Ghanaian history deserves a separate study. I suspect one reason was due to the protection of gold on The Gold Coast.

Other than the militant Akan, the Igbo and Madagascar people also brought significant values to the table during slavery with their language, proverbs, folklore, food, music, and mannerisms. The Igbo people are credited for idioms like having a *long* or *big eye* (meaning you want everything you see), the Jonkonnu celebrations, and the sucking of teeth and cutting of eyes Jamaicans are known to express with. Words such as "Unu (you all)" and "Se (say)" and arguably the introduction of Obeah that the Akan are also said to have brought to the island, are Igbo-influenced.

The Igbo people often demonstrated their resilience by committing suicide, pledging that they'd rather die and have their spirit returned to Africa than to become an enslaved African. It is said that slave owners paired the enslaved Igbo women with enslaved Akan men to control and subdue the latter as an attempt to filter out the Akan. They believed that Igbo women were bound and loyal to the energy of their first-born sons' birthplace.[82] This reflects the awareness Europeans have always had of energy levels and its effects on others. A Jamaican reflected on his educational trip to Madagascar, making a connection between their people and Jamaicans, "Malagasy people, like the Jamaican people I grew up with, display a level of resilience that is unparalleled. This resilience, combined with a deep love for and extensive knowledge of the environment, results in unique harmony with nature."[79] And later in the 19th and 20th centuries, other non-African people from Europe and Asia, such as the Indians, Chinese and Lebanese, contributed their strengths and vigor to the already-resilient Jamaica. Together, every group has earned prosperity on the island and has made contributions to cultivate Jamaica's uniqueness.

Africans in Jamaica were forced to use new resources to adapt and create a new life. They retained their militant and resilient attitude by forming a collective that increased their forces to fight for freedom. During the First Maroon War, enslaved Africans who did not run away into the mountains to join the Maroons still fought on sea level. When most of the Igbo arrived in the 19th century, following what appeared to be an ironic, apparent, unofficial (from a colonist's perspective) ban on the Akan importation to the Americas, they accounted for having the most runaway enslaved Africans. The Second Maroon War from 1795-1796 occurred due to the British not keeping their word. This war had a different turnout.

The British defeated the Maroons and took many of the Maroons as prisoners and deported them to Nova Scotia as a form of punishment, where they were forced to begin a new life.

The Baptist War (also known as the Sam Sharpe Rebellion, the Christmas Rebellion, and the Christmas Uprising) from 1831-1832 led the British to abolish slavery. What was intended to be a peaceful rebellion led by deacon Sam Sharpe in hopes of being compensated for their plantation work ended in a brutal war between colonizers and enslaved peoples. This war cost England $52 million from significant damage to sugar plantations. It is important to note white missionaries served on Sam Sharpe's rebellion, although they did not receive the harsh punishments Blacks received. Maroons served on the side of the colonizers as part of their joint treaty. Another notable revolt was the Morant Bay Rebellion, led by Jamaican National Heroes, Baptist deacon Paul Bogle and businessman George William Gordon. What started off as peacefully protesting widespread poverty, and injustice with living conditions and voting rights, resulted in hundreds of Jamaicans being killed and arrested in St. Thomas. The many uprisings and rebellions that took place in Jamaica made life for the British more difficult. Paul and George were caught and immediately hanged after trial. There are monuments and statues dedicated to their courage and service in the St. Thomas parish. In 2021, the new chief of the Maroons of Cockpit Country (Accompong), Chief Richard Currie, released a valuable document and shared some shocking information on his Instagram hidden in the archives by unsaid parties about who Paul Bogle really was. Apparently, he was an Eastern Maroon from Hayfield, St. Thomas who was being guided by Maroon elders on how to approach the war with colonizers. This is important because the Maroons have historically been blamed for being traitors of their people, further causing division between the Maroons and all other Africans. They are meticulously making steps to close that gap.

In North America, there were six successful slave revolts that were victorious. The San Miguel de Gualdape War in 1526 under Spanish Florida, The Gaspar Yanga's Revolt in 1570 under Spanish Veracruz (Mexico), The First Maroon War from 1730-1739 under British Jamaica, the Haitian Revolution from 1791-1804 under French Saint-Domingue, the Amistad ship rebellion in 1839 off the Cuban coast, and the 1841 Creole case ship rebellion off the Southern U.S. Coast. The First Maroon War was the first and only victory under the British Empire.

As a result of maintaining strong connections to African roots, Jamaicans turned a physical battle into a successful spiritual one through African religion, folklore, and music, eventually with reggae music's aid to fight what has now become more of a spiritual battle. Although music has been discussed previously, it deserves to be noted here because of its integration into the culture. Reggae music is the artistic and creative result of an oppressed people's view on freedom. It reflects the level of freedom Jamaicans are familiar with through their spiritual victories, although the fights are not entirely over. Jamaicans continue to silently win the spiritual battle that has been going on for centuries. Its best example is reggae, a music genre that continues to grasp and influence people and other genres all over the world with its powerful words for peace, equality, and unity. Whether it's the brutally honest lyrics playing on a melodic Roots rhythm, or a dancehall tune on heavy bass that warrants erotic and energetic connection between two or more people, Jamaicans have turned what was once a physical battle into a non-violent one. Jamaicans have proven themselves to be one of the most potent human groups regarding their offerings and energy towards spiritual warfare the world continues to fight. Reggae is one of the most dangerously effective and overlooked tools for spiritual fights in the universe that continues to stand up for the oppressed worldwide, especially for the African diaspora whose ancestors were stolen off their land over 400 years ago.

Below is the actual verbiage from the Peace Treaty of 1739, that both the Maroons and Colonel John Guthrie, a Jamaican planter, signed. It allowed the Maroons to self-govern, in addition to being given acres of land by the British government to continue their autonomous society.

The Peace Treaty

(taken from the Kress Collection of Business and Economic Literature, Baker Library, Harvard Business School [75]

Articles of Pacification with the Maroons of Trelawney Town, Concluded March the first, 1738 (1)

In the name of God, Amen, Whereas Captain Cudjoe, Captain, Accompong, Captain Johnny, Captain Cuffee, Captain Quaco, and several other Negroes, their dependents and adherents, have been in a state of ware and hostility, for several years past, against our sovereign lord the King, and the inhabitants of this island; whereas peace and friendship among mankind, and the preventing of effusion of blood, is agreeable to God, consonant to reason, and desired by every good man; and whereas his Majesty George the Second King of Great Britain, France, and Ireland, and of Jamaica Lord, Defender of the Faith, &c. has by his letters patent, dated February the twenty-fourth, one thousand seven hundred and thirty-eight, in the twelfth year of his reign, granted full power and authority to John Guthrie and Francis Sadler, Esquires, to negotiate and finally conclude a treaty of peace and friendship with the aforesaid Captain Cudjoe, and the rest of his captains, adherents, and others his men; they mutually, sincerely, and amicably, have agreed to the following articles:

First, that all hostilities shall cease on both sides forever.

Secondly, that the said Captain Cudjoe, the rest of his captains, adherents, and men shall forever hereafter in a perfect state of freedom and liberty, excepting those who have been taken by them, or fled to them, within two years last past, if such are willing to return to their said masters and owners, with full pardon and indemnity from their said masters or owners for what is past; provided always that, if they are not willing to return, they shall remain in subjection to Captain Cudjoe and in friendship with us, according to the form of a tenor of this treaty.

Thirdly, that they shall enjoy and possess, for themselves and posterity forever, all the lands situate and lying between Trelawney Town and the Cockpits, to the amount of fifteen hundred acres, bearing northwest from the said Trelawney Town.

Fourthly, that they shall have the liberty to plant the said lands with coffee, cocoa, ginger, tobacco, and cotton, and to breed cattle, hogs, goats, or any other flock, and dispose of the produce or increase of the said commodities to the inhabitants of this island; provided always, that when they bring the said commodities to market, they shall apply fist to the customs, or any other magistrate of the respective parishes where they expose their goods to sale, for a license to vend the same.

Fifthly, that Captain Cudjoe, and all the Captain's adherents, and people now in subjection to him, shall all live together within the bounds of Trelawney Town, and that they have the liberty to hunt where they shall think fit, except within three miles of any settlement, crawl, or pen; provided always, that in case the hunters of Captain Cudjoe and those of other settlements meet, then the hogs to be equally divided between both parties.

Sixthly, that the said Captain Cudjoe and his successors, do use their best endeavors to take, kill, suppress, or destroy, either by themselves, or jointly with any other number of men, commanded on that service by his excellency the Governor, or Commander in Chief, for the time being, all rebels whosesoever they be, throughout this island, unless they submit to the same terms of accommodation granted to Captain Cudjoe, and his successors.

Seventhly, that in case this island is invaded by any foreign enemy, the said Captain Cudjoe, and his successors hereinafter named or to be appointed, shall then, upon notice given, immediately repair to any place the Governor, for the time being, shall appoint, in order to repel the said invaders with his or their utmost force and to submit to the orders of the Commander in Chief on that occasion.

Eighthly, that if any white man shall do any manner of injury to Captain Cudjoe, his successor, or any of his or their people, they shall apply to any commanding officer or magistrate in the neighborhood for justice; and in case Captain Cudjoe, or any of his people, shall do any injury to any whiter person, he shall submit himself, or deliver up such offenders to justice.

Ninthly, that if any negroes shall hereafter run away from their masters or owners, and shall fall into Captain Cudjoe's hands, they shall immediately be sent back to the chief magistrate of the next parish where they are taken; and these that bring them are to be satisfied with their trouble, as the legislature shall appoint. [The assembly granted a premium of thirty shillings for each fugitive slave returned to his owner by the Maroons, besides expenses.]

Tenthly, that all negroes taken, since the raising of this party by Captain Cudjoe's people, shall immediately be returned.

Eleventhly, that Captain Cudjoe, and his successors, shall wait on his Excellency, or the Commander in Chief for the time being, every year if thereunto required.

Twelfth, that Captain Cudjoe, during his life, and the captains succeeding him shall have full power to inflict any punishment they think proper for crimes committed by their men among themselves, death only excepted; in which case, if the Captain thinks they deserve death, he shall be obliged to bring them before any justice of the peace, who shall order proceedings on their trial equal to those of other free negroes.

Thirteenth, that Captain Cudjoe with his people, (Repeat: subjects, peoples.) shall cut, clear, and keep open, large and convenient roads from Trelawney Town to Westmorland and St. James's, and if possible, to St. Elizabeth's.

Fourteenth, that two white men, to be nominated by his Excellency, or the Commander and Chief, for the time being, shall constantly live and reside with Captain Cudjoe and his successors, in order to maintain a

Fearless

friendly correspondence (Not dominance, correspondence -- see "waiting". These are ambassadors, not governors) with the inhabitants of this island.

Fifteenth, that Captain Cudjoe, shall, during his life, be Chief Commander in Trelawney Town; after his decease the command to devolve on his brother, Captain Accompong; and in case of his decease, on his next brother Captain Johnny; and, failing him, Captain Coffee shall succeed; who is to be succeeded by Captain Quaco; and after all their demises, the Governor, or Commander in Chief for the time being, shall appoint, from time to time, whom he thinks fit for that command.

In testimony, &c. &c.

CHAPTER SIXTEEN

The Power of Consciousness

Jamaicans Master Awareness

♪ *Dre Island – We Pray (ft. Popcaan)*
♪ *George Nooks – God Is Standing By*

Jamaicans master awareness. Jamaica is a unique place made up of exceptional people from different cultures. The island inhabitants set an example of what it means to allow differences to create unity and harmony. The energy cultivated over the last four centuries is a result of the strong connection to African roots; in spirituality, religion, music, and dance. Jamaicans accept their royalty. Their pride is indicative of how Africans saw themselves before Europeans arrived in Africa. Today, Jamaicans bury the dead in tombs like kings and queens once did in Egypt.

Jamaicans are aware of their power as humans that can overcome what is unjust. Overtime, the acceleration of their consciousness has contributed to their abundance of pride. They have experienced loss but challenge their drive to grow stronger and improve instead of deterring and being fearful. As we recall, it was the original Africans that courageously fought for their freedom who opened the gateway of awareness. Akan was the first import of enslaved Africans from Africa to Jamaica, bringing their militant attitude and ways. Some decades later, Igbo came to add and further conquer spiritual warfare in Jamaica.

Jamaicans remained deeply connected to their roots. As a result, the mastery of consciousness became a way of life and remained so until this day. They believe in asserting what is just and encourage others to do the same. If we speak to Jamaicans today that were alive to remember the island's vibe before independence from England in 1962, they will tell us that the word 'nigga' never existed in Jamaica. There was oppression based on skin color, but racism was not like elsewhere. When James Baldwin famously said, "No one was white until they came to America," it implies, along with my grandfather's observations, that identities and roles changed once people of different ethnic backgrounds hit American soil.

I have gathered that the Jamaicans' connection to spirituality instilled fear amongst the colonizers. I believed Africans fearlessly voiced their truths about their rights to live in a free world. Their courageous and militant tones spread throughout the island. We will rarely find a Jamaican who does not speak their mind; a reserved and timid Jamaican is questionable and highly unlikely to find.

"A clear conscience allows you to live in the present without being distracted, both mentally and emotionally, by your past. You'll find yourself encouraged by the truths that no failure is permanent, and no life is beyond God's power to bring about change."[102] If we recall from *Chapter Two: Making The Best Out Of Reality*, I explained how the enslaved people accepted their reality to move forward, despite the tragedy of the circumstances that brought them to Jamaica. Africans understood the value of life before they were kidnapped and held onto that understanding with the aid of their collective actions. Today, the customs and ways of survival they practiced showed they had extensive knowledge and high regard for the earth's natural resources. They cherish their physical ability to generate income, take care of family, praise God, sing, and dance. Gratitude is the foundation of life on the island. While greed is not of concern amongst the majority, there is a lack of opportunity on the island, which contradicts a place with such an immense amount of energy.

Jamaicans have proven that we can maintain, restore, and develop the necessary energy to influence other people, and especially expected so in Jamaica, to exercise their consciousness. While doing my research I read an interesting observation from a white man of how he looked at the Africans he was encountering in Jamaica. "Of this qualification the Negro congregations, with their African background of tonal speech (though Bridges did not know and certainly did not admit this), were 'naturally most extraordinary judges."[21] This is a high value that one would say is godly, mirroring their zeal to do the right thing. A point in their evolution is reached in which exercising their consciousness is nearly mandatory and expected in Jamaican society, though not lawfully as it is more of an undeclared law in Jamaican society. As a result of the oppression Black people faced, which was not in God's plan, movements arose to restore royalty. Resilience is demonstrated in the Akan enslaved Africans having to spread their energy of power despite the suppressed rebellions in Jamaica. Even with the existing limit of the number of reggae musicians traveling outside of Jamaica to perform and generate a higher income than Jamaica, due to the government and the guidelines that must be followed, the Akan energy still has made a global impact. Beenie Man, Bounty Killer, Mavado, Aidonia and Ricky Trooper, Popcaan, Busy Signal are just some dancehall musicians whose visas have been revoked since 2010. Public affairs officer at the United States Embassy in Kingston, Joshua Polacheck, says that the revoking of visas has more to do with the artists' involvement in criminal activities and less to do with the content of their music.[103] It is also speculated that this was the result of a quarrel between the US and Jamaica when the government at the time refused to extradite Christopher "Dudus" Coke in 2011.[104] Jamaicans still seek clearer answers as to why obtaining visas is such a difficult and costly feat, mostly resulting with denials.

Women freely express themselves through dance without being demeaned, influencing the dancehall queen-force in places like Japan, China, France, and Italy, just to name a few. There have been many attempts throughout time to suppress the Akan energy. However, the influence of the Rastafarians, reggae, hip-hop, and Jamaican dancing's increasing influence amongst other cultural influences continue to inspire people well beyond the island's border.

All movements mentioned above, since their inception, received backlash from the government, cultures outside of Jamaica, and from members of the African diaspora. Could, we in fact, still have oppressors who are aware and afraid of the Akan energy that is still foundational in Jamaica? The attention I am bringing to Jamaica is just the beginning. Most notably for the descendants of Europeans who brought this curse upon them, the world is going to shift into re-exploring Africa. This time, with a more fearless, relentless, and honest approach; finding and utilizing alternative tools and knowledge accessible outside of Westernized culture and teachings that was imposed on African descendants who essentially aren't from the west, to know who we are and the ways of life of where we truly come from.

When Jamaicans say they only answer to God, they live by every word. Due to the level of confidence Jamaicans carry, one would think they have what is called a 'God complex'. Instead, I believe it is their unwavering belief in God, and what is promised to them is what generates this contagious boost in self-esteem and purpose. "In Jamaican history, God has been imagined and re-imagined constantly. As Garvey duly notes, 'God may be the limit of Jamaicans' creation of self as what they want to be, though interestingly, at the same time, God also seems to be limitless in the way he is utilized in Black Jamaicans identity. He (or She or They, depending) always seems to be there though because he is the strongest identifying agent and tool of rebellion."[41]

They protect God best through actions, showing that sometimes we must bring fire to defend our spirituality. The intensity of one's fight reflects the level of dedication to God, making it acceptable to do things one normally would not have to do, like kill to survive or protect one's freedom. *Jungle justice* is a more common method to handle situations than in Westernized cultures. Time and time again you'll hear about a farmer who retaliated against a cow-thief, or rapist being retaliated on by family or communal members of its victim. The belief in whether God is a man, a woman, Mother Nature, the Big Bang, the universe, or our highest Self is not being examined here. The universe and all its' inhabitants and nature, including fire, water, earth, and air, are from the same source of energy. What is most important to recognize is Jamaicans viewing that source as God, God being a power higher than the human Self. Jamaicans see God as the ultimate limit of where the Self should strive to be. This belief directly connects to the high and palpable energy in the air as there is a widespread national belief and pride in a Higher Entity.

Christianity might be the most dominant religious force in Jamaica and once was thought of to be the most potent tool for Africans during slavery. Akan spirituality is heavily based on tributes to ancestors. The Akan, likely to have migrated to Ghana from Egypt, freely practiced their religion on Jamaican plantations.[83] The English mistakenly recorded Nyame's wife, Asase Ya, as Asarci, giving us reason to believe the Bono spiritual system was dominant on the plantations when the Akan arrived. As mentioned before, Akan believed in a God named Nyame, who was thought of as the creator of the universe and spiritually visible everywhere. Nyame is synonymous with other names found throughout different African cultures and likely used to name the same God. Asase Ya was the goddess of fertility and favored the Bono people of the Akan for their skills as occupational workers in agricultural fields neighboring the Ashanti tribe. Due to Jamaicans' characteristics of Jamaicans work ethic today, we have sufficient evidence to believe there may have been some contribution from the Akan people and their characteristics passed down through generations. However, it's important to note the Igbo was the primary group from Nigeria who dominated in numbers in Jamaica after the Akan. The Yoruba people (being mentioned for the first time) also had a strong presence on the island. They dominated a large portion of Nigeria, Benin, Togo, and the Ivory Coast and are said to have been the descendants of Yorubaland's original people, a civilization that existed during the first millennium BCE and the same period the Assyrians took the conquest of Egypt, that forced the original to move West. The Yoruba people left an influence in Jamaica, for instance, with the name of living settlements in Jamaica such as Naggo Head and Abeokuta in Portmore.

The Igbo people are credited for being the original practitioners of Obeah that the Akan also practiced. Obeah was thought of as a significant defining tool to combat slavery. Another similarity between the Jamaicans and the Akan included what Edwards called the 'prevalence of Obi' which is witchcraft now often called Obeah. Edwards argued that, like all nations of Africa, the Jamaican Maroons believed the older men were wizards or Obeah-men. These Obeah-men were extremely intelligent and would use special herbs and medications to perform weird acts. For example, they would pretend to raise someone from the dead by giving them something to slow their heart down, causing people to believe they were dead, and then the Obeah-man would pretend to resurrect the corpse.[17] They used Obeah to make others, including colonists, believe they had a type of magical power.

There are speculations on the authenticity of Obeah. Concerning indulging in psychological games, I believe an influence could've came from the famous Jamaican story of Anansi mentioned earlier on in this book. The story says Nyame and Asase Ya had three children Bea, Tono, and Anansi - the trickster. Anansi bragged about his intelligence to do anything he wanted to do. Nyame became weary of Anansi's boasts. Simultaneously, Nyame received complaints about a python terrorizing the Akan people, so Nyame challenged Anansi to kill the python as punishment. Anansi tricked the python into eating a lot of food and drinking substantial and large amounts of wine until it went unconscious, upon which he summoned the villagers to beat the creature until they drove it away. This is symbolic of how the Akan people in Jamaica were able to win the First Maroon War, in which they say spirituality played a pivotal role. Maroons most notably "used" Obeah.

Fearless

Obeah is distinguished from its counterparts (like Voodoo and Santeria) as only being a communication tool with spirits and ancestors; no gods were worshiped. Could it be that Obeah is not real at all, and perhaps what colonizers thought of as being real was just a psychological play on their minds? Could this part of the perpetual fights for freedom just have been another re-enactment of Anansi tricking the snake that symbolized Europeans to drive them out or drive them mad? Maybe it was only used as a tool to instill fear. Perhaps Obeah is very real and derives from more profound knowledge and practices traced back to our earliest roots in Africa and beyond. There are existing Obeah practitioners who certainly say the modality is natural along with a plethora of sources that point to its compelling authenticity. On the contrary, there are enough Jamaicans that would label Obeah as false and inauthentic, a tool Queen Nanny is said to have used against her oppressors to secure freedom for her people. Interestingly enough, the word Obeah in the Akan language means woman.

The symbolism of the mongoose animal in Jamaica is something to take notice of. The mongooses are indigenous to Africa and Asia only, and they are among the handful of animals that can kill snakes. Snakes have always been connected to evil spiritually, like the serpent in the Bible. The Mongoose, characterized by cleverness, similar to Anansi, can attack by itself, but usually a group of Mongeese will attack one snake and use it for food. Additionally, they can withstand the spewed poison up to a certain point! Killing or driving away the snake is an important and recurring tale in Jamaican culture.

In such a patriarchal-ruled world, respect for women and femininity is also something to take notice of. The Akan were a matrilineal group that believed because Nyame was able to create, he must have had feminine and masculine principles. The Akan being a matrilineal people is reflective of how Jamaican men behave towards women in and outside of the home. In the dance hall, women express themselves on the dance floor without judgment. Women, through dance, show an awareness of emotions through creative, intimate, and energetic movements. During parties, both men and women take over as personal MCs to encourage their female peers to embrace their femininity through empowerment phrases like "bruk out my girl!" or "walk out my girl, walk out!" This practice is dedicated to the women while men also encouragingly pursue the support. The Akan being matrilineal is also symbolic in the way Jamaican women operate, often taken up both feminine and masculine duties by both caretaking and being the breadwinners of the household.

The name Nyame itself is androgynous. Embracing the feminine means embracing emotions and creating more, commonly not associated with masculinity. The duality of the Jamaican is reflected best in music. In Jamaica, it is common to see men tap deeper into their creativity and emotions, which is noticeable in reggae music. They express their feelings by singing or deejaying about their traumatic pasts, sharing their present, and expressing their heartfelt views on worldly affairs. The same goes for women. Dancehall legends like Lady Saw, Patra, Diana King, all demonstrate this with their ability to switch from a hard flow to a very feminine tone when they feel necessary. The fearlessness to tap into both sides broke barriers for Jamaican women and the freedom to express what they wanted, including their sexuality. I have personally witnessed Lady Saw work a machete to do her own yard work with ease alongside workers she employed. These qualities are rooted and therefore expressed in daily life through their own creative and unique ways.

Refamiliarized value for Black women from oppressors was somewhat evident during slavery, with Europeans often courting African mistresses and putting them in pivotal positions over their white female counterparts. For example, Cuba Cornwallis, a descendant of the Ashanti Empire and former enslaved African, became the mistress of Cornwallis and was freed by him. Cuba was a master healer known to use natural remedies and speculatively, Obeah. Whatever type of intangible power she and other Jamaican women possessed throughout history was magnetic enough to attract men of all backgrounds. What also factored into women making decisions to advance their powerful stance in society was the general will for ultimate freedom, so the African women in Jamaica took advantage of whatever opportunity possible to secure the trust of white men. White men were said to have sometimes preferred Black women because they were less expensive, cleaner, and more able in caretaking areas; I can imagine these preferences were easy to overlook in the quest of one's freedom. This is important to take notice of because the patriarchy has ruthlessly taken general domination of the entire world, simply put, since women were to blame for the fall of humankind after Eve took a bite of the apple. This is a story that continues to to put women at an odd advantage today,

The certainty of the self and pride in our roots creates more space for masculine and feminine balance. Consciousness in life presents us with multiple dimensions and possibilities to exist in. Perhaps the art of honoring the masculine and feminine invites both energies to arise, giving us more control over our destiny. Jamaican people have a strong sense of pride individually and collectively. They understand everybody is important and everybody has a purpose.

The importance of the middleman or middlewoman is highlighted throughout Jamaican society, a term I am using to in order to keep the role to be perceived as human as possible within this context. Another term I equate with middleman or middlewoman and could be used to describe these people are *children of God*, with no judgement. So we can get a better understanding of my direction, I do not want to convolute individuals passionate about religion, with individuals passionate about the well-being of a human being. So, I am using a term I believe can represent the bridge between God and God's children, middlemen and middlewomen. The importance marked on this aspect of Jamaican society is reminiscent of that of Jesus, although this doesn't account for all the reasoning. The Akan themselves created an army of these middle-people through the Maroons. "They were granted semiautonomous government status and land in return for halting all hostilities against whites, obligating themselves to assist in case of foreign invasion, destroying any new maroon communities, and capturing and returning future runaways. Thus, on the fringes of the slave-plantation economy established by Europeans, semiautonomous communities of free Blacks developed, with their own economy and culture partially based on African traditions." This provides a perspective on what enslaved peoples were able to accomplish during unimaginable times for us in 2021. Bob Marley's *One Love Peace Concert* and his joining of hands of two oppositional leaders in Jamaica, Michael Manley of the PNP and Edward Seaga of the JLP. Bob Marley himself famously stated, "My father was white and my mother Black, you know. Them call me half-caste, or whatever. Well, me don't deh pon nobody's side. Me don't deh pon the

Black man's side nor the white man's side. Me deh pon God's side, the One who create me and cause me to come from Black and white, Who give me this talent." Musicians in general assume the middlemen or middlewomen role in society, spiritually through music, and physically through giving back to the community. When it comes to the infamous *don dadda* life in Jamaica, the drug-dealing lifestyle where drug dealers are dubbed dons (or creatively so, *don-dadda*), the common people are often still connected to don-like figures primarily because Jamaicans individually are strong people that take pride in being impenetrable, and able to face people and dangers of all sorts. Jamaica is one of the many countries with corruption as a topic of discussion. Instead of looking at it from a negative perspective where politicians or religious followers are purposefully incriminating themselves by engaging with corruptive activities, which certainly happens, it would also be fair to look at it from a perspective where one may simply know themself so well that they won't allow the affairs of another to interfere with their integrity and their ways of life. Still living by a standard that exemplifies doing the right thing and not being easily-influenced. I think an approach like this would contribute more to an upward trend of less crime, than adhering to the judgmental attitude we are expected upkeep on one another; which in my opinion, causes more division than unity. Environments where middlemen and middlewomen positions are socially accepted to maintain and uphold standards creates a desire for something higher to attain; a small view of how society could be less system-based and more self-ruling.

Nyame, the Akan people's God, is the energy that originally created the universe in the Akan culture.[84] Asase Ya, his wife, was the goddess of fertility, and she favored occupational workers in agricultural fields. This may have some connection to the respect Jamaicans have for working or going hard. The Akan people seemed to have value for energy as a currency. We live in a world where money is the greatest asset to have, or rather something tangible. What would happen if energy was prioritized as the most valuable currency in the world? It would be worth it to make a set into showing that we can value energy as much as we value money. This idea is foreign to many people because energy is intangible. As a result, energy is not overly popularized, nor are the abundant ways this universe is shared. Just like we acquire knowledge to climb up the ladder to make more money, it would make sense to climb to build up positive energy and powerful boundaries in our system to have a more fulfilling life. When we value energy first, we see a difference in human behavior. Energy is God's favorite currency. Money is a human's favored currency. Putting a universal value on energy is a direction that needs more attention. The more we get our energy into the rhythm and flow with the universe, the more connected we are to God. Energy is of high value. Perhaps this special vibe people feel when they arrive in Jamaica can be attributed to the extensive preservation efforts. The energy of Jamaica is a symbolism of spirituality, which lincludes music and dance, from the various groups indigenous to the island.

In re-visiting the Akan people, they had such powerful energy that shaped and advanced their environments. The militant Akan had significant influences on behavior, communication, and speech. They influenced survival methods for other people to adopt to master the environment. The energy that drove them was transferred to everyone around them without force. Their only concern was their freedom.

Fearless

One thing that palpably connects all the island's inhabitants, no matter the color of their skin or the shape of their physical features is their energy. The spirit which Jamaicans carry today proves that evolution can also come from energy transfers., just by being in the same environment with an individual or a group. Not everyone has Akan or Igbo roots in Jamaica, which is apparent amongst the non-Africans. Yet, the energy can be felt and seen in action collectively.

Peeling back the narrative layers in Africa before European arrival is a necessary task that deserves ongoing attention. It is crucial to the eradication of racism and balance regain that systemic injustices have disrupted. As blessed as Jamaica is, she is cursed with strategically pre-written agendas designed to keep the African race at the lowest points of a hierarchy. In different aspects of Jamaican society, holistic indigenous movements such as the Maroons and the Rastafarians prove, in action, that they seek peace and freedom. In environments where expressions are more vulgar and sometimes criticized, such as dancehall, we begin to see a shift within the dancehall world's dynamic. The change in a recent sound clash direction, a significant form of entertainment in Jamaica, saw a different lens of warring with The Beenie Man vs. Bounty Killer's historic battle on Versus TV in 2020 during the Covid-19 pandemic. These two dancehall legends had an in-person standoff on the popular platform Swizz Beats and Timbaland started in 2020. As Bounty said, "on the streets we par and on stage we war." The show was symbolic of the greatness that happens when opposing African forces that have been musical enemies off the grid come together for a higher purpose in real life. The pride resulting from it was abundant across the island, sprouting a deeper winning connection amongst the people. This newly respected understanding of how everyone can win gives me a reason to believe Jamaica could be soon possibly be entering into a new dimension if solutions can continue to be found nfor society development and applied to their current downfalls, especially the handling on crime.

Jamaicans operate in life believing the real fight is between self and fear. They realize the real battle was not between self and any human being. Their belief has a direct connection to why their most important relationship is with an unseen Power (God, ancestors, etc.) and to their confidence in knowing that if they could outsmart fear, then they could triumph over any system that operates from fear. Much of the world operates off of fear which brings light to how the spirit of Jamaica can have global influence. Jamaica's highly spiritual and godly grounds were initially fermented by the different groups that coexisted there since the Spanish first encountered the Taínos on the island in 1492. This unique foundation gave birth to Jamaica's spirit today. Enslaved peoples deliberately challenged the incessant imposition of religion from the British by spiritually counterattacking with their ancestors' customs. Pocomania was an example of how the African spirit still lived through the teachings of Christianity. They were always able to find a way to live above the ways of life imposed on them and remain spiritually connected with their creative way of thinking. In essence, this is what continues to make Jamaica the "heartbeat of the world."[106]

CHAPTER SEVENTEEN

Peace

Jamaicans Believe All People Are Equal, And Everyone Has Something To Bring To The Table

♪ *Dennis Brown – Here I Come*

♪ *Bob Marley – One Love*

Jamaicans believe all people are equal; 'Out of Many, One People' or 'One Love'. Jamaica's belly, the Akan people, migrated to Ghana from ancient Egypt/Nubia (also known as Kemet/Meroe, respectively).[89] Their ancestors of the Akan people were once called Kemets (Blacks). Israelites is said to have ultimately became the Akan tribe after migrating to Nubia-Egypt. Nubians-Egyptians became Bono once they migrated to what is now Mali to establish the empire of ancient Ghana, until a group of Muslim regimes invaded the territory almost 1,000 years later. The Akwamu group was said to have come from the Bonos that settled in ancient Ghana and were considered the Akan genesis. Thus, the Bonos may have been the descendants of Egyptians/Nubians that left the Sahara area after the fall of Kemet. There have been connections found between hieroglyphics and the Akan language.[85] If true, this means the Akan ancestors could have descended from the Egyptian Empire that lasted from 3100 BC to 30 BC. Christ, was of course born towards the ending of that fall.

Though the majority of the Akan enslaved Africans were taken to Jamaica, the Akan, or what a writer refers to as Israelites, occupied the British West Indies, Dutch West Indies, Danish West Indies (Virgin Islands), South Carolina, Guyana, Suriname, Belize, and interestingly, the East-West Indies (Indonesia). At one point, Egypt was very diverse, making the territory a possible connection between Israelites, the Akan, and Jamaicans plausible. I connect the vibe in Southeast Asia, specifically Bali, to that of other Akan descendants around the world in places like Jamaica. I have experienced Bali and the incredible vibe the world has come to love there. In terms of vibrancy and respect for people, it is much like Jamaica, and in my opinion, even better. They believe in karma and one can easily tell through their actions. While there, I saw a sizeable Jamaican flag on a house in the mountains shortly after leaving Mt. Batur, a famous volcano, and seen countless products promoting Bob Marley, eventually buying a Bob Marley painting myself. I had conversations with residents on Bob Marley's significance and how his memory is kept alive in Bali and I remember one of the hotel workers, who actually posed the question to my brother and I first, saying that it was the vibe. He couldn't find too much to say otherwise.

The terms Akan or The Gold Coast are not used in Jamaica, instead, Ghana is used since it is how it's referred to in today's world. No one uses the name 'Nubia' anymore, and that area is now called Sudan. These types of changes sometimes keep distancing Black people from our original roots, though not always done with malicious intent, or intent at all. It makes one wonder. Albeit, the Akan was just one of the powerful groups in Jamaica with an extensive history. The Akan, Igbo, and the Yoruba, all descendants of the Niger-Congo family (the world's third-largest language group), bathed over 1400 languages with many structural similarities. The Niger-Congo family connections are amongst the African diaspora, which I found to be not heavily researched enough. Jamaica's largest enslaved African population came from the Igbo people, who migrated from Israel to Meroe. Meroe continues to exist despite the attempted takeover of its roots by first the Assyrians from the region of Babylon, the Persians, the Macedonians in the BCE (before Christ), and the Arabs in the CE (after Christ). Egyptians are said to have been the first civilization to exist where their architecture, arts, and religious and spiritual beliefs were a model for societies, such as Greece and Rome to follow suit later. By 500 AD, the original ancient Egyptians and Nubians were gone, and nearly all of their cultural practices.

All Akan subgroups are matrilineal. This is important when looking at Jamaica's beauty as it embraces feminine principles such as creativity and displaying emotions without being judged as "too" masculine or feminine. Among these subgroups was the Ashanti tribe, as previously mentioned in this book. The name *Ashanti* possibly comes from *Ashan* in the Kingdom of Judah when one reads the Bible. When the Akan finally settled in Ghana, the Ashanti tribe was divided into around ten clans to develop surrounding countries. Both Islam and Christianity were forced upon Black people at different points in history. Initially, the Akan people ran from having to convert to Islam when the Arabs conquered Egypt-Nubia around 640 AD. The forced imposition of having to follow another religion prompted groups to migrate to other parts of Africa. This chronologically could make sense because the Akan were said to have migrated from Egypt in the 11th or 12th centuries, around 1000 -1100 AD.[89]

"The ancestors of the Akan people did not originally inhabit the modern lands of Ghana and Cote D'Ivoire. Instead, they are thought to have migrated south during the 11th or 12th century. Their origins before this migration are somewhat unclear, but they likely began as citizens of the older Ghana Empire. In addition, some historians maintain a much earlier link to the ancient rulers of Egypt and Nubia. Whatever the case may be, these settlers soon established trading kingdoms such as Bono, which grew alongside the Akan gold trade. The soils of the region, later labeled by the Europeans as the Gold Coast, contain plentiful deposits of the precious metal. From Bono, the Akan diversified into many smaller kingdoms and cultures, including the Akyem, Asante, Akuapem, Abron, Kwahu, and Fante."[89] The Akan and the Asante were the two subgroups that made up most of the Akan tribe brought to Jamaica.

Europeans were in contact with Africans long before arriving on West Africa's shores in the 1400s. I want to note an infamous connection that occurred during the late 4th century BC with Cleopatra of Egypt and notable figures of the Roman Empire. Cleopatra forged political alliances and personal relations with Rome's ruling class in order to maintain peace between both civilizations. She bore kids with Julius Caesar before his assassination, and she had children with Marc Antony, his friend, after Caesar died. Egypt came under Roman rule after Antony's and Cleopatra's joint suicide. Kemet, also known as Egypt-Nubia, fell 30 BCE, just about 30 years before Jesus Christ was born. Christianity then came to Egypt in 33 CE.

The Akan group is estimated to have a population of <u>20 million</u> spread throughout present-day Ghana and parts of the Ivory Coast and Togo. Some of the subgroups within the Akan, such as Ashanti, Fante, Bono, have been mentioned throughout this book. From the 15th to the 19th centuries, the Akan people were among the most powerful groups in Africa due to a gold boom between the 12th and 13th centuries, which initially attracted European traders.[87] We have little-to-enough evidence to believe the Akan people migrated from Nubia-Egypt.

The spirit of Jamaica is inarguably mostly Akan-driven. Although redundant at this point, it is an important and bold point to prove. The Jamaican Maroons have shown how the Akan spirit has survived from invasions in Africa to be tossed into the Americas forcefully. The Maroons, still in existence in Jamaica today, remain separated from the government of Jamaica, self-governing their estate, and have recently been using Maroon identification cards which states, "THE BEARER OF THIS INDIGENOUS PEOPLE MAROON ID IS NOT SUBJECTED TO NO BRITISH COLONIAL GOVERNMENT AGENTS BUT SUBJECTED ONLY TO THE MAROON STATE LAW." I have made friends at Accompong and was recently sent a copy of the picture ID through the popular What's App service used widely in the Caribbean (we're probably wondering if Maroons have phones and if they use technology, yes! They do! And by the way, not a bad thought). The ID is a real thing. The Akan principles have been able to survive the longest on the island. It seems as if the Akan's militant history added a necessary fuel for Africans to retain their power back in Jamaica. And although we hear Rastas mostly talk about Ethiopia, the Akan principles are evident within the Rastafari movement with their direct and militant way of thinking. This is also a movement that was engendered by the general idea of acknowledging, sharing, celebrating, and defending our African roots.

Fearless

I chose to include the connections mentioned above to further define the phrase "Out of Many, One People." Presenting Akan links to Egypt-Nubia, and daringly, Israel, provides more detail into the Akan people's resilient journey to Jamaica and their widespread influence. Rich and controversial biblical connections to Jamaicans' ancestors deserve extensive research and a deeper look, which would have to involve educational voyages throughout Africa. Before I embark on that feat, I use my book research and personal experience to provide justifiable conclusions for now. This claim of the Akan being Israelites comes from oral traditions on personal accounts from descendants throughout the world, or people who have studied the history on their own and provide their own account. I, too, like to tie in my personal experiences just for the reader to be reassured of a fact, or understand how connected I feel to information perceived to be skeptical, and then give the reader the opportunity to draw his or her own conclusions.

Jamaicans are proud of how the Akan fought and disrupted colonial society in the 18th century, and the island continues to show its respect to Ghana. In the past, the government of Jamaica and Ghana have joined forces to establish a visa waiver agreement, and there are plans for Ghana to invest in Jamaica. The Jamaican Maroons and Ghana have also reconciled past relations; Ghana gave an official apology in 2006 for their ancestors' role in selling their own to Europeans. Through an Ancestry DNA test, I discovered that I represent different African tribes: 22% Benin/Togo, 20% Cameroon/Congo, 18% Ivory Coast/Ghana, 8% Mali, 1% Nigerian. Because of the mixture of different African tribes and inter-relationships that was going on in Jamaica from the very beginning, these findings give more credibility to the non-significance of color or ethnic background in Jamaica. Energy is available for all who, regardless of skin color, will show reverence to it.

The peace agreement between the Maroons and the colonists restored Black power in Jamaica. The Maroons had support from all classes of whites in society in the 18th and 19th centuries when the hatred towards rebellions was still intense. John Tharp and General Walpole, considered amongst the elite whites in Jamaica, expressed their disagreement with the Maroons' treatment, and even took drastic actions directed towards the colonial government. Helen Mckee, the author of *From violence to alliance: Maroons and White settlers in Jamaica, 1739–1795*, additionally shared accounts of lower-class white settlers who described their maroon friends with a "friendly nature".[23] They were described as a "quiet innocent people" and transparency continued to be a fundamental feature of the seventeenth and eighteenth centuries. This transparency element was cultivated after the bulk of the Transatlantic Slave Trade to the Americas and is symbolic of the race relations between whites and Blacks, Jews, Chinese, Indians, Germans, and the Irish in Jamaica today. Mckee highlights that there was little to no motivation for violent interactions from both local white colonists and the Maroons during the most tumultuous years of war in Jamaica. Instead, disputes and murmurings were rampant between the colonial government and the Maroons. This is symbolic of the relations between the Jamaican people and the Jamaican government today, still working towards completely separating its ties from the British colonial government. "Jamaican culture is a product of the interaction between Europe and Africa. However, terms such as 'Afro-centered' and 'Euro-centered' are often used to denote Jamaican cultural traditions and values' perceived duality. European influences persist in public institutions, medicine, Christian worship, and the arts. However, African continuities are present in religious life, Jamaican Creole language, cuisine, proverbs, drumming, the rhythms of Jamaican music and dance, traditional medicine (linked to herbal and spiritual healing), and tales of Anansi, the spider-trickster."[92]

Positive vibrations are essential, and light (in its literal and spiritual sense). To be *badmind* (jealous and/or characterized as speaking ill of another) is a recurrent theme heard in Jamaican music and it is a reminder to stay far away from that energy as much as possible. That energy is contagious as it is evident in dancehall music. Jamaicans make creative routes that make it easier to exercise their consciousness and maintain their happiness without letting the current conditions of the world influence their consciousness. Pride contributes to be a mass external influence, feeding the Jamaican pride globally and even amongst non-Jamaicans. Consciousness has proven to be a solution to regaining one's power back and was the Akan people's tool to dominate the island and shake the world with their energy. Jamaicans may be the most advanced humans on earth regarding their evolution and how they respond to the world's pace, regarding the eradication of racism, as exemplified by the Maroons and Rastafarians. The higher energy on the island contributes to the Jamaican pride and is derived from the basic understanding that we are all freedom fighters. Jamaica has yet to reach its pinnacle, but confidence from the people continues to restore order. What will accelerate restoration will be the respect and awareness of consciousness. Outer peace truly begins with inner peace. Only when the cultivation is mastered inward first, can one exemplify peace outwardly to its environment.

The peace agreement between the Maroons and the colonists is what I believe set afire to Jamaica's current motto, "Out of Many, One People"—though the saying came centuries later. The Maroons, the

Rastafarians, and believers in God are the groups that give Jamaica its spiritual glow the most today. These are the most dominant protectors of that strong, one-love, higher dimensional vibe that Jamaicans have. Most follow the basic moral codes of their respected religions or personal beliefs, which are usually rooted in love and fighting for freedom. It is a combination of different people, including the youths in the most impoverished communities, that show hope and resilience with attitude and action. Raising the bar for vibrations between the Europeans and Africans' descendants in countries where the tension still bears is going to be necessary for battles where people are being oppressed.

The fight for love is what patriarchal-dominated nations are afraid of. Being a fighter for love, essentially, is what it means to be a Jamaican. Jamaicans have consciously shared their focus on love with the world. They have been able to influence the world through love in two obvious ways. One is direct, meaning Jamaicans have direct contact with other environments outside of their own, and the energy is transferred through fundamental human interactions, working, dancing or talking with one another. And two, indirectly from Jamaica's products, like listening to reggae music, and engaging on other popular forms of entertainment that foreigners have come to love. Energy is the biggest export out of the country. Although Jamaicans have achieved respect globally, the benefits are not reflected in the Jamaican ghettos and poor communities where this energy is at times, most high. Though racism is non-existential, poverty isn't and has never been eradicated in Jamaica. Fingers are often pointed at the government with a lack of opportunities and overall attention to lower-class issues, or at music and the lyrics. As this awareness and respect for energy grows amongst humankind, the focal point Jamaicans take on energy will be an increasingly respected value from outside cultures.

Jamaicans will not work with someone, often no matter what is at stake, if one's attitude is disrespectful or demeaning. I only hope this incredible human value could one day aid the government and the Jamaican community in the fight against crime. Energy multiples amongst like-minded forces, so I am eager to see what happens in the world when more environments start to mirror Jamaica's energy, and when Jamaica's energy expands tenfold for her own good.

The combination of different ethnic groups being able to coexist with each other and having a majority African-based population heightened and accentuated Jamaica's reputation globally. Dancehall is said to have been the catalyst behind afrobeats, an African-based music genre. This initially raised my eyebrows because although reggae's principles are African-based, the genre itself is indigenous to Jamaica. But Jamaica reflects what happens when we allow the spirit of Black people to lead outside of Africa, a nation where different groups of people can coexist and not discriminate because of ethnic origin. We now know the Jamaican spirit is heavily influenced by the Akan nature, always leading no matter the circumstances. Though a tiny island, Jamaica is proof and an important example that the world can vibe to the beat of the African drum, contrary to the Westernized domination that has taken control of most of the world.

It is likely that any characteristic we hear when speaking of Jamaicans will always be related to high energy. When we Google who Jamaicans are, we'll come up with articles with descriptions that say things such as, "Jamaicans are eccentric, colorful and always the life of the party."[15] In a video my aunt shared with me knowing I was in pursuit of this journey of learning more about my Jamaican roots, I watched an enslaved African port tour guide describe the people as "aggressive" (in a non-offensive manner)— and have been so since they've existed.[1] Being loud, aggressive, hardworking, or being the life of the party, are all actions that require having a lot of energy. If you are Jamaican or know of a Jamaican, see if this still holds weight. With my own experience and now extensive research, I have concluded that there is absolutely a baseline attitude we must have to live as happily as possible in this world. And it is possible, no matter the century or country we're in, no matter our sex, no matter what color we are.

Out of many, one people.
One love.

PART FOUR

Controversy

CHAPTER EIGHTEEN

Crime & Violence

♪ *Richie Spice – Earth a Run Red*
♪ *Romain Virgo – Mi Caan Sleep*

As a second-generation Jamaican, I take pride in the country my parents come from, and the values instilled in me as a result. I am also aware of the troubling aspects of Jamaica that obstruct the essence of the country. As a Jamerican (a person born in America but with Jamaican parents), the term Jamaicans most often use to describe us is a *yankee*, as opposed to a born-Jamaican that is referred to as *yawdie (yardie)*. I address the not-so-beautiful facts based on my experience, interviews, and research as a *yankee*.

As highlighted previously, Africans kidnapped and sold each other to Europeans amidst civil wars. Today, crime and violence are highly linked to poverty. Narcotics trade, lottery scamming, and other illegal activities trouble lower socio-economic areas. Crimes are most often committed by people who lack access to opportunities yet seek to achieve a better way of life. Poverty has led to the rise of dons and kingpins since the 80s. Dons and kingpins can be used interchangeably and are criminals in charge of a criminal organizations, often working their way up the ranks like the godfather role in the mafia. I stand with the basic codes of morality where we each know right from wrong and have the ability to choose, but to ignore that making the right choice can be more difficult in specific environments would not be fair. With that said, I have great respect for the Rastafari movement and how they exemplify the ability to upkeep their Black mind in a conscious state, impenetrable by systematic structures and temptations already of no help to the African diaspora. The Maroons have a long history of no violence, which makes a case for self-governing communities a viable option in Jamaica.

Crime and violence have taken a heavy toll on Jamaica's image. While tourists can assure safety in more places than none, the tainted images by real life situations have caused enough damage to keep tourists and Jamaicans abroad worried of going back home. The youth who live in the ghettos often feel stuck on a tiny island with no access to resources to help them evolve skillfully or academically. Other than the capital, tourist areas, and affluent areas of Jamaica, the island has many Third World infrastructures as the old Spanish and British style of doing things can still be seen throughout the island; which, also, arguably adds to the island's uniqueness. It is said that 'barrel children' are just one of many causes that increase crime, but what is the cause of barrel children's prevalence throughout the last several decades? Barrel children's primary guardians often go abroad to work for an income but have to leave their children behind, and as a result, sends barrels from abroad of necessary goods as a tool to sustain the long-distance relationship, and of course take care of their family. We can combat this by creating more job opportunities and "sustainable living conditions" so Jamaicans don't feel the need to leave the country (this might sound easier said than done for some). I read that "the impact on these children of this type of neglect includes a range of emotional and behavioral problems including run-away behavior, withdrawal, depression, and, in some cases, acting-out behavior," an article published in Newsweek by Brook Larmar called *Barrel Children.*

The lack of opportunity leading to crime is not just a problem for children; it affects entire families. "The cardboard barrel has been sitting empty in Marsha Flowers's backyard for more than a month now, but the Jamaican teenager hangs onto it as though it was a sacred totem. And in a way, it is. Five years after her mother immigrated to the United States, leaving Marsha and two sisters to fend for themselves in a Kingston slum, the barrel is one of the few tangible signs of her mother's love - and of her own frustrated desires."[107]

Violence surged in Jamaica after gaining independence from England. When I first interviewed my grandfather on his views on modern Jamaica, I did not understand why he was so adamant about the old Jamaica (England rule) being better than the new Jamaica (with no England rule). He stated that Jamaicans did not have a problem gaining employment under English control. "Today," he says, "the youths are lazy, and they are not the same." I had to laugh at my grandfather's ancient way of thinking, but I also was observing what he was trying to convey. He said violence was at a low, "the things they carry on with today could not happen back in my day," as there would be severe punishments. He even mentioned the guillotine still being necessary! I wonder how many people from his time feel the same way. From my grandfather's perspective, a Britain-ran government provides better order and structure than independent Jamaica, who is not independent from European rule. The majority of Jamaica's inhabitants are of African descent, where in Africa, the societal structure and social order looked different. To leave a predominantly African-based population that was once heavily British-influenced for over 300 years, to figure out the next steps for their independent nation, it sounds like it could perhaps have to be a well-thought out process with things in order. Nearly 60 years have passed since Jamaica's independence from England, which is not a long time. Collectively, the island has work to do as every political party faces obstacles to get society under complete control, and they must do so with their ever-unruly Jamaicans. As the tension between both major political parties, the Jamaica Labour Party (JLP) and People's National Party (PNP), remain constant, I see how the tension also benefits the Jamaican people at times, as parties always have to answer to public cries and will be under scrutiny by an opposing party and the public if not. I think it's a genius mechanism to have two powerful parties in play. Jamaicans support politicians that they believe act on their behalf, simply put. They are very vocal and passionate about politics as a result. And it seems like the political parties have continued to develop solutions to societal needs as every new term commences and there's a new prime minster in place. With only nearly 60 years independent from England, I think we have been doing gradually well, and I think we can do gradually better. The fear of energy from the 18th and 19th-century rebellions, although now out of the British government's hands, I assume continues to keep the government accountable for major societal needs. The energy of the people has not much changed from that of their ancestors. By 1962 when Jamaica gained its independence from England, the island had long already won the fight against racism. Classism and colorism, which will be discussed more, became the new predominant 'isms' in Jamaica. Still unacceptable, it's a step.

Despite the weight of crime and violence on this island, this is a society that has managed to popularize the outcasting of rapists, child abusers, and women-beaters. Musicians have helped with this by getting involved with the government for the best interest of the people and creating accompanying music. While Jamaica is actively and gradually addressing crime on the island, some express concern that the government is not doing enough in its efforts or that the Jamaican police force is unruly and corrupt. What doesn't help is the role of the *informer* being looked down upon. Being an informer or a snitch is popular to be uncool. People often fear for their lives, so they won't share information that could help authorities protect their families or community. This also poses difficulty for Jamaica's government to do its job for the public as best as it could. Several factors lead to the crime and its disruption to Jamaica. Unfortunately, attention is shifted from other important factors that need to be addressed, such as education, human development, and creating more job opportunities.

Aside from notable movements like the Rastafari and Maroon movement, whose ideals have been able to grasp people's minds and actions, the people of God in Jamaica are the most noticeable force in Jamaica that combats crime. In Part Two, I introduced the idea of the *middleman* being a valuable tool in the development of Jamaican society. These *middlemen or middlewomen* are grandparents, parents, aunts & uncles, teachers, neighbors, and even amongst the younger population who were brought up by these types of people. Jamaicans, especially those living in rural areas where land has been passed down through generations, will attest to the communal vibe that gives truth to the adage "it takes a village to raise a child." It wasn't long ago that teachers were allowed to punish students. These types of people are pivotal for as long as their alive and even after death, but especially so in a child's prime when they are navigating through life. My mom and aunts also have countless stories of getting disciplined by their parents because neighbors quickly reported their mischievousness. My family heavily influenced my spirituality and faith in God. They are un-formidable middlemen and middlewomen despite any negative environment they may be in, and this is a common trait amongst many Jamaicans. In the *Man Free* documentary, there was a sweet woman by the name of Ulalee who was referred to as "granma" by locals and tourists, and when asked about the effects of neighborhood violence on her, "well I don't find it such a violent neighborhood. They have shootings sometimes and so, but that doesn't affect me, and that doesn't affect my work…I just have confidence and I come knowing that God will protect me, so I am not scared. I just feel that God's will and God's keeping will keep me."[70] I would absolutely think of Ulalee as a middlewoman, growing physically old as the days go by, but showing no loss of spiritual strength no matter how many days go by. Her words mirror a common belief among many Jamaicans' attitude towards crime.

CHAPTER NINETEEN

Classism

♪ *Bounty Killer – Fed Up*
♪ *Morgan Heritage – Tell Me How Come*

"*Everyone should come together and say it's our time. Everyone could have a farm, you know. And you help me and me help you, to build unity, but unity is not there. One man Waan [want to] drive all five cars. That's why I love Cuba, you know. Mi loves Castro. Yeh. He said, 'equal share for everyone.' He doesn't put [a man] bigger than no man because every man is just a man to him.*"[70] Classism is a prevalent and important issue in Jamaica. The lower class are very vocal about their need for more opportunities and keep a steadfast attitude of what they believe their society should have access to. There is no serious tension between the upper, middle, and lower classes, yet the vast difference between the living circumstances would say otherwise. Instead, the anger is directed towards the government. It is common to find strong connections between social classes, and sometimes these links can provide opportunities in strong industries like tourism or entertainment where opportunities are increasingly lucrative. The relationships, however, do not solve the income disparities.

The lower class looks toward the government for help in closing the income gap. It is common to see reggae musicians and its subgenres, quite notably dancehall, advocating for poor people, in and out of the studio. Who is to blame could at rare times turn into direct and public exchanges between the government and music, with music often representing most what people think. One thing is for sure, classism in Jamaica is a result of the residue from systematic British-influenced aspects still in existence.

Just short of five years ago, Black people were recorded to make up nearly 92% of the Jamaican population which is relative to the number of Africans to other races since their inhabitation on the island.[108] They only accounted for 30% of the wealth then in 2016. The reasons for this perpetual issue are extensive; but they popularly include colorism, the government not doing enough, the content of certain types of dancehall music that promote rogue lifestyles, the rich, and even the poor.

It is often shared that people are preferred for a job or any opportunity, or even treated better because of the color of their skin. Jamaica differs from the US in the sense that racism doesn't exist in Jamaica, but colorism is alive and well. In addition to the color of the skin, other attributes such as residence location and assets such as cars is said to influence employers on their decisions to hire. "The evidence from sending out over 1,000 résumés suggests employers prefer applicants perceived to be from high-income backgrounds."[108]

I read in an Observer article that dancehall is often the go-to for those seeking a better life. It made me question whether there are enough resources for other types of education or arts that continue to put Jamaica on the map, in these poorer communities that give people an alternative other than music? It would be fair to argue that if these resources existed, especially in excess where people can exercise options, the fight dancehall music gets from those primarily in charge of maintaining and developing society can easily wane when the government is reminded of the people's conditions. "Dancehall reflects, reinforces, and celebrates the often-necessary way of life of many very ordinary and often very poor Jamaicans."[110] Seeing as music is a strong pursuit for Jamaicans due to the success of reggae worldwide, it is understandably a go-to outlet if all else fails.

The government gets a lot of backlash from Jamaicans for outsiders coming in to profit off Jamaica, and sometimes jeopardize the environment in the process. At the same time, these ventures provide opportunities for more Jamaicans to work and contribute to the development of Jamaica overall, like the Chinese coming in to build highways that have proven to be favorable. Although they don't receive as much heat as outsiders, the rich can at times experience more indirect anger for their more privileged lifestyle while many suffer. There is a noticeable difference between the upper-class and lower-class communities, or in Jamaican terms, uptown and downtown communities, and the poor people still outnumber the rich. In her article, *Who is to be blamed for classism in Jamaica*, Sashakay Fairclough noted that "the elite have made attempts to separate themselves (no fault of theirs as some places are quite violent), but they were failing miserably as garrisons seemed to pop up close to a lot of these so-called 'uptown' communities in Kingston."[109]

There is also a notion that poor people are a part of the problem, at times being called lazy and dishonest. Although this may be true for some, one can also arguably question if honesty is the best policy as George

Graham questioned in his article.[111] "Did all the members of Jamaica's "upper class" behave according to these [honest] standards? Of course not. Some abused their positions of privilege."[111] In this same article, George shares a forgotten yet more prevalent group of the poorer class, the 'decent people' who don't take advantage and demonstrate integrity. The decent people who do the right thing.

Everyone has their own justifiable opinions based on their life experience, but that is not to say the entire upper class or lower class share the same beliefs. There are Jamaicans like Sashakay who believe both social classes should be blamed for the prevalence of classism. "Poor Blacks should be blamed for allowing this to continue for as long as it has because they accept that they are inferior. If we did not agree that lighter is better than darker, or that rich is better than poor, then a lot more would have been done to eradicate the classism that is keeping us down. We have to stop playing the victims."[109] The view that everyone has work to do is also a courageously popular shared sentiment that outs accountability on all social classes. Also exemplified throughout the island are lower-class individuals overcoming their struggles with their own unique ways and attitudes and will judge their own for not doing enough; and amongst the upper class, there are a number of people who strategize how to further create more opportunities for poorer Jamaicans with their own unique ways and attitudes and will judge their own for also not doing enough. Perry Henzell, the white Jamaican film director, can perhaps support Sashakay's sentiments. "Now you'd never find a Jamaican, no matter how rich, who feels that a poor man in Jamaica shouldn't have ambition. You won't find that. The rich in Jamaica might want to lose their money so that poor people can be better off. But they most certainly, would never feel, that they don't want poor people to get richer through their own initiative. And they would never feel that poor people shouldn't have the chance to get richer if they have ambition."[70]

These disparities exist and are prevalent all over the world in nations where the Black diaspora populate, and even where they don't populate, but I believe the little, tiny island of Jamaica is in one of the best positions to do something about it sooner than other nations because of their attitude, and their track history when it comes to overcoming societal and systematic struggles. On an end note for this quite controversial topic, Sashakay challenges Jamaicans, "We all want a better Jamaica, so the mentality of every single person needs to change. Is that possible? Only time will tell." This perspective means that collective effort is required from all Jamaicans, and fearlessly starting at the root is a definitive way to take on such a pervasive problem.

CHAPTER TWENTY

Colorism & Bleaching

♪ *Nardo Ranks – Dem ah Bleach*

♪ *Spice – Black Hyprocrisy*

During slavery, there was a massive movement of manumission, where whites were freeing Blacks at an exponential rate. There was an increase in colored people on the island, who also received special treatment over their African kin. "Despite the intensifying hostility directed toward free Blacks and free people of color during the 1760s and 1770s, a small number of whites continued to manumit (voluntarily free) individual enslaved people. Title grantees, merchants, plantation attorneys, white tradesmen, spinsters, and widows persisted in liberating select enslaved people for a variety of economic and personal reasons, including (1) paternalistic generosity; (2) the reward for loyalty and hard work; (3) 'love and affection' for sons, daughters, liaisons, and other family members; and/or (4) financial compensation for the loss of the manumitted person's labor. Further, the island government continued to consider manumission a tool for controlling enslaved people by offering freedom to those who revealed conspiracies or defended the colony from external enemies."[67] For the British to retain some type of power, they fueled colorism by giving special privileges to Africans with lighter complexions. They created different levels of colored people or those mixed with white to discern the biological differences; mulattoes were half-Black and half-white, samboes were three-fourths Black and one-fourth white, quadroons were three fourths white and one-fourth Black, and mestees were one-eighth Black. The British ceased to use those terms once it became harder to detect those mixed with white. By the time Marcus Mosiah Garvey was born, Jamaica's population of six hundred thousand was made up of three distinct groups of people. The upper class who comprised Anglo-Saxons made up only two percent of the population. Most of this group descended from former slave owners or Europeans who had administered the British colony. Eighteen percent of the population was of mixed Black and white ancestry, known as mulattoes. At seventy-eight percent, the majority of Jamaica's citizens were Black laborers.[25]

The impact colorism has had on today's society is deeply rooted in a direct power link. Today, a significant amount of Jamaicans bleach, both men and women, and more so amongst lower classes. Although there is no official consensus of how many people engage in the method, it is at times notable when walking populated streets. It is said that the cause for many to start bleaching is the discrimination they regularly face. The belief exists that the lighter your skin, the more privileges you have. The idea of colorism is so deeply rooted it has affected the minds of the African diaspora. Bleaching is generally looked down upon, and it is prevalent amongst all sexes, but especially so amongst the lower class, and sometimes even musicians. Vybz Kartel, a musician who famously bleached his skin at one point in his career, adding fuel to a growing-society of bleachers, decided to be "Black again" as he proudly stated in an Instagram picture. This was a significant announcement for the culture because of the influence musicians have on Jamaican people.

Still using Garvey as an example, his parents, for instance, only trusted the darkest skin of people. With his awakening on racial awareness, "Mosiah learned that Blacks needed a better education, more economic opportunities, and renewed pride in their Black history." He thought unified action was the only thing that would improve Blacks' lives.[25] This consciousness has not ceased to exist. The love for Black skin is still popularized in Jamaican culture, especially by the Rastafarians, and holds its dominant place in society despite the phenomenon of bleaching.

CHAPTER TWENTY-ONE

Rigid Mindsets

♪ *Toots & The Maytals – 54-46 That's My Number*
♪ *Sizzla – No Time to Gaze*

This entire book up until Part Four highlights both the origin of the unruliness of Jamaicans, and its role and effectiveness in human evolution when it comes to facing systematic pressures. In that case, rigid mindsets could be a blessing, but in the following context I share how it can perhaps debilitate our journey to freedom. The passion for religion can get in the way of human evolution, as making judgements on others often cause divisive behavior. Jamaicans have a locked belief system which can be a blessing and a curse. Their belief system can be a blessing because they have an effective formula to share with humanity for world peace; exercising love, consciousness, and tools like sound and dancing are unifying. Do good, don't do bad things. The system can be a curse for being close-minded and not allowing room for new ways of thinking. We see this with homophobia present amongst certain groups in Jamaica, most notably the Rastafarians, but certainly not limited to.

Homophobia seems to be fueled by ancestral trauma. In Jamaica, they had many seasoning plantations where they would conduct a process called *buck-breaking*, where white slave owners would rape Black men to break his spirit and show dominance against him. To control the enslaved population, slave owners raped men to emasculate and remove respect.

That horrific act was done to scare the enslaved population into submission and limit those who rebelled.

The close-mindedness has led to tragic deaths, as gay men have been targeted for their choice of sexual orientation as detailed by recent documentaries by the Human Rights Watch. This is not to say people should not have their beliefs, but if the actions to follow include harassment, bullying, and worst, death, there is no basis of reason and not an effective solution long-term for what they consider wrong. Today, homophobia seems to be more directed towards men than women, although women experience it. Homosexuality imposes no physical threats to anyone, what two people choose to engage in is between those two people . If Jamaica wants to be a nation that stands for heterosexuality, then do so, but people should not be treated differently because of their personal beliefs. With a society facing so much crime, including domestic violence, rape and the murdering of women, I think Jamaican men, especially those who are homophobic, should focus on being the example they want to see in their society first, before condemning others for their lifestyle choices. No matter how passionate we are on a topic, nothing will be as defining and exemplary as the way we actually live our life when trying to prove a point to anyone. Jamaica being homophobic and women being abused, raped and murdered in numbers make no sense. Be firm in one's beliefs, share them in peaceful ways, but I think redirecting one's energy from hating to loving and understanding is a better approach, if one cares so much about seeing this type of change. Change has been unfolding with newer generations and adaptive mindsets. The country is seemingly becoming more accepting of gay culture. In my early 20s, I regularly visited Kingston. I did not know of a scene where gay people had their area to assemble and hang out. It was not until a visit in 2016 that I started seeing popular scenes like this emerge.

Although the relations between the Jamaican government and Rastafarians seems to be getting better overtime, Rastafarians have suffered a great deal of discrimination in Jamaica. The same goes with the government and the Maroons. Both groups are integrated in society, the former more than the latter, but still go through their fair deal of feeling outcasted in Jamaican society. Ganja is now a herb that was legalized in 2015 for medical, scientific, therapeutic, and sacramental purposes for groups like Rastafarians. This was great for Rastas who have been discriminated by this very thing just decades ago in Jamaica. They also still are discriminated against for their dreadlocks. In 2020, there was a young child banned from attending a school because her parents would not concede to cutting her dreadlocks. This was asked of by the girl's school, and additionally was backed by a Supreme Court of Jamaica ruling. This is still an ongoing issue. The Rastas, the Maroons and other free villages in Jamaica continue to stoically hold their stance on their beliefs.

Rigid belief systems in Jamaica have also pushed science away. Universally, science has always been pitted against religion worldwide. There is an infinite number of connections between religion and science that is worth considering and accepting. Astronomy and astrology were both considered science until Western 17th-century philosophers rejected astrology. Jamaica, with its very religious grounds, doesn't give much attention to these sciences either. Instead, God is the only thing that makes sense to them. When I asked my mom if she'd ever considered learning more about astrology or cosmology, her response was, "No! Bianca, my God is my God!" While I absolutely respect her passion and beliefs, I believe there are strong connections between science and religion, and one does not triumph over the other. Life is relative, and we can assume the same with all of God's creations, including the universe, the planets, and dimensions that will be discussed in further chapters.

One of the first disastrous disagreements ever to be had by humans started with the question: Where did it all start? Religion says it was a Higher Force (most often God); science says it was The Big Bang. There is somewhat of a divide amongst Jamaicans, though not apparently socially, who believe in God and those who practice ancient spiritual practices, as spiritual practices are typically linked to obeah. I ask the question, Why can't God and The Big Bang have a connection? There isn't a large portion of Jamaicans outside of Rastafarians who advocate for ways of life before Christianity, at least notably. Let's remember Egyptians believed in astrology and heavily relied on that system for direction. Our African ancestors had systems we believed in before western religion sought to dominate. We should remember this, and reasonably look further back into our roots before slavery as slavery was not the beginning. This is the case for both Indians and Chinese who also have similar ancient spiritual practices. Some Jamaicans do not want to entertain the idea that there's an alternative to what they were systematically taught, an example of cognitive dissonance. The idea that there was African religion and spirituality before Christianity is not willfully a topic of discussion.

CHAPTER TWENTY-TWO

Society & Development

♪ *Vybz Kartel – Life We Living*
♪ *Chronixx – Smile Jamaica*

We lightly touched on how society is set up in Jamaica, and we will mention a bit about the living conditions. Jamaica is a beautiful island that continues to develop better infrastructures throughout its parishes as the years accumulate. There are areas where people are accustomed to living in one-bedroom shacks or zinc-made shelters. In 2020, the unemployment rate was at 8.4%, a decrease from previous years, and the poverty rate was below 13% in 2020.[112][113] The upper class is a smaller group in Jamaica, but the disparity between the upper and lower class is wide. There are about 2,000 homeless people estimated to be in Jamaica with about 700 alone in Kingston of St. Andrew, and the rest are spread throughout the other thirteen parishes.[114]

In Jamaica, there are three generic names to describe different communities in Jamaica that Jamaicans use themselves. *Uptown* is the more affluent areas in Kingston, the capital; *downtown* or often the *ghetto* is known to be the poorer sides of Kingston; and *country* is basically everywhere else in Jamaica. Even though there are affluent areas throughout different parishes, I presume because Kingston, the capital, has a wide disparity between social classes, these terms are more necessary to use in those areas.

To a Kingstonian, poor or rich, everywhere else besides Kingston is *country*. As mentioned previously, there are also many Rastafarian villages and several Maroon villages on the island. It is important to note other than the Maroon villages that exist in St. Elizabeth and Portland, there were a number of free villages, or settlements, established across Jamaica for freed enslaved Africans. To combat the plan of plantation and estate owners wanting to retain enslaved people as agricultural workers after slavery was abolished in the 1830s, English Baptist missionaries worked with locals to secretly buy land through agents in London, in order to not be detected. This land would later be used to establish free villages independent of plantation and estate owners. A popular free village that still exists today is Sturge Town in the St. Ann parish, not too far away from the area of Bob Marley's birthplace, Nine Mile.

Jamaica, one of the leading bauxite producers in the world, and tourism, are Jamaica's top sources of revenue. Developments in technology, healthcare, education, politics continue to be on the rise to meet the demands of the very outspoken population, though at times it seems like it's not happening fast enough. Jamaica does not have systems in place where poorer people can benefit to aid their struggles, like how Americans have food stamps to help with food or welfare to help with accomodations. Jamaica has a long way to go before it finds its way being structurally First World. Initiatives continue to be created to assist with improvements and are often shared through the Prime Minister's social media and his cabinet. One, in particular, and a new favorite, is called The Global Jamaica Diaspora Youth Council (GJDYC) created by the Jamaican government who closely works and engages with its members. The GJDYC has been instrumental in connecting young Jamaicans from largely the UK, Canada, and the USA who want to make a change. This is amazing to me as I see how it can be most instrumental in the continual development of Jamaica. Once one joins, it feels very invigorating to hear what other Jamaicans around the world feel like they can contribute to their home in Jamaica or their homes abroad as a Jamaican. Members of the cabinet have made appearances during seminars or meetings, such as Minister of Foreign Affairs and Foreign Trade, Kamina Johnson-Smith, sharing pertinent information and listening to projects being implemented by Jamaicans worldwide for their community home and abroad. The council was created to discover more ways to contribute to the development of Jamaica, their own influence in their respective communities outside of Jamaica, to educate the diaspora, and to offer the diaspora a uniform platform to use their voice on making a stronger Jamaica. Many Jamaicans leave the island to look for opportunities elsewhere understandably, so this method of staying connected is great. It is a resource available to those of us who want to add to the island's developing infrastructure within our abilities, and with the knowledge and skills acquired abroad that could be collectively useful. The current government's efforts to increase opportunities have attracted an influx of both the Jamaican diaspora and the non-Jamaican diaspora. The government has started heavily utilizing social media to update the Jamaican public and those abroad with the internet being so largely accessible.

The Jamaican diaspora has a more significant population outside of the island than on the island itself. This means the diaspora on all continents exceeds the number of Jamaicans living in Jamaica. Emigration was first initiated by employment opportunities abroad like with the construction of the famous Panama Canal in the late 1800s. "During the economic transition from slavery to wage labor, Indian-Jamaican migration to former enslaved industries (like sugar production) allowed select Black Jamaicans to find work in more skilled industries and attain more respected social statuses."[116] Additionally, job opportunities aimed at Jamaicans in Britain in post-war reconstruction in the 1940s, unemployment during the 1950s, and rising crime following the country's independence in 1962, as well as slow economic growth contributed to Jamaican emigration, as stated in Gene Tidrick's, *Some Aspects of Jamaican Emigration to the United Kingdom 1953-1962*. The U.S. Department of Homeland Security's website records around 800,000 Britons are of Jamaican origin. 700,000 people of Jamaican origin live in the United States, mainly concentrated in New York City (416,000), Connecticut, Rhode Island, Massachusetts, and South Florida. Immigration, especially so to Canada, Britain, and USA contributes to thriving Jamaican communities that make it easy for new Jamaicans to settle and adapt to.

The United States had more Jamaicans than all other countries combined during the 19th and 20th centuries. In the USA, New York City, Boston, Philly, Jersey, Connecticut, and as we start to go south, Baltimore, Atlanta, Miami, and Houston are heavily populated with Jamaican people. As far as the West Coast, cities in California such as LA tend to have a growing population of Jamaicans. The United States and Canada continue to be the primary destination of Jamaican immigrants. Canada has 300,000, Trinidad has 15,000, the Bahamas has 5500, Cuba has 5000, Germany has 1600, and Australia has 1000. Costa Rica, Nicaragua, Panama, China, Japan, Italy, and Amsterdam have growing Jamaican populations as well.

Human connection is a part of the human evolution process, and it involves using a certain level of emotional intelligence for a group to prevail passed heights comfortable to them. Emotional intelligence is not something I have heard popularized here in the US, nor is it encouraged, but it seems to be the way Jamaicans even in the poorest conditions get by day to day. The current prime minister shared an idea public event for his political party that left an impression on me regarding what Jamaicans strive for and the potential for what can be for Jamaican society. "That is the kind of Jamaica we're going to build. Where people have the emotional intelligence to treat justly, and fairly, man to man, woman to woman, children to children."

PART FIVE

Attentively & Courageously Entering Higher Dimensions

"It will show Jamaica in its true light, and not in the midst of prejudice and ignorance, which have maligned not only the climate, which is not pestilential but salubrious, but the people, who are progressive and proud of their land, and even the fair face of the island, which will compare for beauty and fertility, with the fairest spots on the earth's surface. That Jamaica is "awakening" may be shown in many ways; but the success which has attended the extension and improvement of the railway service since the Government bought the railway in 1878 will exemplify the progress of the colony, and, at the same time, the wisdom of the late Governor, Sir Anthony Musgrave [1883]."[22]

CHAPTER TWENTY-THREE

Trace Your Roots

♪ *Garnett Silk – Hello Africa*

♪ *Freddie McGregor – Africa, Here I Come*

I mentioned in the introduction that researching this book has elevated my understanding of how necessary it is for us to journey into our roots. We can do our best to make sense of the information passed through generations and what historians have gathered. For the African diaspora, it's more complicated with much of it being erased out of history books. Information on African history is challenging to assemble. This brings light to how much the African diaspora have been misled through the ambitions of westerners by irresponsibly not teaching us everything we should know; the American education system is an example. What is so important about our history that it had to be hidden, changed, manipulated, erased?

There were ancient wisdom and traditions in place that Africans were forced to leave once they became enslaved. Although Africans are one, the uniqueness is vast due to the amount of different African cultures making up the continent. The more we are willing to take on this deep dive into African history, the more we can all make sense of our forgotten past and make connections to who we are today.

I don't believe we should limit ourselves to just one way of acquiring knowledge. Let us remain open, exhaust all possibilities, and use rationality to make sense of all the information gathered, which is what I have tried my best to do in this book. If one grew up in nations like America as I, we have not been taught everything we are supposed to know about the world's history. For a race that makes up such a large percentage of America, significant time should be allocated to educating students on African history during their primitive years.

Once we gain back control of knowing our history, I believe it is a tool that can start to balance some of the extreme polarities that exist in many of our environments. We must seek consciously higher consciousness. In the *Soul of Black Folks*, Dubois talks about double consciousness; Black people have to live two lives. This is due to Blacks having to follow and upkeep with the standards of a constitution or a system not created in their favor, while still staying attentive and committed to the journey of their Soul; spiritual ascension.

Marcus Garvey fueled the most impactful Back to Africa movement. Countries such as Ghana and Ethiopia granted special privileges to Blacks interested in coming back to Africa to live; a large portion of Jamaicans once migrated to a city in Ethiopia called Shashamane, still saturated with Jamaican influence today. Even today, countries like Ghana and Jamaica have made special arrangements to make it easier for both societies to access each other better. As hereditary descendants of Africa, we must ask ourselves how far will we go to gain equality and truly be free? Do we want to go back to Africa and help our brothers and sisters build? Do we want an American lifestyle in Africa? Do we want to live and work in a society that doesn't uphold us with value, most evident in the treatment we still receive because of the color of our skin? What do we want? I learned "town slaves had opportunities to escape from the island by ship and to pass themselves off as freemen, especially if they possessed skills permitting them relative freedom of movement. But…the urban slave saw greater opportunities for re-establishing himself successfully as a free man within the context of a slave society."[23] Perhaps this a recurring generational thought people down the line entertain; and what propels or deters decisions from being executed lies in both the matter of environmental influence and personal will. These are thought-provoking questions we must ask ourselves. While I crave more knowledge about Jamaica, I aim to do further research and become aware of more fearless stories from other cultures to make further connections and subsequent solutions.

I recall a conversation I had with one of my mentors, Jerry Saunders, who at the time was the highest-paid African American employee in an organization we both worked in. I shared with him that I was working on this book and offered some discoveries I had uncovered. At the time of our conversation, he was in his sixties and approaching retirement. He shared some of his rich experiences upon encountering more people of the African-diaspora from a Caribbean background when he moved up North of the U.S. He was from the South and immigrated up North decades prior. It was his comment on how his first interactions with people of Caribbean descent was marked with a distinctive energy and vibrancy. It made me understand how much more we need to understand each other and our history to advance as a unit. When my sister moved here from Jamaica, it was then I learned American history (including Black history) is not taught in Jamaican schools. On the contrary, while growing in America, I have learned that schools in general omit or give little focus to pivotal Black heroes from other countries, like Garvey from Jamaica, Toussaint from Haiti, and Prince Hall from Barbados, from our Black history education;

unless it is a focus in tertiary education, sometimes, even shedding them in a negative light. My sister had little knowledge of Martin Luther King, which was shocking, just as I had little understanding of who Marcus Garvey really was until I started to do research on my own.

In the southern states of the U.S., a vibrant Black culture exists that I have been fortunate enough to experience. There are two places in America I have traveled to where I have felt the most connected to my roots and I'm sure there are more; Atlanta and New Orleans. Atlanta has many successful Black business owners amidst a vibrant culture. Black power is noticeable there. There are a sufficient number of Black people in power in Atlanta that were able to ease the tension during the 2020 Black Lives Matter protests, compared to other cities. I visited Martin Luther King Jr. (MLK) and his wife, Coretta Scott King's tomb and MLK's childhood home and church, and countless sites relevant to Black history that the city does a good job of preserving. I could not help but connect the energy I felt there to the influential people that emerged from there and gave it its strong platform for Black voices, like the emergence of Marcus Garvey and Bob Marley from Jamaica.

CHAPTER TWENTY-FOUR

Striving For Unity Amongst The African Diasporas

♪ *Shabba Ranks – Roots & Culture*
♪ *Bob Marley - Africa, Unite*

W*elcoming, understanding, and respecting each other's differences that have evolved within each our borders is what it's going to take for the African diaspora to unite.* Unity is a powerful tool in fighting racism and understanding that the enemy is the systemic structures that suppress people. Holding the people accountable that perpetuate the employment of outdated laws is essential to our freedom in countries like America, and the UK. Mental freedom from the enslaved-like systems must be the priority for every individual of the African diaspora. This freedom comes by first, learning about our own culture and others' history, and can be an easy way to fuel that shift as one can do this on their own. Bob Marley reminded us of this in *Redemption Song* when he sang, "emancipate yourselves from mental slavery, none but ourselves can free our minds," originally taken from a Marcus Garvey speech. Preserving the African culture was essential for the survival of the enslaved, no matter how difficult it was. The President of the Association of Nigerians, Dr. Ibrahim Ajagunna, while living in Jamaica, spoke on the importance of building relationships with our roots. "Being a Nigerian is a task and being a Nigerian in Jamaica is a project." When he told people in Nigeria that he was going to Jamaica, they asked, "why are you leaving one Third World country to move to another Third World country?" He had no answer for this other than to say it would have been too easy to migrate, like so many others, to the UK, Canada, or the U.S.[93] Building relationships with our ancestral nations is essential. Ghana and Jamaica started reparations during the 'Year of Return' movement by scrapping the need for entry visa requirements for Jamaicans returning. I foresee moves like these as the predecessors to something bigger, whether that's in a matter of years, decades, or centuries. Although these moves might not seem like they are creating waves right now, the current is there.

In addition to learning more about other cultures primarily if we were raised in American or European environments, the idea of adapting to more practical ways of life (while finding ways to enrich life for those in less fortunate situations), has been romanticized more than ever; as the poor treatment Blacks receive in these First World countries, in lieu of a more spiritually-privileged lifestyle than our Black brothers in sisters in the Caribbean, South America, and Africa, feels like it is getting to an end; as it is no longer just an idea but action. An end, and thus new beginning, that has been challenging to fathom for many of us accustomed to a certain lifestyle. Many Jamaican-natives come to America for the opportunity to make more money so they can support their relatives better and return to Jamaica to build stronger infrastructures; dismissing the notion that living in a First World country is the most ideal.

For those of us in the African diaspora, while starting or continuing the journey into our roots, we must not ignore the current state of how we treat each other. Black people are the most notorious for killing each other.

Fearless

Violence was happening in Africa amongst Blacks before the Transatlantic Slave Trade began, this is not something that can be altogether blamed on oppressors, at least not to a point where one forgets the gravity of their own behavioral and attitudinal role towards a sensible society. When Europeans arrived on the African shores in the 16th century, they found Africans fighting, kidnapping, and killing each other. Before Europeans kidnapped Africans to board the Middle Passage, Africans sold each other to them when capturing each other during internal battles. Europeans only did what they did because they saw Africans were weak when it came to these battles, and they took advantage of that weakness. Africans gave them that power.

Regarding Jamaica and the first importation of Africans from West Africa, wars between tribes were witnessed by Europeans in Ghana (the Gold Coast). Two of the most potent subgroups of the Akan ethnicity that lived in Ghana were the Fante and Asante (sometimes called Ashanti) peoples. These powerful tribes were at war with each other while there was a British presence on the land. Asante people (also known as Ashanti) became angry with the Fante because they assumed some of the Fante people were digging up Asante graves for riches; this angered the Asante elders. The Asante launched attacks on the Fante people who sought refuge with the British. After witnessing the attacks on the Fante group, the British became allies with the Asante, and then sold the Fante refugees to the Americas. The British took advantage of the two weakened Black powers fighting each other. This is reminiscent of many predominant black societies in First World countries today. Could the mental inabilities and lack of sensibility that plagued our ancestors then still haunt us today? Though we could've never prepared for the evils that lay ahead of Africa's borders, perhaps things would've been different if we were. After all, when finally learning what was happening to our sold brothers and sisters did we begin to fight both the British and Dutch back on our African soil, forcing them to eventually forgo their empirical rule and return to us our autonomy.

So, what do we do to combat this problem? We are sensible people who understand we need to focus more on becoming our best selves. 'Best' has many possibilities, but specific tools could accelerate the entire African diaspora's unity. Some tools will lead us to higher awareness and deeper levels of consciousness. The most powerful tool to date, since its inception, is music. Music followed by dance is essential to the evolutionary process of each of us individually and collectively, especially conscious music. Bob Marley said, "when the music hits, you feel no pain." While pain may not disappear overnight, we can find ease in the process with music and movement.

There is a correlation between the energy behind the sounds produced and the people who favor those sounds in certain societies. The Caribbean was predominantly Black, unlike in the U.S. where Black people were outnumbered. I look at the music produced to connect to the African state of mind and how much of their Soul was stripped in their day-to-day environments. When looking at how many enslaved Africans were brought to each region; there was North America: 0.5 million, Caribbean: 5 million, and South America: 5 million. This is very important to keep in mind because it seems like the further away from Africa the enslaved were placed in, the more likely they lost connection with their African identity. "Historians have speculated that the Spanish slavers, who first set up colonies in the Americas in South America, and had at that time not long expelled the North African Moors after 800 years of Islamic rule back home, preferred not to import Afro-Muslims. Thus, a higher concentration of people from the Sahel/Mali/Senegal regions, many of whom were Muslim, ended up in North America, bringing their more vocal and string-based traditions. While more people from the Congo/Ghana/Nigeria regions arrived in South America and the Caribbean, with their more extensive drumming traditions."[76] But there was an exception in America, "due to the Catholic laws in Louisiana being different from the protestant ones in Georgia and the Carolinas, drums were not banned in New Orleans, the center of the American slave trade, until much later, in the second half of the 19th Century." I carefully suspect the sounds produced by each group of the African diaspora tell a story that can be traced back to their realities as enslaved Africans and their roots from Africa.

"...it is absolutely necessary to the safety of this Province, that all due care be taken to restrain Negroes from using or keeping of drums, which may call together or give sign or notice to one another of their wicked designs and purposes." — Slave Code of South Carolina, Article 36 (1740)

The Caribbean and the southern U.S. are interwoven in their historical foundation from Africa with their rhythm and sounds. In the Caribbean, the drums were kept alive through Kumina's practices in Jamaica or Voodoo in Haiti where the Haitian Rada Drum was used to call in ancestral spirits to assist with daily life struggles. In South America, drums were kept alive through sounds like Samba in Brazil. However, there was no heavy usage of the drums in the southern states, except New Orleans. "In an atmosphere of relative tolerance and less repressive laws, for much of the 19th century. This opulent melting pot city was host to a vibrant nightlife, exotic rituals, tribal dances, pagan festivals, funeral marches, and all kinds of parties that never seemed to stop."[76] Southern Europeans were already heavily influenced by African culture because their countries of origin were closer to Africa. They had somewhat different ideas from the Northern Europeans in their treatment of enslaved people, so other states in the South weren't as lucky as French-ruled Louisiana (until the U.S. acquired it in 1803).[76]

Most Africans came to colonial America from West Africa, and some from the Caribbean. Only a small fraction of Africans transported throughout the New World were brought to four main areas in America: the Chesapeake (33%), the Carolinas and Georgia (54%), the Gulf Coast (6%), and the North (7%). This launched the beginning of the African American story, where Africans merged their culture with their new environment, creating thriving all-black communities such as Tulsa in Oklahoma and Eatonville in Florida. They resisted enslavement while creating new ways of life that contributed to the physical, cultural, and intellectual foundations of America. But that did not stop the ambitions of the racist white America to keep the country segregated and justify the mistreatment of black people, who were outnumbered. From the 1800s well into the 1900s, it was common to find racism depicted in everyday items such as advertisements, toys, and household items, as it was a common notion to believe that black people were lazy, slow and untrustworthy, but still loveable and growable under the supervision of white people. This attitude and mistreatment of black people could be reflected in the music they produced. We produced genres like ragtime, spirituals, salon music, jubilee, blues, and gospel (which has been called "percussion music without drums" by historians). Sweet jazz sounds noticeably ring loud in Louisiana until this day, taxis and bars alike can be heard playing classic tunes. Gunther Schuller noted in his book, *Early Jazz, Its Roots & Musical Development*, that "it is probably safe to say that by and large, the simpler African rhythmic patterns survived in jazz ... because they could be adapted more readily to European rhythmic conceptions." Gunter's quote illustrates the control and input white people had over Black music in America. I make these observations to draw attention to the omitting of the drums in America. The absence of drums gave way to Minstrel shows. These shows consisted of white people who painted their faces black while performing musical and dance acts that made a mockery of African descent people.

Drums were successfully banned in the Caribbean for their association with slave rebellions across the Americas, including Jamaica, Haiti, and even Trinidad in the late 19th century. What Trinidadians did with this ban was impressive, and forever changed their culture. Africans improvised with frying pans, dustbin lids, and oil drums after the ban, forming the Trinidadian tradition of Steel Pan and Steel Drum music.[143] Even though they banned the drums, the Trinidadians still found a way to preserve a rhythm reminiscent of their homelands and we hear the many different instruments melodically flowing through their signature Calypso and Soca music today. Like Trinidad, drums were taken away from enslaved Africans in Cuba at a later time. Cubans also got creative and found a way to keep the beat of the drum going. As David Peñalosa shares in his book *Rumba Quinto*, Afro-Cubans used household items for instruments. "The side of a cabinet functioned in the role of the present-day Tumba or salido (the primary supportive drum), while an overturned drawer served as the Quinto (the lead drum) and a pair of spoons played the cáscara part on whatever was available." Despite the banning of drums, Africans in the

Caribbean and South America were able to preserve their roots by maintaining their drumming traditions in creative ways, "unlike African Americans", who Robert Palmer, author of *Deep Blues*, says, re-invented their African musical heritage through memory and forgetfulness in a completely new context. In many states, African Americans were not permitted to gather in groups of more than five. Like the Caribbean, this did not stop people from gathering to dance, worship, celebrate and express themselves in their preferred ways in secret areas.

As a Jamaican-American, I find myself in multiple music worlds. My dad managed and worked with several reggae artists on many international shows, such as Everton Blender, Richie Spice, and Frankie Paul. My childhood was spent in band rehearsals and on tours to nearby states that our mother would permit us to travel to. I witnessed the effects reggae had on people from all nationalities. The artists promoted Black consciousness, Black unity, so I experienced richer dimensions of living at an early age. In the same sense, my experience in America has pulled me closer to another genre that has been able to capture a conscious focus from the mass: hip-hop. The efforts Africans have made in America to combat racism since slavery began is immense. The unlimited list includes the organizing of major black movements such as the NAACP or the Black Panther Party; the prioritizing and organizing of systematic structures like homes, churches, educational institutions, and overall productive systems that led to generational wealth; the courageous nonviolent sit-ins; major rebellious movements such as the Million Man March; and the impact both women and men had behind them. Early hip-hop focused on the inequalities Black people faced in America.

Fearless

The 1990s saw a growing influx of Caribbean and African immigrants that led to Black America growing more diverse culturally and an international rise of black activists and entertainers on the world stage. Hip-hop emerged and began to shed a more aggressive (and necessary) light on important issues such as police brutality, like the famous hip-hop group NWA (Niggas with Attitudes) which highlighted Rodney King's beating with the hit song *Fuck The Police*. Artists like Tupac developed timeless music because themes specifically addressed social ills that were being ignored, but that the people resonated with. Now with today's hip-hop, I have to be the conductor of what music I listen to instead of the radio so I can control what I am intaking; because what is on mainstream, I don't always find educational or uplifting, especially after realizing how our ways of life have been manipulated here. "American music is still without a doubt the best for expressions of anger, frustration, and resentment in a modern world filled with injustice."[76] This is a sentiment I can relate to. I believe we will continue to find a correlation between energy and mindset amongst the American people and the music we gravitate to the most, and why.

I have noticed the conscious hip-hop sound has not achieved popularity in America as reggae does in Jamaica. The older genres that preceded hip-hop dominated by Blacks didn't highlight too much recognition of Mama Africa; if there were an excess it seems as if they were hardly brought to the forefront of Black music culture, and of, course with non-Blacks in charge. "If one accepts the seminal, foundational influence exerted by transplanted African culture, this legacy of drum-less evolution might just be the most important piece of the puzzle, the main answer to the question of how the Duple came to dominate American modern music."[76] Hip-Hop started to bring the importance of the drum to America which is why I believe it still has such a profound impact on American culture. As we learned in earlier chapters, it was a Jamaican credited to have found hip-hop. This can likely be an example and proof that energy is authentic and quite transferrable.

Energy's intangibleness makes it difficult for those existing in lower dimensions to understand its value. Jamaicans have mastered putting hard truths to melodic beats. Their ability has been birthed through generational trauma and a deep desire for fairness and liberty.

I am convinced sound has the power to individually empower us, and thus unite us all. Hariett Tubman carried around a now-famous, wear-and-tear hymnal, and as a result of the condition, it is said that she must have loved it and used it frequently as an aid and source of strength for her missions. I imagine sound can strengthen and make people move together (synchronicity) in combination with words of consciousness, for further evolution; it is what gives a tune its magic. Music can be a weapon for Souls to ascend to fearless heights and higher dimensions. Who knew words so simple as "one love, one heart" could be so powerfully felt throughout the world? There is beauty, peace, and power in reggae that makes it so adaptable. With the metamorphosis of music by the African diaspora in America (blues, jazz, rock & roll, blues, funk, hip-hop, rap, trap, etc.), we see how the energy has increased in our musical production and perhaps in our social environments overtime as well. I believe the American musical taste is going to change as people's desire for unity increases. I envision the desire for unity will be coupled with the desire for a sound that focuses on unity and consciousness, as Jamaicans do with reggae. "But in many ways, explicit use of African polyrhythms is returning to African American music, from the self-conscious attempts to reconnect with Motherland culture made by musicians in the 1960s and 70s to the Chicago Juke/Footwork of today. It seems unlikely only one type of rhythm can sustain all these different kinds of music for long, and I think we are currently in the process of a global polyrhythmic revival."[76] Whatever these new rhythms will be, the African diaspora's mass movement connecting more with their roots will contribute the most to that direction. The African rhythm thrives even in the most oppressive environments.[76]

CHAPTER TWENTY-FIVE

Evolving Pass Black Oppression

♪ *Gyptian – Serious Times*
♪ *Junior Reid – One Blood*

White people are speaking out against inequality more than ever with the help of the media letting us see what's happening throughout the world. They are examining harmful paradigms and mindsets that were passed down from their ancestors and are advocating for change. White people are becoming more aware of the hidden and overt injustices that plague America. I have witnessed this in-person in Boston as they have shown support of justice movements like Black Livers Matter by joining and making their voices heard at the protests. I feel we are experiencing a phenomenon where everyone is examining truth and looking deeper within themselves and generational line. People use rationale to uncover and understand information never popularized because they are wary of the same injustices happening repeatedly. Following George Floyd's death and the resulting of the heightened, already-present Black Lives Matter movement, I have never seen white people so self-reflective. It has been increasingly hard for *everyone* to be at peace as injustices that have always existed are coming more into light, and as people are becoming more conscious.

Detrimental mindsets began with the Portuguese greed for sugar. They stole the Canary Islands off the coast of Africa and used it as a base to further raid the Western coast of Africa. When the Europeans arrived in Africa, they also found themselves in the middle of tribal and civil wars. The Portuguese formed an agreement with African kings that would put the slave-trading system into effect, taking advantage of immoral situations for their own greed.

During 18th century Jamaica, "peace with local whites brought an opportunity to end the persistent strain of being a society incessantly at war. It brought opportunities to solidify their freedom, have safer access to resources, and the chance to form a more stable environment to encourage natural reproduction."[23] We find this pattern to be true throughout American history as well. For instance, Harriet Tubman in her historic voyages to free the enslaved had white allies all along the routes. When researching Jamaica's history, I found after Africans, the Irish had the largest population on the island, accounting for about 25% of Jamaica's population with 300,000 people. Still, I could not find a surplus of stories where Africans didn't get along with the Irish, which I was expecting to find, especially since they were brought to Jamaica around the same period. "There is no evidence of violent clashes over land, no instances of kidnapping, and retribution for crimes was seemingly non-existent."[23] Even in a new millennium, centuries later, First World nations like the USA cannot bring herself to a space where racism is non-existent. It has been a continuous struggle despite strides being made.

Growing up in America, there is a plethora of information about American and European-based history taught in schools and not nearly enough about African history. Just recently, we have discovered (or instead accepted) both Jesus and Beethoven were Black. What is perplexing more than anything, and what should raise eyebrows from both my Black and white peers, is why there has been so much concentrated, diligent, and successful effort into hiding, faltering, and nearly erasing information on African history? History taught in the schools presents information on slavery and the Civil Rights Movement, but nothing in-depth beyond that. The information regarding Egypt, the pyramids, and the dynasties is only taught off the strength of its connections with European empires such as Rome and Greece, it feels like. After the history lessons gained in school from the periods of 2000-2013, I viewed the American Revolution as a victory and the British Red coats as pure evil. Now that my history and knowledge have been broadened, I see the American Revolution was just the beginning of a weary and deadly fight for freedom passed down to Black people throughout generations.

It was not until 2020 that states started to recognize Juneteenth, the holiday that marks the day West Virginia abolished slavery, the last state to do so. As of summer 2021, Jamaica plans to demand 10.6 billion dollars from the British government for slave trade reparations. These types of moves are signs to me that we are collectively trying to get to the same goal. During the 2020 Black Livers Matter protests, one of the recurring quotes I saw on social media was, "This isn't white vs. Black. This is everyone vs. racists." That is right. Right and wrong have no color. Treating everyone justly involves standing for what is right no matter what ethnic background the person is.

We must face the reality that the idea of slavery was able to be conceptualized, and we need to steer ourselves away from this type of thinking. The normalcy of slavery has had long-lasting repercussions in our societies, disrupting stability and peace in communities. For peace to be possible, perhaps we should study and take note of both the mindsets of the normalized role of the oppressor and the victim, and then consciously choose to realign with our highest selves. This presents an opportunity to revisit the personal beliefs and morals that drive us, often coming from a religious source, a spiritual source, or neither. We must really ask ourselves what type of thinking led to these non-evolutionary behaviors and decisions in American or European history that have produced such a divisive society. And would we categorize those types of thinking as mental illnesses, as we are quick to do for so many afflictions today?

The God complex, or similarly, the superiority complex, that has plagued white America for generations is sourced from the belief that God is white, rather than God being colorless and being the Source within us all. I have learned through experiences that people do not know what they do not know. It is essential to be aware of this perspective, so we don't get caught up in an emotion. Once I started to become aware of this and exercised emotional intelligence more, the research of my ancestors begun and augmented overtime, eventually producing this work. Everything started to become clearer in a non-judgmental mental space.

White allies have always existed, and they have always been growing in numbers. Every significant movement to fight Black oppression has always had white allies in one way or another. Otherwise, the fight would be next to impossible, especially in America where Blacks are the minority. America needs to rewrite its constitution. The constitution was created in a way that disproportionately affected Black people and still does. The authors did not understand their egos' long-term effects on their descendants, nor could they anticipate how their irrationalities would affect race relations in America, even nearly 400 years later. Though white people have perhaps outgrown the ways of their ancestors, the laws infused with inequality are still here. When Black people speak up with a force of supporters, laws are changed. But what happens if not? Who is our voice when we can't use ours, or when ours is ignored?

White Trash: The 400-Year Untold History of Class in America does an interesting job exploring poor white Americans in rural areas and their role in a non-evolutionary America. I don't know what the author meant by poor, but I take it as having poor mental states rather than it just be related to socioeconomic backgrounds. Slavery was made illegal in Britain in 1772 and was abolished throughout the empire on August 28, 1833, and it went into effect a year later. Britain benefitted the most from the slave trade, but their number of enslaved Africans brought to the country was relatively low compared to America. There are injustices in Britain against Blacks today, as I've learned through the media covering their Black Lives Matter protests, but not as deep-rooted as it is in America. Forgive me for comparing such an evil and let me be clear that both nations have work to do, but it seems as if Britain has been assuming accountability earlier on.

    I believe white people are afraid of accepting accountability and ownership of their ancestors' actions due to misunderstandings, or they might feel like their ancestor's actions have nothing to do with theirs, or even shame, which is understandable. They are often at times not aware that they perpetuate systems and mentalities from passed generations. This realization and accountability could lead to breakthroughs. The fight must be a spiritual fight. I believe physical fighting is going to send us back to old patterns and behaviors; history will repeat itself and we don't know what that outcome could look like. America, "the home of the brave?" — "The

Fearless

land of the free?" We need to be braver; we all need to be free. We're now in 2021, I believe there are too many conscious white Americans for a revolt to be necessary. In the past, uprisings occurred because Europeans were not using their conscience appropriately and refused to when confronted about it. One's voice as a white person can be the most pivotal voice against white oppressors who don't favor equality, because they have more respect for their color of skin, it's as simple as that. The mentality of a racist that justifies his actions is so weak that the color of one's skin is what warrants the level of respect or attention said person is going to give, one's character is not even considered. It's daunting. White men, like Andrew and Chris Cuomo, are the great examples today of how far white Americans can expand their consciousness even in the American, political realm. They also had a father who dedicated himself to human rights like they do today; energy being transferable is applicable for everyone. I personally do not like categorizing white people when we use the term 'white people' because I have white friends who live by energy, not by color. These types of white people that exercise morality instead of bigotry or capitalism have always existed but are always overshadowed especially when some nonsensical things happen by peers who share their same skin color. America has such a long way to go. So, I suspect that part of creating a new narrative is to find more definitive terms for clarity while on this spiritual fight the world is facing if we choose to use divisive terms, instead of 'white people' to describe the people we're up against or 'Black people' when in reality, energy knows no color. This is no longer a battle over the color of skin, it has always been a spiritual battle and the more time goes on is the more this becomes obvious.

It is vital to embrace all cultures. Through studying abroad, I have learned we can benefit from the good of any culture without forgetting our own. I wish I could live in a Jamaica with New Zealand's crime rate, while making American money, while receiving Canadian free healthcare, while getting a free French college education, with Indian cuisine at my convenience all the time. Imagine if we made a practice of finding beauty in each other and each other's customs, so we may learn and adapt ways that could best serve us as a whole. I grew up with the understanding that people are all equal. I did not understand racism until after college where I had my first and only experience of being called a nigger while volunteering at a nursing home during my freshman year in New York City. Growing up in Boston exposed me to many cultures and different backgrounds, similar to NYC. Traveling has opened my eyes wider and my heart, larger. I can separate the negative and positive things about any society and culture when I remember the route to world peace is about understanding one another and expressing respect and gratitude.

A logical approach to ending racism anywhere is to review places where it has existed and has been eradicated. By writing this book, I am hoping to provide some tools for America to follow. We must understand it is the energy a person or people carry, how they treat one another, that makes a country great, not just the things they have or produce. Focusing on consciousness and energy will solve so many issues beyond the -isms, global warming, population control, immigration control, and wherever else injustice lays.

Another great start to work from is for us to recognize what is fueling the "garbage" music that labels are capitalizing on. What "garbage" means to so many can vary but for this book's sake I'm going to equate it with musical content that deters us from evolving peacefully with one another. Is it the people and their inabilities? Is it the environmental circumstances? Is it a lack of resources? What is it? And what better systematic approaches can we take to make it better? The people who profit off music who promote violence are rich, and the artists as well, and maybe family and a couple of friends benefit, but that's it. The music goes right back into the ears of young people in these impoverished communities who aren't fully matured adults yet, it motivates them to do things how they've seen and now hear it to be done, and then they replicate it. One or two of the bunch then gains a considerable amount of popularity more than others, feuds are likely to be had, and the cycle continues. When music points us more to a fifth-dimensional direction, with powerful messages by musicians like Lauryn Hill, Kendrick Lamar, and J. Cole (who keep us connected to the motherland and our roots outside of reggae) is played as often if not more than music that keeps us on a more third-dimensional level where material matter, we will start to see a shift in human behavior. I think music, and especially what is rotated heavily on the radio and in the media beyond our control, can be correlated to human behavior, especially when an environment has little direction or control over themselves. Systems and people can play their parts by choosing not to be a part of this cause-and-effect. Even with similar battles in Jamaica as dancehall music is said to have negative impacts in certain communities, one thing Jamaica does have is the popularity of reggae/roots reggae whose messages never change. Reggae is still the biggest genre to come out of Jamaica despite dancehall's continual success, and I look at this with a sigh of relief. If it were the other way around, as much as I love dancehall, I would be worried, and I'd start to look at crime trends in congruence with what dancehall messages are hot at the moment. But because of reggae's growing, firm stance in Jamaica and in the world, the spiritual battle being fought in Jamaica is a less of a fight to endure for many. When I think of reggae artists like Sizzla, Buju Banton, and Chronixx, the spiritual battle in Jamaica is being fought with much more powerful tools than in America.

Our foundation is everything, and we can restart cycles or continue them. White men must face white men and white women. White women must face white women and white men. In public, and in private. When someone loves and values us, we can use this to our advantage to correct them or share our opinion on something we might not agree with, we're in a better position to use our voice without being ignored. This is a tool I believe parents use to help their kids mature. This same method can be applied to people confronting their racist family and friends to help them mature. We have come such a long way already, and with the help of newer generations and new ways of thinking, people cherish the freedom to think for themselves. We need more laws that protect Black people against injustices. Perhaps even a peace treaty in America between the ruling white class and everyone discriminated against because of their color of their skin or their ethnic background could be a step in the right direction, as Jamaica still has in place. I am encouraged by the awareness that continues. To increase, like states mandating Juneteenth as a holiday and by the talks of reparations for Black people for America's role in slavery.

We live up to the roles that the system keeps. This means we really need to challenge ourselves to figure out what's right and challeng the system where they are wrong. German historian Erwin Rusch said he did not view the beginnings of the slave revolt as a conscious effort on the part of the Blacks to fight for their freedom portions, "the negroes had not yet awakened to a racial consciousness and racial pride.... They are still very far from an awareness of their equality among nations."[21] This is a white man realizing Black people aren't aware of their excellence, and so many like him knww this, and chose to take advantage of it. Black consciousness is essential for us to evolve into newer dimensions. We must understand our history and where we're coming from in order to know where we are going. The American people have done incredible things to advance human evolution in the medical field, in science, heck we even flew to the moon! It's also a nation known to save the day for other countries experiencing what is portrayed as upheaval at times. This is always a nice gesture, but the best example America can give to the world to prove they are qualified for such a heroic and godly position is meeting the needs of minorities and people-in-need in their own country. Only at this point will America be truly a land for the free. We can't undo the past, but we can look forward and create a new narrative for the future.

CHAPTER TWENTY-SIX

Executing The Steps For Ascension To Higher Dimensions

♪ *Steel Pulse – Your House*

♪ *Buju Banton – Destiny*

The education on dimensions for me begun in my late 20s, years after receiving my rudimentary education in America. Without this knowledge being readily accessible in our primitive years, I can understand how coming upon it in our later years can almost seem alien-like, like it was for me. Ascending through different dimensions requires the tolerance of others and their beliefs while journeying through our higher self with key principles and values in tow. The spiritual dimensions exists, our home isn't only physical. The former has a greater impact on ourselves and our environment.

The spiritual dimension is a topic people shy away from, as the subject is an intimidating one to delve into. However, once we start, it's hard to unlearn, and in fact, we want to learn more as we start to make sensible connections with our life up until this current phase.

The first dimension is marked by self-awareness. There is only one point with no awareness of separation. There is no individual identity nor time, there is only *me*. It is associated with the root chakra, our first chakra and an earth element, which represents grounding, security, and manifestation. It is focused on the most basic needs for survival. At this first point, we simply exist.

The second dimension is marked by polarity and it invites us to our second point. It now increases our awareness of separation, duality, and polarity. This dimension now involves the first trials of using our senses and using them to carefully and curiously understand the world around us. The second dimension is associated with the sacral chakra, the second chakra and a water element, representing creativity, nurturement, sexuality, emotion stability, and flexibility. Historically-speaking, it can represent the engenderment of civilizations and societies; technology, sexuality, individuality are all expressions of the sacral chakra in their most fundamental phase. Second dimensional beings were the influence in discovering us having a pair or two sides of mostly everything on or in our bodies, as well as material things like wheels on cars, two sides of a street, two sides of bread, and tons of real-life examples to brainstorm on.

The third dimension is an experiential phase marked by matter. It introduces a third point where the past, present, and future exist; exploring ourselves and others now with our (1) body, (2) space and (3) time. This makes way for discernment, comparisons and judgments, which then leads to the emotions we experience everyday like desire, fear, and worry. It is associated with the solar plexus chakra, the third chakra and a fire element representing power, purpose, and confidence. We can connect this to our history. Every 2,000 years or so the universe is said to shift into a new age in astrology. During the Age of Aries from 2000 BC to 1 AD was a period marked by fire, symbolizing transformation, which was the spiritual energy that ignited the Bronze Age, Heroic Age, Iron Age, Golden Age, and the Silver Age during this quaternary human time period; and additionally, many of our life-changing wars. There was a lot of separation going on here. This makes sense because this is when civilizations really started to expand and have deeper interactions with one another. The Thinkers: Socrates, Plato, and Aristotle lived during these times and the Romans started building their famous empire. There is a noticeable decline in wars after this period. This was also right before the birth of Jesus Christ's and the Age of Pisces from 1 AD to 2000 AD, where the Pisces' gift of understanding and unconditional love is exemplified with notable figures emerging; Gandhi, Nelson Mandela, John F. Kennedy, and Martin Luther King just to name a few. We begin to differentiate self-care and service to others here in this time period. I'm sure we can probably make more connections to other worldly events from this time. If we could learn any lesson from this time period, it is pivotal to understand that every good or bad event that happens in our life is just an experience for us to learn and grow from. Unconditional love for our environment is necessary to acknowledge and develop here for us to ascend through the higher dimensions.

The fourth dimension is a transitional period marked by time. It is very similar to the third dimension, except it now starts to tap into the spiritual realm. It is associated with the heart chakra, the fourth chakra and an air element, representing the seat of the Soul, love, emotions, and empathy. It is engendered through interactions between our first dimensional self and our second-dimensional self. However, instead of a 3D focus on physical reality, 4D steers us more towards our non-physical selves, introducing a fourth point in this realm. This dimension challenges us to be who we truly are. I know it to be a dimension we don't want to linger in for too long because we can get stuck and feel stagnant in this dimension for our whole life, and never ascend because we don't want to leave behind our ego (or where our id takes control of our ego and our collective lack of attention to what happens once the id takes lead with pleasure, rather than the superego pulling the ego in a moral direction). Even though we may have body space, and time, we additionally have a very strong and developed ego through our 3D phase. Here is where we are forced to master both love and fear since everyone has higher powers here, both good and bad. It is said that humankind has been entering a fourth-dimensional phase and the evidence lays in the worldwide growing interest in ascension.

This abundance of love and a greater lack of fear now brings us to the fifth dimension. The fifth dimension is marked by spirituality. It is a level of interaction between our self (1D) and our other (2D) that has moved beyond the physical reality of body, time, and space (3D) into an almost entirely non-physical reality (4D). Human beings in the fifth dimension are focused on spiritual advancement for themselves and the universe, this is where our highest 4D self resides. It is associated with the throat chakra, the fifth chakra and a space element, representing, self-expression and communication. Contrary to the third dimension, the fifth chakra allows us to consciously create our own reality. Because the past, present, and future all exist on the same plane here, their co-existence broadens our experiences and gives us deeper insights on life that make our journeys smoother. This is where our Soul manifests what our thoughts and actions have been geared to. The energies we choose to ingest as far as food, music, people, you name it, all gets lighter and lighter. There is no physical body here (or the importance of it is now meaningless). Instead, our emotional energy within dictates what is seen on the outside from others, and how we also see the world. In order to exist in this realm, we must have the fundamental understanding that we are all one.

The sixth dimension and up begins to solidify a group-form based mentality where the idea of separation becomes gradually non-existent and the idea of oneness increases. These realms become lighter and closer to The Source gradually as well. Where we are is a lot denser with energy than it is in the higher dimensions, this is what makes it more of a challenge to feel and connect with the energy of spirits in higher dimensions from down here, including loved ones that have passed on. The fifth dimension and up have become symbols for a "heaven" people want to experience while here on earth. Nothing is good or bad, everything is an experience. This is an improvement from lower dimensions where systems are in place to maintain the physicality of a material world.

It is important to remember that in any dimension one can feel the bliss of experiencing their highest self in that dimension before moving on to a lighter dimension, in fact it is necessary to. All dimensions have their unique challenges for each person. What is key to experience in every dimension while we're on our ascension is awareness, this is the bliss of it all that sort of gives us a roller coaster ride to our next level. We can be happy at any level, and the higher vibrations individuals experience are pivotal for the world in any dimension. We need human beings in every dimension operating at their highest frequency possible in any given moment to maintain the momentum we all need to keep ascending collectively.

It is said that the human race is currently ascending from the third dimension onto higher dimensions. A little research will show us that some believe we are already collectively in the fourth. The pandemic that has devastatingly took away so many lives from us has also shown us many third dimensional things about reality we don't like about ourselves and/or our environment and galvanized us into paying attention to things that really make us happy. This is just one mere sign of ascension. In reality, we have always been moving up the ladder for a substantial period of time, with notable setbacks throughout history. The collective pace depends on the indepedent thinking and actions of every individual.

- 1st dimension: I am.
- 2nd dimension: I feel.
- 3rd dimension: I do.
- 4th dimension: I love.
- 5th dimension: I speak.
- 6th dimension: I see.
- 7th dimension: I understand.

We live in a 3D world, and those who are not familiar with dimensions in the spiritual realm might refer to the 3D world as the 'material world'. This is the phase where material matters, and we can't seem to get passed that phenomenon. Aspects of the 3D world plague us in ways that make it hard for us to realize what's really going on, much less make the right decisions and do the right actions because the focus is on the production and worship of material things. Less attention is given to the world within us and around us, thus giving the outside world more control over our minds. Diamonds, golds, houses, cars, clothes, shoes, body sizes, skin color, they all matter a lot in 3D environments. Our Soul and spiritual growth are compromised when we are not aware that there are realms beyond the 3D to experience. We don't even know that we're stuck in a dimension sometimes because the way our external environment was created has very little to do with us, and more to do with systems that have been in place for too long. We're only following what appears as normal. Instead of giving attention to our 'energy account' as we would need to ascend into higher realms of life, we are conditioned to worry about our bank account. It's often only all about the 'benjamins' in a 3D world. We likely all have 4D or 5D experience at random times, possibly even higher for some, it's the sign of consistency that eventually make us feel our ascension.

With ominous resources planted in and beyond the universe for our guidance and protection, energy is undoubtedly the world's most valuable currency that serves the human evolution best. This doesn't mean that other currencies have no value, but valuing energy affects human behavior in a more positive way than valuing material, like money. The more our energy is aligned with the universe and its grandeur, which I believe includes the cosmic world that existed long before geology started to form here on earth, the more we will collectively be aligned with All That Is. It's a good idea from time to time to reflect on what currency on this earth we value the most. It can lead to important breakthroughs internally and externally.

"Jamaica is a crossroads. There is a connection between the north and south. Black and white. You know, I mean I've said it many times. A Jamaican will understand a European better than an African ever could [or an American], better than an African ever could. A Jamaican will understand an African, better than anyone could. In other words, he is in the middle. He's in the middle, he's seeing it both ways."[70] To be so courageous and sure to share this belief in his documentary, *Man Free* highlights important points that give credibility to my theory on Jamaicans possibly being able to tap into higher dimensions collectively. Perry Henzell was a Jamaican-born director, whose ancestors were a combination of Huguenots escaping from religious persecution by the French and English plantation owners in Antigua. He has a background of ancestors who have fought for their freedom and coexisted with other cultures peacefully, therefore perhaps familiarized with this type of energy that so vibrantly shows through his thinking and actions, like many other Jamaicans.

A sizeable amount of Jamaicans may have collectively left the third dimension where material matters. An example of this is seeing how Maroon and Rasta societies do not put value on material things, best reflected in how they live daily. And when in this dimension, "the lower mind is designed to receive, interpret, and process higher channeled knowing through our clairvoyant, clairaudient and clairsentient (psychic) skills. So now we know what to do. The question is how to do it? If our authentic and creative action does not get side-tracked, the gathering energies are next passed into our subconscious or 'lower mind'. The lower mind then helps us to 'connect the dots within the co-creative weave. Through the clairvoyant, clairaudient, and clairsentient skills of the lower mind, we notice rhythms and patterns of synchronicity in our 'consciousness landscape' and have clear visions of the 'garment' to be created. As Right Action clicks into place moment by moment, it becomes abundantly clear what we are being invited to do and how to do it."[86]

The process described above is ties in with what I would define as exercising emotional intelligence. Emotional intelligence is the ability to understand, utilize, and manage our own emotions in positive ways. It has been mastered by groups indigenous to Jamaica such as the Maroons and the Rastas. Redemption is also a favored value in Jamaican society. In higher dimensions, wrongs are correctable if we have a conscience and yearn to evolve. Although one doesn't want to stay in any dimension for too long, each one is necessary to experience in order to ascend.

The chakra system, a system originated in ancient India, is another way to understand our body at a spiritual level so we can unlock energy and improve our overall well-being. The last two of the seven chakras assosociated with these higher dimensions that have not yet been mentioned are the third eye and crown chakras. The third eye chakra is a light element; marked by intuition, an inner vision and enlightenment beyond what the physical eyes can see. It precedes the last step of mastering our crown chakra, or our ability to understand reality from a different perspective. This crown chakra, a thought element, represents enlightenment and detachment from the ego, where one can see the light in another, feel peace, and make sound decisions even while under pressure. Mastering the ascension of the seven chakras builds our energy and personal character; when aligned they bring us peace. Intuition, imagination, vision, consciousness, spirituality, and inspiration are all associated with these higher dimensions.

With the crown chakra representing spirituality, consciousness, and inspiration, perhaps their militant way of behaving somehow manifested itself in an energy that allowed the Maroons and Rastas to use their conscience collectively. The value of energy in Jamaica creates an exciting and clear direction for these types of discussions.

In relation to the Jamaican connection to chakra balancing, I believe one connection is activation through dancing. Movement brings awareness to the body and can help achieve alignment of the chakras to bring about advancement to higher dimensions and the overall awareness of spirit. The fifth dimension is characterized by synchronicity in spirituality. 'From authentic being arises authentic creation. The purpose of the higher mind is to harmonize with the divine flow of synchronicity and initiate "'Right Action' aligned with the universe. Through the power of the celestial body, we have noticed how to be within the external world, and now is the time to experience this through creative action. At this stage, the creative impulse is quite abstract and undefined; the purpose is more about creative intent, and co-creating with other sentient life, rather than an actual creation itself. The Soul now acts through higher mind, gathering 'elementals of consciousness into a directional flow of Right Action, like swirling clouds in the heavens."[86] Synchronization is a power that gives life to more power. It is a power for eternal unity.

In Jamaica, the power of music and dance are two common denominators in religion and spirituality. With Jamaica's vibrant churches, already dubbed for having the most per square mile in the world, one might think they are at a party when going to certain churches in Jamaica. If it wasn't for the difference in musical content and the messages being shared, it would be hard to tell the difference from particular social events by the way people still joyously dance and celebrate from a religious or spiritual perspective. The Rastafari movement, as explained earlier on, is recognizably a facilitator of one of the world's most powerful genres, Reggae, and they too incorporate spiritual celebrations in their regular life. "Some of the principal aims of the Rastafari movement were to purge

Fearless

Jamaicans of their inferiority complex, instill self-pride in them, and create a bond of unity between them and their African brothers and sisters. In the course of resistance, many Africans of the diaspora re-constitute their history, a history that has been battered by slavery and colonialism...Reggae artists narrate the story of slavery and economic exploitation of the poor...[They] expose all forms of social injustice, especially White domination, capitalist exploitation, police brutality, corruption, and political intimidation."[41][42] The Maroons, Rastafarians and many Jamaicans incorporate sound and dance in their everday life. The Jamaicans love for sound, especially the drums, correlates with the human connection to The Big Bang that happened over 13 billion years ago (billions of years before Christ was born); the beginning of everything from a scientific scope. With this love for sound so remarkably felt throughout the island, I believe they enrich their powerful connection to the Source.

For the fifth dimension, sound and the subsequent rhythm becomes a fundamental part of its foundation. This simply reminds me of the music and dance culture we've dissected within Jamaican society. Phrases Jamaicans use like "energy!" or "tun it up!" can be heard in the dance halls, inclfuencing more or higher energy into the environment. The acceptance of the party lifestyle reflects a respect Jamaicans have for energy and the awareness that there are always dimensions we can vibrate higher to. As addressed previously, visitors immediately feel a "special vibe" when their feet touch the island. I have connected this to the possibility of many Jamaicans being able to tap into the fifth dimension from earlier centuries. The most popular contributing factor joining the Maroons, especially with higher numbers in population, is the Rastafari movement that gave back oppressed peoples control of their minds in the ever-changing times of the

20th and 21st centuries; regardless of their ethnic, social or financial circumstances. The Maroons and Rastafarians do not believe in materialism and it is evident in their minimalist lifestyle. Both groups expose the possibility of being able to observe life from higher dimensions and understand that there is more knowledge available to us beyond the Westernized plane.

The minimalist lifestyle is embraced and largely felt in Jamaica, and this is a simple example demonstrating the appreciation Jamaicans have for more simpler ways of living and exhibiting less greed. My only observation of seeing food wasted in Jamaica is while at all-inclusive hotels, where the guests are usually more tourists than locals and are used to certain lifestyles and expectations that the hotels must accomodate. The act almost seems nearly forbidden in Jamaican households, and social class holds no exemption. Food is never wasted, for instance, it's always saved for the stray dogs or cats and other animals that are around one's area, who sometimes sort of adopt homes on their own. This is a drastic difference from the environment I was brought up in in America where throwing away food we don't want or doesn't sell is normalized.

Even after having to move to the States for better healthcare once making a name for herself as the most famous Jamaican poet, writer, and folklorist coming from the island, Miss Lou's Jamaican pride never ceased as she saw Jamaica as a more spiritual realm than a physical place: "Any which part mi live — Toronto -o! London -o! Florida-o! —Jamaica mi Deh!"[59] I share the same sentiments and notice many Jamaicans do too, in addition to the visitors that can't get enough of the island. There are so many examples I've experienced overtime. It really is a phenomenon to me looking at white or Asian Jamaicans and how they are more Jamaican than they are a color. Energy speaks louder than color on that island.

Experiencing different dimensions by traveling back and forth from the rural parts of Jamaica to the ever-progressive towns and boroughs of Boston and New York City has afforded me a different outlook on what's important; the former being looked at from a more Third World point of few, and the two latter, First World. In Jamaica, the concept of time does not exist, or rather, it is far less respected there than my experience in the very systematic America. Jamaicans do things on their own time which is quite known within the Jamaican community. Even Jamaicans despise Jamaicans when it comes to customer service because it's just so bad when it comes to the level of attention they care to give you. It's even worse when there is little-to-no-care shown, as it can feel brutal if you're used to certain privleges in First World environments (if you couldn't tell, I've had my experiences). But in a more positive light regarding their outlook on time, this is a sign to me that many Jamaicans really are living in the fifth dimension or higher, where time no longer exists, and material no longer matters because personal peace and happiness presides. My limited expertise on dimensions won't allow me to make an accurate judgement on where the Jamaican group truly is spiritually (and I really think that's a job for God), but with my experience and the knowledge I am progressively gathering and connecting, I believe it's worth it to keep exploring.

Reggae is often fifth dimensional in the sense that it omits the need for material things, and instead focuses on the need for spirituality, consciousness, and unity. Reggae is therefore an example of a fifth dimensional weapon against racism, and the fifth dimension is a realm people experience when listening. It is often why people gravitate to the genre and the country it was birthed in without consciously realizing it is fifth-dimensional. When singer Mikey Dread described the legendary King Tubby's role in the development of Toasting, he said, "King Tubby truly understood sound in a scientific sense. He knew how the circuits worked and what the electrons did. That's why he could do what he did." To me, this is indicative of King Tubby's ability to tap into a higher dimension even in his times, and representative of so many producers, engineers, and artists who were and still are able to do the same. People have been tapping into higher dimensions since time, it's just a topic that has become very alienated in Westernized environments.

Jamaica's stoic honoring of God is also an act I can connect to a fifth-dimensional experience. I like what Elizabeth Nelson wrote in her *Rhetoric of Reggae* piece about Jamaicans and their connection to God. "God has been imagined and re-imagined constantly, at the same time, God also seems to be limitless in the way he is utilized in Black Jamaicans identity. He (or She or They, depending) always seems to be there though because He is the strongest identifying agent and tool of rebellion."[41] Jamaicans have an unequivocal respect for God that is impenetrable. The calls for equality and peace and becoming more self-sufficient have been a popular way to go for Jamaica since the 19th century. Before there was Marcus Garvey, there were people like Alexander Bedward of August Town in Kingston. Bedward was a preacher that called for a change in race relations in the late 1800s. He advocated for his 30,000 followers to be self-reliant. His followers subsequently followed Garvey and his similar ideals when he emerged. "Garvey, like the slaves, held on tightly to Africa because it was in this land that they were understood to be fully human. Garvey's cry was a cry of self-awareness. He felt that an important ingredient in Jamaica's journey to make peace with Blackness or Black consciousness was the affirmation of a sense of self-worth and self-esteem as crucial aspects of a healthy national psyche."[41] The Rastafari movement growing as big as it is on that island should be no surprise with the preceding movements that existed before it and the values they've all held. This is a humble recommendation from me to my readers to look into spiritual practices like Rastafarianism's works that specifically promote the *I & I* lifestyle; and other similar spiritual movements, like Hinduism and Buddhism. Every man and woman is responsible for his or her actions, but a community is there for us to fall back on when we need it. I have not seen a movement unite so many African diasporas harmoniously, and even including those outside of the diaspora, as much as I have with the Rastafari movement.

With fear leading the way, we sink ourselves to lower dimensions subconsciously to fit in and feel a part of a group because being lonely can be hard, and we're not taught the value in it because spiritual dimensions don't hold too much weight in our First World systems or our material world. It seems like people do not want us to find out that we can be happy without the aid of anyone or anything, like we must depend on a thing, person or a system for happiness. When I see Jamaican entertainers not being allowed to obtain or re-obtain their visas after being revoked, I can't help to think of the influence reggae music has on people outside of the island and how it may disrupt agendas. It gives credibility to those that believe only certain music is promoted in certain First World environments to have better control over our minds and put more money in pockets that don't understand the effects music has on our mind. There is a reason why artists like Lauryn Hill, Erykah Badu, Common, Talib, Jill Scott, and a long list of musicians are not the faces of American music like how Bob

Marley is lastingly to Jamaican music. What is the message in their songs? How far and deep does the effect take us to our roots, our heights, our peace? If we sit with reggae music long enough, the words will have a strong influence on our minds and, eventually, our bodies with the instruments used. It's like a spiritual, natural order that First World environments are lacking.

The most complex battles have already been fought, yet the condition of Africans and their diasporas have systematically remained the same in many places. What more do we need to do for equality in our countries, like America and the UK, where racism is rampant? The entire human race must be fearless in the pursuit of peace. We are coming into a more collective, conscious state of mind of realizing what it takes to make real change in the world. We would not physically harm ourselves to become better, so why do we continue to take the physical route on each other as an approach to world peace or personal happiness? Redirecting the war from physical to spiritual is essential for further human evolution, with the spiritual way always proven itself to be the most powerful in the long run. I believe the way to win spiritually is through consistent practice of good actions as often as possible despite our circumstances, which is what I think makes Jamaican people a worthy component in this world's spiritual warfare. Discovering that the real war is between our earthly selves, which compiles the habits we have often innocently gathered, and our godly self, is necessary for every individual.

The conscience is the most powerful weapon we each have on earth, and we can use it to win a fight before it has to get physical. It takes patience, an unfavored value in Westernized environments. It takes technique, with the ability to excerise emotional intelligence and evolve in denser environments. It's important for us to pay attention to how someone communicates with us, specifically the energy that's behind it. More than we realize, people already show themselves, reveal their true character, and/or demonstrate a lack of fundamental understanding on what the point of communication is; to teach, chellange and learn from one another. Disagreeing with something does not have to equate to negativity, but the manner in which we communicate with each other can derail a potential learning experience or further it to a point where we can learn from each other. Conquering fear includes having to look fear in the eye. It's the most important staring contest we'll ever have in our life. When we know something is the right thing to do, and we exhibit no fear, there's a confidence we feel that leaves us without a will to fight or argue; especially with particular foundational beliefs. This is a force many Jamaicans carry collectively, where words are spoken of God and actions are individually followed, strengthening the collective force. This does not mean there are not pockets of Jamaican people tittering in third dimensional activities. There are people there that can't live without ideals from that dimension (mostly younger people heavily influenced by the media), not realizing there is more to life to experience. But Jamaica's spirit is saved time and time again because of these three dominant groups there; the general people's widespread belief in God (no matter the religion and its denominations); the ever-growing Rastafarian community; and the resilient, legendary, Jamaican Maroons.

Each person, or group, owning their accountability and position in this fight for peace is essential for our collective advancement as human beings. Dismantling the system's power over the human Soul is crucial for our future as it was for the Maroons and the British at a point in time. "The mutual recognition of the benefits of an alliance between Maroons and local planters reminds us that interactions and relationships…were shaped as much by free, non-white communities as by colonial forces." [23] White people are becoming less afraid to address injustices. They are speaking out. Progressively, they realize their power in this pursuit of freedom and peace for all. There is a logical approach to ending racism anywhere; a practical approach could be looking at places where racism once existed but has been eradicated. This book is not only a model for ancestral discovery, but a model fow how Westernized environments can evolve from racism.

I always dream of racism being eradicated in America during my lifetime. I remain hopeful by observing younger generations as we become more conscious and courageously overcome old mindsets passed on in hopes of having better tomorrows. White Americans are still the majority, comprising more than half of the U.S. population, followed by Hispanics, Blacks, Asians, Native Americans, and Hawaiians. Power should be equally distributed amongst all groups, in the positions within the system that affect everyone's well-being. There should be more of a pull rather than a push on the topic of African or Caribbean importation into America. I believe the increase of such a thing could influence a balance of energies in areas where racial tension and inequality are greater in Westernized environments, leading to a vast cultural exchange and connection. Black Americans who don't travel and experience other cultures and/or who have also been most distant from their African roots through generations, strategically so by the American system, could become more familiar with their power through such a cultural exhange.

Racism is not fifth-dimensional. Racism is not progressive. Racism is inharmonic and marked by discord. Racism gains its strength off the degradation of a human flesh's hue, adding to the credibility of our infatuation with material in this very 3D, material world. Our entire evolution is delayed when one group chooses not to progress, because we are all connected; we are one. We need to maintain momentum as a collective so that there is an equal exchange of vibrations; there needs to positive reciprocity for us to make strides together. It's against the core of who we are not to stay connected. Life can be hard, but it is designed for us to be able to reach higher realms, whether that be Heaven for us, Jannah, or whatever utopia we believe in. We can reach these heights mentally while alive. Many of us never get to understand this truth, because we were taught to believe what is most powerful is outside of ourselves and within our mental reach.

The only way to defeat racism in a non-physical manner is to fearlessly and relentlessly serve the oppressor's conscience with facts. Who the oppressor is varies from person to person, from situation to situation. The conscience is where all the power lies, and there's no color on a conscience. It is intabgible, it is unseeable; one can only discern it being used by observing one's actions. Historian, Professor, and Director of the History Design Studio at Harvard University, Vincent Brown, argues that the Jamaicans rebellions did more to end the slave trade than any actions taken by white abolitionists. At this point in our ever-evolving history, I do not think physical activity is needed as much as enlightenment. I pose two questions to consider when developing solutions to end racism. Was the human trajectory of the Jamaican maroon a pinnacle of what ended racism amongst Europeans and Africans? And was the threat of violence, to protect one's human rights and freedom, the only way to end racism? America is a more diverse society today compared to the past in so many ways. Yet racism is still the root of unlawful and inhumane actions in America, enabled by its system. With a more varied environment, could having this be a tool in developing a higher-dimensional way of thinking? Let us learn from our past to advance instead of reliving it.

America has managed to keep energy levels low through government assistance, materialism, and the media to keep us dependent and distracted. The government has given out food stamps and other forms of help that can be fruitful in our individual pursuits of life, but it also can keep our energy at baseline by giving us just enough to be comfortable and unwilling to evolve if we don't have control over our own minds. Black people in America were already at a disadvantage with numbers when brought here as enslaved Africans. When Africans were brought to America, Europeans (or who would become some of the first Americans) spread them throughout the states to prevent them from uniting and potentially rebelling. In America today, unity is lacking, which is indicative of an environment stuck in a 3D way of thinking. In heavy 3D environments like these, we can lose ourselves easier even while trying to ascend, depending on how heavy the influences are around us, because we can lose and possibly never gain control of our own minds.

The media, specifically the entertainment industry, presents to the American people fantasized reasons to remain in 3D. In this plane, we are trapped between what we would like to be and what we are. We cannot begin to become what we would like to be until we honestly ask ourselves why our lives in First World countries, or having a 3D state of mind, could at times feel so empty and lonely. Not facing these realities and developing these understandings weaken our inability to deal with the world as it is — ourselves, as we are.

Fear has been ever present in America. We need to dance more. We need to listen to good music more. I know we are entering new dimensions because the warfare is getting more spiritual and less physical, more internal and less external, and more focused on the individual and their mental health instead of targeting a group. I believe it is in higher dimensions that we will see our ancestors again. I was reminded by my good friend Tiffany, that because our ancestors are in higher dimensions, we must do the inner work to raise our vibrations to be able to have any form of communication; and it will never be direct. Our ancestors heed our call in our most challenging situations. This type of communication is not taught in our primary and secondary institutions. Libations, white candles, meditation are just a few ways to stay in contact. Especially in Westernized environments, we have gotten comfortable with not understanding something and then giving it a label that often ends up having a negative connotation, like mental illnesses or spiritual practices. As Africans, once we get deeper into our spirituality and stay in touch with ancestors like Chinese and Indian traditions, and other spiritualities around the world, many things we have not been able to make sense of with a Westernized state of mind will start to make sense.

Transition is never easy; whether that's from one life to the next, from one country to the next, or from one dimension to the next. In any case change and growth is never easy, but we cannot be afraid to distance ourselves from energy that does not serve us. It is a life or death situation. We are in control of our energy, and our environment is powerful enough to build or tear it down.

Research shows that human beings have tapped into the fifth dimension here on earth. There are higher dimensions, but it seems as if we have been stuck in one particular dimension for a long time where a lack of respect for others is acceptable. We are the blame, and we are the solution. Many -isms have developed throughout time because of our ego. A type of order or Godly element is lost when we allow the ego to rule over God. Once upon a time, this world began with Love, God. Then the ego took the lead, everyone wanted to do their own thing, and life became complicated.

There is a famous quote that goes, "in many shamanic societies if you came to a medicine person complaining of being disheartened, discouraged, or depressed, they would ask one of four questions. When did you stop dancing? When did you stop singing? When did you stop being enchanted by stories? When did you stop finding comfort in the sweet territory of silence?"

Although this book heavily highlights the roots of Jamaican pride due to my experience of being raised by Jamaicans and the further curiosity I had about my roots, I found there are similarities between all peoples with my experiences traveling around the world. We will soon realize the characteristics we often think are unique to our culture and its people are shared and/or valued by others, and they can even contribute to our evolution. Our backgrounds may differ in ethnicity or language, foods we eat, or music we listen to, but the fact that we share more common roots than not is best expressed and proven in our ways and behaviors today. Ultimately with a stronger view and understanding on how similar we really are, we can mentally ascend to higher planes and dimensions together.

Epilogue

There is no amount of fun, no amount of trying to do/be good, no amount of accomplishments that can erase the pain from your loss. The memories of your pain cannot seem to move out the way from my ascension to the peace I want. It was so grave, it led me on a journey that took me beyond this 3D world we are living in. The experience I had with your energy was so special, that your loss recalibrated my energy and instantly sent me off on a journey I couldn't imagine then, with one-too-many detours, just so I could one day find you again. Now finding you was obviously physically impossible, but spiritually it was not, I discovered. Ultimately, I understood this to be more truth and less fantastical as I collected information I never came across in educational institutions, and I wouldn't have come across if I didn't lose you. And thus, I wouldn't find it so important to do the very hard research these last five years, just so I could prove a life-changing point in this book through my experience with you, mommy, and the ever vibrant, but fearless Jamaican population. Dimensions are real. What's best is I now have produced a tangible that not only helped heal me, but could change people's lives, and even societies, whole nations, including the one you decided to rest your physical body at after years of building yourself in America. If Jamaicans, like you, weren't vibrating as high as you always have, and for it to be such a common trait amongst so many of them, I wouldn't have a reason to simply find out, why? I couldn't ever imagine this quest until I experienced it. Many people experience the powerful vibrations, they'll make positive comments and show their appreciation in many different anyways, but not many have asked, why? Or how? I did. Perhaps everything does happen for a reason and this notion signals real, true new beginnings. Finally. Thank you, daddy. I hope you are proud.

Postscript

Common resources used for ascension:

- Sacred texts (ex. Bible, Quran, Tanakh, Tipitaka, etc.)
- Meditation (ex. Prayers, Insight Timer, Calm, Headspace, etc.)
- Books on dimensions (ex. Waking Up in 5D by Maureen St. Germain)
- Tracing roots (ex. Ancestry DNA, 23andMe)
- Social environments or gatherings with empowering music

A note.

Like Nanny is on the $500 Jamaican dollar bill, her fellow Akan sister Harriet should be on an American bill by now. This would stand for a symbolic and powerful move within America, giving the respect to an extraordinary African freedom fighter as Jamaica has done with Queen Nanny. This parallel to Jamaica seems logical, and a further step in an empowering direction, as both Harriett and Queen Nanny are treasured freedom fighters amongst their respected believers.

Fun Facts:

Jamaicans are not bystanders and assert themselves on all things from politics to music, sports, and more. Their militant characteristics have had some influence in other societies outside of Jamaica around the world. Many freedom fighters and politicians are of Jamaican descent, including Louis Farrakhan - Leader of the Nation of Islam, Colin Powell — the 65th

U.S. Secretary of State, and Kamala Harris, the first female vice-president of the United States, all who have used their platforms to advance on humane issues, such as racism, in the United States of America. Jamaicans continue to rise and be recognized on powerful platforms internationally.

In the arts and entertainment fields worldwide, we have multitalented supermodels Grace Jones, Tyson Beckford; and Naomi Campbell, who founded two charitable organizations and raised millions of dollars for the sub-Saharan children of Africa, Hurricane Katrina victims, and poverty in Brazil by supporting local artisans.

We also boast internationally-known actors like Madge Sinclair, Gloria Reuben, Sheryl Lee Ralph, Christopher Reid, Kerry Washington (cousins to Colin Powell).

Award-winning writers & poets Festus Claudius "Claude" McKay from the Harlem Renaissance era and Opal Palmer Adisa; Barrington Watson, John Dunkley, Albert Huie, Gloria Escoffery, Nari Ward, Ken Spencer, Cecil Cooper, Laura Facey, Dawn Scott, and Ebony G Patterson are just several figures out of a long list of pivotal Jamaican artists.

Our list of radio personalities continue to have an impact outside of the tiny island as well; with the likes of animated and intelligent entertainers like Ragashanti and Fluffy Miss Kitty,

The list of notable Jamaican musicians probably runs the longest: Harry Belafonte, Biggie Smalls, Busta Rhymes, Missy Elliott, Uncle Luke, DJ Kool Herc, Heavy D, KRS-One, Alicia Keys, Safaree Samuels, Justine Skye, Sean Kingston, Bobby Shmurda, Tyga, Young M.A, YFN Lucci, and both the late XXX Tentacion and Pop Smoke. In other fields, we have business executive Ann-Marie Campbell, executive V.P. of the Home

Depot stores who has been listed in Fortune's 50 Most Powerful Women in Business several times; Maurice Ashley is the first Black person to become a grandmaster in chess; and the late Yvette Francis-McBarnette who pioneered antibiotic treatment for pediatric sickle cell anemia in the 70s. I could go on not only with a list of Jamaicans making an impact around the world in influential areas, but the mentioned and many unmentioned people here deserve to be researched. Most, if not all, stories start with some personal or societal struggle and a yearning to follow their dreams.

Everyday Jamaican sayings that remind that relate to energy (just a few):

"Mind yuh hurt yuh self!" or "mind how yuh talk to me" — Be mindful of hurting yourself or how you talk to me

"Easy yuhself" — Relax or find balance of self

"Level" – Return to balance

"Energy!" – a popular MC saying in the dancehall to acknowledge the energy in the room

"Mi deh yah" – I am present, I'm here [chilling]

"No long talking" - No need for many words, action and energy speaks louder

"Everything criss" - A new way of saying "everything irie" meaning everything is good

"Crosses" – A situation or a person characterized by bad energy

Acknowledgements

My family all over the world for the inspiration they give to not only myself, but our worldly environment through their continuous positive vibes; Boston, Jamaica, New York, UK, Florida, Connecticut, California and everywhere else in the world we're scattered throughout. My mom, Uncle Bobby, Aunty Angie, Aunty Pat, Aunty Lark, Aunty Pauline, my cousin Adora, and all of the elders, including my Grandma in St. Elizabeth, Jamaica and my Grandad who migrated to Buffalo NY, for keeping the Jamaican family heritage alive through descriptive storytelling.

My non-Jamaican friends, and all my regular encounters with people outside of my culture, throughout the many different environments I've found myself in for my 30 years of life thus far, who show me time and time again that energy has no color, no ethnicity; it is boundless.

My dear Aunt Betsy in Buffalo, an extremely kind Black American woman my granddad married in America. She has taught me so much about my own family, even more so than my grandfather who is known to have an extensive amount of knowledge on the family. If she didn't take her time out to go on her own quest in her prime to learn about his Jamaican history, I wouldn't know a lot about my father's paternal side to draw conclusions with the historical patterns I wanted to connect with my personal life.

Dainjamentalz, Junior Rodigan, DJ Ghetto Hype for the passionate conversations on music.

Bibliography

1. "Jamaicans were never slaves." YouTube video, 3:14, January 24, 2017, https://www.youtube.com/watch?v=XJFDVMoZKJk.
2. Atkinson, L. G. (Ed.). *The earliest inhabitants: The dynamics of the Jamaican Taíno.* University of West Indies Press, 2006.
3. Rampersad, Sabrina R. *Targeting the Jamaican Ostionoid: The Blue Marlin Archaeological Project.* Caribbean Quarterly. Taylor & Francis, Ltd, 2017. https://www.tandfonline.com/doi/pdf/10.1080/00086495.2009.11829757.
4. *Caciques, Nobles, and Their Regalia.* Wayback Machine. http://web.archive.org/web/20061009090513/elmuseo.org/Taíno/caciques.html.
5. Researchers of ANU Museum of the Jewish People. "The Jewish Community of Jamaica." Dbs.anumuseum.org.il. https://dbs.anumuseum.org.il/skn/en/c6/e227517/Place/Jamaica.
6. Minority Rights Group International, "World Directory of Minorities and Indigenous Peoples - Jamaica," 2007, https://www.refworld.org/docid/4954ce122d.html.
7. United Nations High Commissioner for Refugees. *"World Directory of Minorities and Indigenous Peoples – Jamaica."* Refworld. Minority Rights Group International. https://www.refworld.org/docid/4954ce122d.html.
8. Zach, Paul. "Insight Guides: Jamaica," 1996. https://www.geni.com/projects/Germans-of-Westmoreland-Jamaica/12326/.

9. Valley Beit Midrash, "Jewish Slave Owners of Jamaica: Prof. Stan Mirvis Interviewed by Rabbi Dr. Shmuly Yanklowitz," YouTube Video, 21:27, May 9, 2019, https://www.youtube.com/watch?v=UNBr2hn6kvY.

10. "How the Lebanese and Syrians Came to Jamaica. Jamaicans.com," January 11, 2020. https://jamaicans.com/how-the-lebanese-and-syrians-came-to-jamaica/.

11. Benitez, Suzette. "Maroons in Jamaica: Their Origins And Development." Slave Resistance. University of Miami, https://scholar.library.miami.edu/slaves/Maroons/individual_essays/suzette1.html.

12. Harris, Howard. "Maroons: Violence and Confrontation with the Planters." University of Miami, https://scholar.library.miami.edu/slaves/Maroons/individual_essays/howard.html.

13. Sivapragasam, Michael. "After the Treaties: a Social, Economic and Demographic History of Maroon Society in Jamaica, 1739-1842." University of Southampton, June 1, 2018. https://eprints.soton.ac.uk/423482/.

14. Campbell, Mavis Christine. *The Maroons of Jamaica, 1655-1796: a History of Resistance, Collaboration & Betrayal.* Trenton, NJ: Africa World, 1990.

15. McLeod, Sheri-Kae. "8 Reasons Why You Should Date a Jamaican." The Culture Trip, November 19, 2017. https://theculturetrip.com/caribbean/jamaica/articles/8-reasons-why-you-should-date-a-jamaica/.

16. Chambers, Douglas B. *Runaway Slaves in Jamaica (I): Eighteenth Century.* University of Southern Mississippi, 2013. https://ufdcimages.uflib.ufl.edu/AA/00/02/11/44/00001/JamaicaRunawaySlaves-18thCentury.pdf.

17. Prendergast, Leanna. "Maroon Culture and How It Came About" https://scholar.library.miami.edu/slaves/Maroons/individual_essays/leanna.html.

18. "Senegal, Guinea, Slave Accounts of Life in Africa before Capture, Freedom, African American Identity: Vol. I, 1500-1865, Primary Resources in U.S. History and Literature, Toolbox Library, National Humanities Center." http://nationalhumanitiescenter.org/pds/maai/freedom/text1/text1read.htm.

19. Newman, Simon P. "The West African Ethnicity of the Enslaved in Jamaica." Taylor & Francis, November 14, 2012. https://www.tandfonline.com/doi/abs/10.1080/0144039X.2012.734054.

20. Brathwaite, Kamau, and B. W. Higman. *The Development of Creole Society in Jamaica: 1770-1820.* Kingston, Jamaica: Randle, 2005.

21. Braithwaite, Edward Kamau. *The Folk Culture of the Slaves in Jamaica.* London: New Beacon Books, 1981.

22. "Jamaica. The Caribbean. Plantations, Slavery, European Rule. Maritime Heritage Project. Sea Captains, Ships, Merchants, Merchandise, World Migration." The Maritime Heritage Project. https://www.maritimeheritage.org/ports/caribbeanJamaica.html.

23. McKee, Helen. "From Violence to Alliance: Maroons and White Settlers in Jamaica, 1739–1795." *Slavery & Abolition 39, no. 1* (2017): 27–52. https://doi.org/10.1080/0144039x.2017.1341016.

24. Bjorklund, Ruth. *Jamaica*. New York: Children's Press, an imprint of Scholastic Inc., 2015.

25. Lawler, Mary, and John Davenport. *Marcus Garvey: Black Nationalist Leader*. Chelsea House, 1988.

26. Dunn, Richard S. *The Demographic Contrast between Slave Life in Jamaica and Virginia, 1760-1865*. American Philosophical Society, 2007.

27. The Boiler Room. "Migrant Sound Documentary." The Boiler Room. YouTube video, 11:17, August 30, 2018. https://www.youtube.com/watch?v=8HdRh3H9a08.

28. Seala Media. *Jamaica's History Told by a Living Taíno*. YouTube video, 14:22, 2017. https://www.youtube.com/watch?v=6GactnhnY9Y.

29. Tortello, Rebecca. "Out Of Many Cultures, The People Who Came: The Arrival Of The Irish." Pieces of the Past. Jamaica Gleaner. http://old.jamaica-gleaner.com/pages/history/story0058.htm.

30. "Jamaican Cuisine From Then to Now." Jamaica Land We Love. https://www.jamaica-land-we-love.com/jamaican-cuisine.html.

31. "Culinary Heritage." Celebrating Jamaica 55. https://jamaica55.gov.jm/culinary/culinary-heritage/.

32. "Captain Bligh's Cursed Breadfruit." Smithsonian Magazine. Smithsonian Institution, September 1, 2009. https://www.smithsonianmag.com/travel/captain-blighs-cursed-breadfruit-41433018/.

33. "How The Lebanese And Syrians Came To Jamaica." The Jamaican Blogs, December 5, 2019. https://jablogz.com/2019/12/how-the-lebanese-and-syrians-came-to-jamaica/.

34. "Jamaicans - Marriage and Family." Countries and Their Cultures. https://www.everyculture.com/Middle-America-Caribbean/Jamaicans-Marriage-and-Family.html.

35. Tortello, Rebecca. ""Out Of Many Cultures, The People Who Came: The Arrival Of The Germans." Pieces of the Past. Jamaica Gleaner. http://old.jamaica-gleaner.com/pages/history/story0060.htm.

36. "International Religious Freedom Report 2008." U.S. Department of State Archive. U.S. Department of State, September 19, 2008. https://2001-2009.state.gov/g/drl/rls/irf/2008/108531.htm.

37. "Religion of Jamaica." Britannica. Encyclopedia Britannica, inc. https://www.britannica.com/place/Jamaica/Religion.

38. Nag, Oishimaya Sen. "Religious Beliefs In Jamaica." World Atlas, May 30, 2018. https://www.worldatlas.com/articles/religious-beliefs-in-jamaica.html

39. Bucknor, Hopeton. "Woman Detained for Obeah, Oils, Sprays." The Star. Jamaica Star, June 6, 2019. http://jamaica-star.com/article/news/20190606/woman-detained-obeah-oils-sprays.

40. "Faith in Jamaica: Learn More About What We Believe." Visit Jamaica. https://www.visitjamaica.com/feel-the-vibe/people/faith/

41. Nelson, Elizabeth. "Religion in Jamaica: Finding the Self through Finding God." Rhetoric of Reggae Term Paper. https://debate.uvm.edu/dreadlibrary/ENelson.htm.

42. Ohadike, Don C. *Sacred Drums of Liberation: Religions and Music of Resistance in Africa and the Diaspora*. Trenton NJ: Africa World Press, 2007.

43. "History of the United Pentecostal Church of Jamaica." Press Reader. PressReader.com, February 29, 2016. https://www.pressreader.com/jamaica-gleaner/20160229/282501477712352.

44. Mill, Mary. "Early 19th Century Jamaica, Church of Scotland and Presbyterian Missionaries." Presbyterian Church in Jamaica early 19th century, 2013. http://www.jamaicanfamilysearch.com/Samples2/PresbyteriansJamaica.htm.

45. *The Orthodox Presbyterian Theological Review and Missionary Recorder*. Belfast: W. M'Comb, 1839.

46. O'Reggio, Trevor. "Exploring the Factors That Shaped the Early Adventist Mission to Jamaica." Journal of the Adventist Theological Society, 2008. https://digitalcommons.andrews.edu/cgi/viewcontent.cgi?article=1016&context=church-history-pubs.

47. Olsen, Ted. "The Island of Too Many Churches." Christianity Today, October 4, 1999. https://www.christianitytoday.com/ct/1999/october4/9tb064.html.

48. "Statistics and Church Facts: Total Church Membership." The Church of Jesus Christ of Latter Day Saints. https://newsroom.churchofjesuschrist.org/facts-and-statistics/country/jamaica.

49. "Jehovah's Witnesses Around the World." JW.ORG Jehovah's Witnesses https://www.jw.org/en/jehovahs-witnesses/worldwide/JA/.

50. Tortello, Rebecca. "Kingston's Historic and Diverse Places of Worship, Religious Icons Part 2." Pieces of the Past. Jamaica Gleaner. https://old.jamaica-gleaner.com/pages/history/story0074.html.

51. Reddie, Richard. "Atlantic Slave Trade and Abolition." BBC, January 29, 2007. https://www.bbc.co.uk/religion/religions/christianity/history/slavery_1.shtml.

52. Williams, Joseph J. "Voodoos and Obeah: Phases of West India Witchcraft." Internet Sacred Text Archive, 1932. https://www.sacred-texts.com/afr/vao/vao07.htm.

53. Tortello, Rebecca. "Old-Time Jamaican Weddings." Pieces of the Past. Jamaica Gleaner. https://old.jamaica-gleaner.com/pages/history/story0064.html.

54. Tortello, Rebecca. "Out Of Many Cultures, The People Who Came: The Arrival Of The Irish." Pieces of the Past. Jamaica Gleaner. http://old.jamaica-gleaner.com/pages/history/story0058.htm.

55. Tortello, Rebecca. "Out Of Many Cultures, The People Who Came: The Arrival Of The Chinese." Pieces of the Past. Jamaica Gleaner. http://old.jamaica-gleaner.com/pages/history/story0055.htm.

56. Tortello, Rebecca. "Out Of Many Cultures, The People Who Came: The Arrival Of The Lebanese." Pieces of the Past. Jamaica Gleaner. http://old.jamaica-gleaner.com/pages/history/story0056.htm

57. Tortello, Rebecca. "Out Of Many Cultures, The People Who Came: The Arrival Of The Indians." Pieces of the Past. Jamaica Gleaner. http://old.jamaica-gleaner.com/pages/history/story0057.htm.
58. Tortello, Rebecca. "Out Of Many Cultures, The People Who Came: The Jews In Jamaica." Pieces of the Past. Jamaica Gleaner. http://old.jamaica-gleaner.com/pages/history/story0054.htm.
59. Franco, Jules. "Miss Lou Liberated Jamaica From the Queen's English." OZY, October 15, 2018. https://www.ozy.com/flashback/miss-lou-liberated-jamaica-from-the-queens-english/88370/.
60. Cauchi, Tony. "Revival in Jamaica - 1860." The Revival Library. https://www.revival-library.org/revival_histories/evangelical/1857/jamaica_revival_1860.shtml.
61. Scott, Shalman. "The Rise of Revivalism in Jamaica." Jamaica Observer, January 21, 2018. https://www.jamaicaobserver.com/news/the-rise-of-revivalism-in-jamaica_122140?profile=1470.
62. Madden, Ruby. "The Historical and Culture Aspects of Jamaican Patois." Debate Central, December 1, 2009. https://debate.uvm.edu/dreadlibrary/Madden.htm.
63. "Rastafari movement." PHILTAR: Overview of World Religions. http://www.philtar.ac.uk/encyclopedia/latam/rasta.html.
64. Harvey, Leroy. Vice Principal of Academics, Moneague College. Interview by contributor - Nasheema Harvey, Jamaica, 2020.
65. "Jamaica - Educational System Overview." Education Encyclopedia. StateUniversity.com.

https://education.stateuniversity.com/pages/727/Jamaica-EDUCATIONAL-SYSTEM-OVERVIEW.html.

66. Trines, Stefan, ed. "Education in Jamaica." WENR, September 10, 2019. https://wenr.wes.org/2019/09/education-in-jamaica.

67. Ryden, David Beck. "Manumission in Late Eighteenth-Century Jamaica." Brill, December 7, 2018. https://brill.com/view/journals/nwig/92/3-4/article-p211_1.xml?language=en.

68. Babb, Stefanie. "Five Facts About Education in Jamaica." The Borgen Project, July 7, 2018. https://borgenproject.org/education-in-jamaica/.

69. "Education in Jamaica." K12 Academics. https://www.k12academics.com/Education%20Worldwide/education-jamaica.

70. *Man Free. Man Free | Jamaican Life Documentary.* Jamaica: Atlas Digital, Kinsey, 2011. https://www.youtube.com/watch?v=xY0BU7MSEyo.

71. "The History of Cocaine - Where Does Cocaine Come from?." Foundation for a Drug-Free World. https://www.drugfreeworld.org/drugfacts/cocaine/a-short-history.html.

72. Grant, John N. "Jamaican Maroons in Nova Scotia." The Canadian Encyclopedia, October 23, 2015. https://www.thecanadianencyclopedia.ca/en/article/Maroons-of-nova-scotia.

73. "African American Ancestry: The Akan States of the Gold Coast." BlackDemographics.com.

74. https://blackdemographics.com/african-american-ancestry-the-akan-states-of-the-gold-coast/.

75. Kopytoff, Barbara Klamon. "Guerilla Warfare in Eighteenth Century Jamaica." Expedition Magazine. Penn Museum, 1977. https://www.penn.museum/sites/expedition/guerilla-warfare-in-eighteenth-century-jamaica/.

76. "Treaty between the British and the Maroons." Treaty between the British and the Maroons. Kress Collection of Business and Economic Literature, Baker Library, Harvard Business School. https://cyber.harvard.edu/eon/marroon/treaty.html.

77. Zhao, He. "No Drums Allowed: Afro Rhythm Mutations in North America." Medium, January 2, 2018. https://leohezhao.medium.com/no-drums-allowed-afro-rhythm-mutations-in-north-america-8230a5a663c0.

78. Bornstein, Avram S. "Dancehall Ethnography in Jamaica," September 2001, 183–85. https://doi.org/10.1353/smx.2001.0015.

79. Chang, Jeff. *Can't Stop Won't Stop: a History of the Hip-Hop Generation*. London: Ebury Press, 2007.

80. Angulu, Hakeem. "From Jamaica to Madagascar: Consistent Meaning of Resilience and Need for Planetary Health." Medium, December 23, 2017. https://medium.com/@hakeemangulu/from-jamaica-to-madagascar-consistent-meaning-of-resilience-and-need-for-planetary-health-78abbaa51295.

81. Web Neal, Aidan. Web log. *What Does It Mean To Work Like A Jamaican?* (blog). Aidan Neal, December 9, 2014. http://aidanneal.com/2014/12/09/whats-funny-jamaicans-two-jobs/.

82. James, Marlon. *The Book of Night Women*. London: Oneworld, 2015.

83. Mullin, Michael. *Africa in America: Slave Acculturation and Resistance in the American South and the British Caribbean, 1736-1831*. New York: ACLS History E-Book Project, 2004.

84. Diop, Cheikh Anta. *Nations Nègres Et Culture: De L'antiquité Nègre Égyptienne Aux Problèmes Culturels De L'Afrique Noire D'aujourd'hui*. Paris: Présence Africaine, 1979.

85. Kama, Lisapo ya. "The Religion of the Akan People." African History. https://en.lisapoyakama.org/religion-akan-people/.

86. Akhan, dwirafo Kwesi Ra Nehem Ptah. *KAMIT HENA NTORO - The Black Nation and Divinity*. www.odwirafo.com.

87. Inner, and Erica. "Understanding the Chakra System and 7 Dimensional Vehicles of Expression." Openhand. https://www.openhandweb.org/chakra-system-and-7-dimensional-vehicles-of-expression.

88. *Africa: A Voyage of Discovery*. Artfilms, 1984. https://www.artfilms.com.au/item/africa-a-voyage-of-discovery.

89. Paige, Krystal. *Ema - The Heart and Soul of Jewish Jamaica*. YouTube video, 6:29, July 31, 2017. https://www.youtube.com/watch?v=2teFewfGbGs.

90. "Akan History." TOTA. https://www.tota.world/article/801/.

91. Fonte, Felipe. "Ethnic Origins of Jamaican Runaway Slaves." Tracing African Roots, April 15, 2015. https://tracingafricanroots.wordpress.com/2015/04/15/ethnic-origins-of-jamaican-runaway-slaves/.

92. Chambers, Douglas B. "The Links of a Legacy: Figuring the Slave Trade to Jamaica." Academia.edu.

https://www.academia.edu/8565814/_The_Links_of_a_Legacy_Figuring_the_Slave_Trade_to_Jamaica._.

93. "Cultural Life." Encyclopedia Britannica. https://www.britannica.com/place/Jamaica/Cultural-life.

94. Goffe, Leslie Gordon. "Africans in Jamaica: A Piece of Africa in the Caribbean." New African Magazine, September 12, 2016. https://newafricanmagazine.com/9633/.

95. Cep, Casey. "The Long War Against Slavery." The New Yorker, January 17, 2020. https://www.newyorker.com/magazine/2020/01/27/the-long-war-against-slavery.

96. Falola, Toyin, and Raphael Chijioke Njoku. *Igbo in the Atlantic World: African Origins and Diasporic Destinations*. Bloomington: Indiana University Press, 2016.

97. Limited, Jamaica Observer. "The Ganja Law of 1913: 100 Years of Oppressive Injustice." Jamaica Observer, December 2, 2013. https://www.jamaicaobserver.com/columns/The-ganja-law-of-1913--100-years-of-oppressive-injustice_15548584.

98. Bilby, Kenneth M. "The Kromanti Dance of the Windward Maroons of Jamaica." Brill. Brill, January 1, 1981. https://brill.com/view/journals/nwig/55/1/article-p52_6.xml?language=en.

99. Hill, Richard. *A Week at Port-Royal*. Montego-Bay Jamaica: Cornwall chronical Office, 1855.

100. Bernard, Ian. "Queen Nanny of the Maroons (? - 1733)." Blackpast, March 1, 2011. https://www.blackpast.org/global-african-history/queen-nanny-maroons-1733/.

101. Raskin, Sam, and Bruce Golding. "NYC Hospital Worker Beats Coronavirus - and Returns to Work." New York Post, April 1, 2020. https://nypost.com/2020/04/01/nyc-hospital-worker-beats-coronavirus-and-returns-to-work/.

102. Ayim, Kofi. *The Akan of Ghana: Aspects of Past and Present Practices*. West Orange, NJ: Kofi Ayim, 2015.

103. Lutzer, Erwin W. *The Power of a Clear Conscience: Let God Free You from Your Past*. Eugene: Harvest House Publishers, 2016.

104. "US Embassy Explains Why Some Jamaican Artiste Will NEVER Be Granted a Visa." Newsbugmedia, October 27, 2016. https://newsbugmedia.com/entertainment/169-us-embassy-explains-why-some-jamaican-artiste-will-never-be-granted-a-visa.

105. "U.S Revoking Dancehall Artist Visas." CelebrityAccess, April 28, 2010. https://celebrityaccess.com/caarchive/u-s-revoking-dancehall-artist-visas/.

106. Long, Edward. *The History of Jamaica: or, General Survey of the Antient and Modern State of That Island; with Reflections on Its Situation, Settlements, Inhabitants, Climate, Products, Commerce, Laws, and Government*. Cambridge: Cambridge University Press, 2010.

107. Myers, Gay Nagle. "New Tourism Slogan for Jamaica: 'Heartbeat of the World.'" Travel Weekly, January 27, 2020. https://www.travelweekly.com/Caribbean-Travel/Brand-slogan-for-Jamaica-heartbeat-of-world.

108. Larmer, Brook. "The 'Barrel Children'." Newsweek. Newsweek, March 13, 2010. https://www.newsweek.com/barrel-children-179978.

109. Spencer, Nekeisha, Mikhail-Ann Urquhart, and Patrice Whitely. "Class Discrimination? Evidence from Jamaica: A Racially Homogeneous Labor Market." *Review of Radical Political Economics* 52, no. 1 (2019): 77–95. https://doi.org/10.1177/0486613419832674.

110. Fairclough, Sashakay. "Who Is to Be Blamed for Classism in Jamaica?" Jamaica Observer, May 1, 2016. https://www.jamaicaobserver.com/columns/Who-is-to-be-blamed-for-classism-in-Jamaica-_59523.

111. Hope, Donna. "Jamaica's Pervasive Class Problem." Jamaica Observer News, November 7, 2019. https://www.jamaicaobserver.com/news/Jamaica-s-pervasive-class-problem?profile=&template=PrinterVersion.

112. Graham, George. "Race and Class Interaction in Jamaica - And Its Impact on the World." Jamaicans.com. https://jamaicans.com/raceandclassinjamaica/.

113. "The World Bank in Jamaica." World Bank, April 13, 2020. https://www.worldbank.org/en/country/jamaica/overview.

114. Scott, Shamille. "Jamaica Records Lowest Poverty Rate in 10 Years - Clarke." Loop News, June 24, 2020. https://jamaica.loopnews.com/content/jamaica-records-lowest-poverty-rate-10-years-clarke.

115. Williams, Andre. "Homeless Horror - Streets Filled with Trembling as Four Chopped to Death in Kingston." Jamaica Gleaner, January 26, 2021. https://jamaica-gleaner.com/article/lead-stories/20210126/homeless-horror-streets-filled-trembling-four-chopped-death-kingston.

116. "Maroon History." History of the Maroons.
https://cyber.harvard.edu/eon/marroon/history.html.
117. Tidrick, G. (n.d.). Some Aspects of Jamaican Emigration to the United Kingdom 1953-1962.
https://www.jstor.org/stable/27853886.
118. https://jamaicagreathouses.com/slavery/maroons.html
119.

www.ingramcontent.com/pod-product-compliance
Lightning Source LLC
Chambersburg PA
CBHW080606170426
43209CB00007B/1341